Presented to

Jackie
_____

By: Ronéll
_____

Date: 12 - 25 - 98
_____

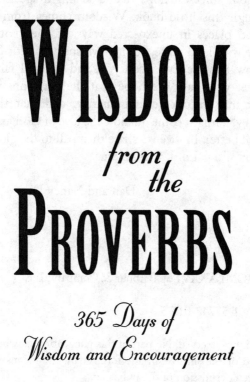

WISDOM
from
the
PROVERBS

*365 Days of
Wisdom and Encouragement*

Dan and Nancy Dick

A Barbour Book

It is our sincerest hope that God might speak to you through this little book. Wisdom comes from unexpected places in unexpected ways. It does not often come with loud noise, but in a whisper. Pray for God to bestow His blessing upon you, and He will faithfully answer your call. We hope that the devotions in this book may encourage and instruct, and that through them you might come to know the love of God just a little bit better. In love we share them, all to the glory and honor of our Lord, Christ Jesus.

Dan and Nancy Dick

© MCMLXXXVI by Barbour & Company, Inc.

ISBN 1-57748-015-5

Published by Barbour & Company, Inc.
P.O. Box 719
Uhrichsville, Ohio 44683
http://www.barbourbooks.com

ecpa Member of the
Evangelical Christian
Publishers Association

Printed in the United States of America.

Also published as *Wisdom from the Bible*.

January 1

The Proverbs of Solomon the son of David, King of Israel: To know wisdom and instruction; to perceive the words of understanding (1:1-2).

There is no easy way to be a Christian. Christianity requires a lot of effort, sacrifice and commitment. The heart of the Christian life is to live the way Christ taught and lived. Though it sounds simple, it is terribly difficult. The temptation is to throw up our hands and say, "I'm not Christ! I can't do the things He did!" Still, Christ himself said that we should "Be ye perfect, even as your Father which is in heaven is perfect." (Matt. 5:48) How can Christ ask such a thing of us?

Christ never for one minute thought that we would be as perfect as God is. He knew that we are imperfect and sinful. He also knew how much God loves us and wants us to grow and to be happy. With His help we can find joy and maturity. To assist us, God gave us His word; the Holy scriptures. If we will be dedicated to reading the Bible regularly, and do it prayerfully, God will help us to understand it, and through understanding we will be able to live more perfectly, the way God intends.

PRAYER: O Lord, help me to know you, and through knowing you, help me to be like you. Make me a faithful and loving follower, and be with me to guide me this day, and every day to come. Amen.

January 2

The Proverbs of Solomon the son of David, king of Israel: to receive the instruction of wisdom, justice, and judgment, and equity (1:1, 3).

A small boy was excitedly opening a toy automobile, but found that it required a good deal of assembly. Try as he might, he could not get the car put together, and with a cry he threw some of the pieces across the room. The frustration of not being able to accomplish what seemed simple was devastating to the boy.

Attempting to live a good Christian life can be just as frustrating sometimes. It seems like it should be easy, but as hard as we might try to live as God would want we find that we can't quite do it. We need help. We need instruction. God gives us that instruction if we only seek it. Through prayer, scripture, and the support of fellow believers we can gain special insights which make living the Christian life much esier and more fulfilling. What seems impossible on our own becomes a pleasure when we have help. We are never alone in our Christian journey. We are given one another, and we are even in touch with God's Holy Spirit.

PRAYER: O Lord, show me how you want me to be. When I struggle with life, grant me your wisdom to lead me through. Open my eyes, my heart, my spirit. Amen.

January 3

The Proverbs of Solomon the son of David, king of Israel: to give subtilty to the simple, to the young man knowledge and discretion (1:1,4).

The saying is certainly true which says, "Experience is the best teacher." It is through day to day living that we come to understand life. What we did not understand as children we come to know as adults. When we start upon a new endeavor we learn slowly, gathering more information and experience, until we finally master it.

Our Christian life is like that. We start out inexperienced and with little knowledge, but then we grow in our understanding and commitment. Christ Himself spent a good deal of His life preparing for His ministry and work. Like Him, we are growing, maturing and preparing for the Kingdom of God which awaits us. When we search for God in the Bible and through prayer we are being made ready for our heavenly home. In this life, we never really arrive at "being" Christian, but we are ever "becoming" Christian. As long as we continue to learn, we continue to grow. In that growth lies wisdom.

PRAYER: Dear heavenly Father, grant that I might continue to learn more about you each and every day. Create in me a real hunger for Your truth. Amen.

January 4

The Proverbs of Solomon the son of David, king of Israel: to understand a proverb, and the interpretation; the words of the wise, and their dark sayings (1:1,6).

It is often hard to listen to someone who tells you something "for your own good." No one likes to hear negative comments, whether they are true or not. It takes a special person to seek criticism and suggestions for improvement. The Bible says that we should be humble and always trying to improve ourselves. This is an important part of wisdom.

The Apostle Paul advised that every person should examine him- or herself to see that he or she is truly living the way Christ would want them to live. Honest examination and evaluation requires a lot of integrity. It is not always easy. Happily, God supports us through our self-examination, and He loves us no matter how good or bad we might find ourselves to be. The love of God is unconditional. God is truly for us, and if He is for us, who can be against us? Wise words may be welcome, or they may create in us feelings of hurt or resentment. Knowing that we are loved by God makes all the difference in the world.

PRAYER: O Lord, help me to be open to the comments of others. Let me face my shortcomings with dignity and open-mindedness. Help me ever to work to change myself for the better. Amen.

January 5

The fear of the Lord is the beginning of knowledge, but fools despise wisdom and instruction (1:7).

Standing on the shore of a great ocean, one is amazed at the force of the waves crashing on the rocks. The vast expanse of water is awe-inspiring, and yet it is beautiful. Only a very foolish person would ignore the dangers presented by the sea, and yet, only a fool would not be attracted by its beauty. The ocean is to be feared and respected, but it is also to be experienced. Despite our sense of awe, or perhaps because of it, we are drawn to the water, to be immersed in it, to become part of it. Our true enjoyment of the surf comes when we enter in, but only when we understand its power.

The same is true of God. We stand in awe before Him, wisely cautious in the face of His power, and yet we long to know Him, to be united with Him. The wise pursue Him with all their heart, while the foolish ignore Him or reject Him through their fear. Once we understand the power of our Lord, this fear enables us to be with Him, immersed in Him, but always respecting His might.

PRAYER: O Lord, help me to know fear in a positive way, and set my feet on the path to wisdom. Amen.

January 6

My son, hear the instruction of thy father, and forsake not the law of thy mother (1:8).

Parents are entrusted with an awesome responsibility. The idea of raising a child, or instructing a young boy or girl in the best way to live, is incredible. Every mother and father questions the decisions they make hundreds of times in their lives. The ongoing prayer of most men and women is that they have made good choices for their children. Their consolation comes from their children's happiness and prosperity. When the Bible says that children should honor their parents, it is saying that children should live in such a way that no dishonor should ever befall their mothers and fathers.

This is true of our relationship with our heavenly Father, also. God wants for us only the best. He has given instruction, not to show His power or might, but to help us live the best life we possibly can. He only wants our peace and happiness. In turn, we should live in such a way that He is honored. Our actions should reflect the quality of our upbringing. We should live as a proof of how much we love God

PRAYER: Dear God, please assist us in our attempts to live as you have instructed. Help us to be a glory and an honor to you. May we do nothing to bring shame to your Holy name. Amen.

January 7

My son, if sinners entice thee, consent thou not (1:10).

Our Lord, Jesus Christ, once walked in the wilderness. He fasted forty days, and when it was past, Satan came and walked with Him. Christ, hungry as he was, refused to be tempted by Satan's charge to turn stones into bread. Christ, poor as he was by worldly standards, withstood the allure of wealth, fame and power. Christ, Holy as He was, refused to put God to a test. In the face of enormous enticement Jesus stood firmly consenting to none of Satan's requests.

It sounds so easy, "consent thou not." Yet many desirous things tempt us. How are we to resist the multitude of temptations we face every day? We resist temptation the same way Jesus did, with the help of the Holy Spirit.

As we grow in our knowledge of God, we feel His presence in our lives, and we become able to rely on His strength to resist enticement when our strength is not enough. Our choice is not so much whether or not to give in to temptation, but whether or not we will allow God to strengthen us when we need it most.

PRAYER: O Lord, be with me in the face of temptation. Grant me the wisdom and courage I need to resist enticement and help me turn to thee. Amen.

January 8

Surely in vain the net is spread in the sight of any bird (1:17).

There was a man whose hobby was taxidermy. He specialized in rare and exotic birds. One day the man's son expressed an interest in taxidermy. The man wanted the son to experience the whole process, so early one morning they set out to trap a bird for the son to begin with.

"We spread a net to snare the bird. We don't want to damage it in any way, so nets are best to use. However, the nets must be carefully camouflaged so the bird won't suspect anything. If a bird senses the net, it won't come down to take the bait."

If only we had the good sense of the birds! "Fools rush in where angels fear to tread." We have a good, basic idea of what things are right and what things are wrong, but we all too often ignore the danger signs and do those things we know that we should not. Alone, we stumble into the snare, finding ourselves hopelessly trapped. With God we receive the wisdom we need to avoid the traps. He liberates us from our foolish tendencies to ignore the signs of peril. As we open ourselves to God, He teaches us wisdom and discernment.

PRAYER: O Lord, open my eyes to those areas of my life, where it is foolish to tread. Protect my steps and lead me in the ways of righteousness and truth. Amen.

January 9

So are the ways of every one that is greedy of gain; which taketh away the life of the owners thereof (1:19).

An important question each person should ask is, "How much do I really need?" Christ is quite clear about the accumulation of wealth. As in the story of the man who built his storehouses bigger to hold his great crops, Christ asks each one of us where it is we keep our treasure. Is it on earth or is it in heaven? Surely, God wants every person to enjoy life and to share in good times, but He does not find joy in the celebration of a few when many suffer.

A good guideline to follow concerning the possessions of this world is to contemplate the question of what Christ might do with the same possessions if they were His. If this rule were followed much more would be given and shared, and fewer people would have to do without. The Bible says that greed is keeping what we don't need. God rejoices in the life of a giver, but has no part of the greedy person's life. With His help and guidance, we all can learn to be more giving.

PRAYER: Oh heavenly Father, open my eyes to the needs of those around me. Destroy the spirit of selfishness in my heart, and teach me to give as you would give. Amen.

January 10

Wisdom crieth without; she uttereth her voice in the streets;
she crieth in the chief place of concourse, in the openings of
the gates; in the city she uttereth her words, saying, How
long ye simple ones will ye love simplicity? and the scorners
delight in their scorning, and fools hate knowledge?
(1:20-22).

It isn't easy being Christian. There is a great deal of
responsibility that goes along with the Christian life.
We have been called of God to show love to everyone we come in contact with. We are even called to
show love to those people that we will never come in
contact with. There are no shortcuts we can take.
Love is a matter of giving everything we are, all the
time.

How can we hope to learn this kind of love?
Through an ever-deepening knowledge of God.
Herein true wisdom lies. God can give us the love we
do not possess on our own. He fills us with more
than enough love, continually refilling us as we share
what we have. Only fools will turn from the knowledge of God which fills our hearts and enables us to
love unselfishly.

PRAYER: O heavenly Father, grant me a deeper
knowledge of who you are. Fill me with an unselfish love.
Let me embrace the intricacies of life, scorning simplicity,
and help me to pursue wisdom all of my days. Amen.

January 11

Turn you at my reproof: behold, I will pour out my spirit unto you, I will make known my words unto you (1:23).

A young woman remembered her girlhood with mixed feelings. When she had been younger she had resisted every effort her parents made to impose rules on her. She resented the fact that her mother and father continually told her what to do. Her usual response was, "When I have children of my own, I'll never treat them the way you treat me."

When she did in fact have children of her own, the words came back to haunt her. She began to understand better why her parents had acted as they had. She began to see the wisdom in her parents' actions and words. Her eyes were opened to the true intentions of her parents: to try to do what was best for their daughter.

The rules and laws of God often have the same effect on us. We resist them, thinking that God doesn't want us to have any fun. If we will only realize that every rule God gives is given out of perfect love for us, we can truly enjoy our lives the way God intends us to. By obeying, we learn more about God.

PRAYER: Dear God, help me to be obedient to your will. Please help me not to question your wisdom, but to always trust you. If I do, understanding will follow. Amen.

January 12

But ye have set at nought all my counsel, and would none of my reproof: I also will laugh at your calamity; I will mock when your fear cometh (1:25-26).

Once, when I was young, I climbed a tree against the wishes of my mother. I got high up in the branches and found that I could neither continue forward nor go back. I held tight to a large branch and began to cry. I yelled for my mother, and I could see her walk out to where I was captive. Instead of being angry, as I thought she would be, she began to laugh, and placing her hands on her hips, she said, "I told you not to try to climb up there. Now look at you. Why do you think I tell you not to do some things?"

All too often, our inclination is to test God. We know what He says He wants us to do, but we do other things instead. We try to get away with things we know we should not. When we find ourselves in trouble we look to God to bail us out, and we cannot understand why He doesn't jump to our aid. Often God allows us to struggle through adversity in order to learn that He means what He says.

PRAYER: Dear heavenly Father, I so often do what I know you do not want me to. Forgive my foolishness and disobedience. Help me to heed your will, not my own. Amen.

January 13

When your fear cometh as desolation, and your destruction cometh as a whirlwind; when distress and anguish cometh upon you. Then shall they call upon me, but I will not answer; they shall seek me early, but they shall not find me (1:27-28).

A little boy waited patiently, day after day, to be allowed to play baseball with the bigger boys on the block. Every game was the same. He sat waiting and never got to play. One day he didn't bother to show up. He found another team on another block where he was needed. His old team came to find themselves short of the number needed to play, so they called on the little boy. The boy said, "If you wanted me so bad, you should have given me a chance to play before. Now it's too late."

Often we treat God the same way. When things are going well we ignore Him, but the minute things go wrong we run to Him, hoping that He will make everything all right. God is not someone that we should turn to only in times of trial. He should be a part of our whole life, both in good times and bad. We must be sure to include God in everything we do.

PRAYER: Dear God, forgive those times when I seem to forget you. Help me to include you in all I do, think and feel. Be with me to guide me, now and forever. Amen.

January 14

For the turning away of the simple shall slay them, and the prosperity of fools shall destroy them. But whoso hearkeneth unto me shall dwell safely, and shall be quiet from fear of evil (1:32-33).

There were once three men who met a thief. The first man foolishly turned to run, and was killed. The second man, a wealthy, powerful leader, tried to bribe the thief, but he too was killed for his troubles. The last man stood fearlessly before the thief, and said, "Of wealth, I have none. The only thing of value I possess is my life, but that is not truly mine, but the Lord's, for I have given all I am to Him." The thief was amazed by the man's courage and faith, and so he let him go.

In the face of trouble, we too often try to run away, or we turn to worldly solutions. These can never be enough. Instead, we must turn to God and rely on His strength to get us through. True wisdom comes from realizing God's greatness and taking it as a freely given gift into our hearts. We may dwell in safety in the Lord, for He is greater than any trial this world can produce.

PRAYER: O Lord, receive me into your loving care. Allow me to dwell in the safety you provide. Help me to place you, and you alone, at the center of my life. Amen.

January 15

My son, if thou wilt receive my words, and hide my commandments with thee: so that thou incline thine ear unto wisdom, and apply thine heart to understanding; yea, if thou criest after knowledge, and liftest up thy voice for understanding; if thou seekest her as silver, and searchest for her as for hid treasures; then shalt thou understand the fear of the Lord, and find the knowledge of God. (2:1-5).

Following Christ requires our all. In order for us to walk in His footsteps we must be totally dedicated; body, mind and soul. We need to listen carefully to the word of God, and we must learn to apply it. We should spend time in contemplation using our minds to gain a deeper understanding of God's will. We should open our hearts in order to feel God's presence in our lives. We should praise God with our voices and shout His glories. We should talk with other believers and share our questions and experiences.

We devote such great energies to the acquisition of material goods. Wealth is so appealing. Yet, we fail to understand that true wealth comes only through a relationship with God. The knowledge of God is worth more than the finest riches. God desires that we pursue Him with the same devotion that we pursue material gain. Let that be our aim.

PRAYER: Lord, God, no matter what I own, what I might possess, without you I have nothing. Turn my sight from this world, dear God, and help me to seek only you, body, mind and soul. Amen.

January 16

For the Lord giveth wisdom: out of his mouth cometh knowledge and understanding (2:6).

A man went to college to gain wisdom, but he came away with facts and figures. He turned to business, and he came away with cunning. He tried a craft, and he learned skill with his hands. The man tried pleasure and he gained a feeling of emptiness. The man felt that he would never know wisdom. He grew weary of his search, but one day he stopped at a church. He listened quietly to what was being said, and his heart filled with excitement. His quest came to an end with the simple words, "Be still, and know that I am God."

Often, wisdom comes without great fanfare. It comes to those who wait with open heart and mind. It comes simply and quietly. It comes in the stillness, when God and his Word can get through. Christ is the Word of God. If we will only open our lives to Jesus, the wisdom of God will be ours.

PRAYER: Open my heart, Almighty God. Give me knowledge which is beyond ordinary knowledge. Teach me more about your love, your Word, Jesus the Christ. Amen.

January 17

He layeth up sound wisdom for the righteous: he is a buckler to them that walk upright (2:7).

A teenage girl found herself continually tempted by her friends to do things she knew she shouldn't. Once she was offered drugs, occasionally she was offered alcohol, often she was approached by boys who tried to take advantage of her. Her constant reply was that she was a Christian. Usually she was made fun of for her faith. One time, however, a friend asked her why her faith made such a difference. The girl replied, "I really want to do what God asks me to. When I do what He wants, I feel better about myself. When I do wrong, I feel terrible. I'd rather feel good inside and have people make fun of me, than feel lousy and give in to temptation."

Faith like that is hard to have. It is easy to give into temptation when it constantly attacks you. But it's good to know that when we resist the temptations that God makes it all worth while. He makes us feel good about ourselves and gives us even more power to resist in the future.

PRAYER: Dear Father, I am faced by so many temptations. Help me to resist them. Grant that I might rely on your will and power. Be with me in every situation. Amen.

January 18

He keepeth the paths of judgment, and preserveth the way of his saints (2:8).

A minister friend of mine recently had a heart attack. While awaiting a procedure to unblock a clogged artery his heart began spasming and he felt himself slip into oblivion. Had he not been in the hospital, he would most certainly have died. The doctors were able to revive him and proceed with the operation. Today my friend is fine.

The most memorable part of my friend's story was his assurance that Christ was with him at all times. He knew with a certainty that he was not alone, and that God moved with him every step of the way. He felt God's guidance for the doctors, and he experienced great peace.

That peace is available to us all. God truly watches over all who believe in Him. Learning to trust in God is the greatest comfort we can ever hope to find. No matter what might happen, know that Christ is with you always.

PRAYER: Thank you for being with me, Almighty God. I need you here in my life. Uphold me and guide me, shine your light before me. Grant me your peace. Amen.

January 19

Then shalt thou understand righteousness, and judgment, and equity; yea, every good path (2:9).

Jesus Christ selected for himself a band of twelve rough, rugged men to be His disciples. These men knew very little of qualities like gentleness, compassion, kindness, and giving. Prior to Jesus' coming to them they had very little reason to consider any of these traits. Their paths were many, but none would have been considered good. None until Christ came along.

During their three years with Jesus, the disciples learned everything there was to know of these qualities. They came to understand all that Jesus tried to show them. They carried these qualities of goodness into the world and taught others to follow them.

If we will take time to spend with Christ, through prayer, Bible reading and devotion, we too will learn these traits. We will learn to follow the good paths that Jesus followed. This is what it means to be a Christian. The key is in spending time with God in order to learn them.

PRAYER: Remind me, heavenly Father, that I should spend time with you today and every day. Make me a disciple of yours, anxious to learn all that you would teach me. Amen.

January 20

When wisdom entereth into thine heart, and knowledge is pleasant unto thy soul; discretion shall preserve thee, understanding shall keep thee (2:10-11).

When I was in school, I knew a young woman who seemed to have everything she could possibly want. She was a straight-A student, she came from a wealthy background, had wonderful looks and dressed beatifully. Her only drawback was her personality. Though she was friendly, she lacked compassion. When other people hurt, she had no use for them. She had the knack of saying all the wrong things at all the wrong times. As long as the situation required a logical mind, this woman performed excellently, but when it called for a depth of feeling she was bankrupt.

Reason and logic are important traits, but there is something more. Many situations call for feeling, not just thinking. Faith is like that. Paul says we should "know the love of Christ, which passeth knowledge." (Eph. 3:19) It is vital that we learn to think with our hearts, as well as with our heads. This is where true wisdom comes from. This is the understanding which God wants each of us to have.

PRAYER: Too often, Father, I try to think my way through my problems rather than feeling my way. Open my heart so that I might know Your love in the deepest way possible. Amen.

January 21

To deliver thee from the way of the evil man, from the man that speaketh froward things; who leaves the paths of uprightness, to walk in the ways of darkness; who rejoice to do evil, and delight in the frowardness of the wicked (2:12-14).

I recently visited a woman in the hospital. She didn't seem too happy to see me, and after awhile she let me know why. "God is doing this to me," she said. "He is punishing me because I'm not a church woman. He just waits for someone to make a mistake, then He gets them."

Isn't it strange that people think of God this way? God doesn't want anyone to suffer. He never punishes people arbitrarily. Nor does He turn His sight from those who do wrong. God will finally be the judge of all people, and true justice will be served, but to think that God acts unfairly and without cause is absurd. God loves all human beings and wants the best for them. His love knows no bounds, and when we suffer or struggle, He struggles with us. God is with us in both good times and bad, but He is never to be blamed for our misfortunes. Instead, He is to be praised and thanked for all the wonderful blessings we receive each and every day. There is no place that we can go that God will not be with us. This is the real meaning of blessed assurance. God is with us. Hallelujah!

PRAYER: O thank you, dear Lord, that I am never out of your sight. You are with me always. Grant that I might feel your presence each and every day. It is good to know I am never alone. Amen.

January 22

For God will deliver thee from the strange woman, even from the stranger which flattereth with her words; which forsaketh the guide of her youth, and forgetteth the covenant of her God (2:16-17).

Society has come up with some wonderful philosophies over the years. "If it feels good do it," "I'm okay, you're okay," "God is dead." Every year there is some new easy belief to buy into. Good, solid beliefs are hard to come by, and they are even harder to hold onto. Someone is always trying to sell us something new to believe in.

It's good to know that God is watching over us and that He is there for us when we turn to Him with our doubts and questions. Prayer is the direct connection that we have with God. When we find ourselves faced with new and different beliefs it is a good idea to take them to God. He will provide the light we need to closely scrutinize different beliefs. Jesus said, "I am the way, the truth, and the life, no man cometh unto the Father, but by me." (John 14:6) If we will remain committed to our Christian faith, God will help us to see the folly of believing in the easy philosophies offered to us by society. God wants us to come to believe in Him with as few doubts as possible. He will always help us to learn as much as we can when our Christian faith is challenged.

PRAYER: God, I think that I know what to believe, but new things come up almost every day. Help me to sort out what is right and good to believe, and what is not. Grant me your wisdom. Amen.

January 23

For her house inclineth unto death, and her paths unto the dead. None that go unto her return again, neither take they hold of the paths of life (2:18-19).

A young man left for college and found that once on his own it was easy to sleep in on Sunday morning. As the weeks passed, church became a memory, and the young man found himself attracted to different activities, not many of them healthy. By the end of his first year, the young man had no connection left with the church. His grades were terrible, his health was ruined, his friends had all turned from him, and he found himself alone and lonely. He felt helpless and hopeless. The young man took his life and wrote in his parting note, "I have nowhere to turn. No one wants me around. I've even slammed the door on God."

How sad that the young man didn't understand God better. This young man is no different from the prodigal son in Luke's gospel story. God waits for us continually, standing ready with open arms to receive us back to Him. It is important that we know that we can always go back to God. All other paths lead to destruction and pain. How wonderful it is to know that the road to God is never blocked. We cannot do anything to make God stop loving us.

PRAYER: Thank you, Father, for extending your loving arms to me. If I should stray from your path, guide me back into your sight and care. I never want to be without You in my life. Amen.

January 24

That thou mayest walk in the way of good men, and keep the paths of the righteous (2:20).

I knew a little boy who was always good when his mother was watching him, but whenever she was out of sight he was a terror. His mother thought he was the perfect child because he never gave her any problems. Other children never wanted him around, though. The other children's parents tried to explain to the boy's mother how her son behaved when she was away, but she would not listen to them.

The woman finally opened her eyes and caught on to the way her son often behaved. She was amazed at the way her son worked so skillfully to impress her by his good behavior. We are often like that young boy when it comes to our relationship with God. When we think that God is watching us we are on our best behavior, but when we forget that He is there, we misbehave. It is as we grow in our knowledge of God's presence in our lives that it is easier to walk the path of righteousness. When we realize that He is with us every moment of every day we are compelled to live good and upright lives. We must admit our weakness and that we need God to motivate us when we will not motivate ourselves to right living.

PRAYER: Guide my steps, O Lord, that I might always, in every way, be found pleasing in your sight. Grant me special insight that I might recognize your presence in my life. Amen.

January 25

For the upright shall dwell in the land, and the perfect shall remain in it (2:21).

My grandmother had a special cedar box that she kept all of her prized possessions in. I used to sit with her at the kitchen table as she would unwrap her treasures. There were old pictures, coins, gems, a lock of hair, a ribbon from a long passed contest, a pair of old glasses, a hand carved spinning top, and a dozen other knick-knacks. My grandmother would tell the story of each and every one, and the love and affection she shared with those memories will stay with me all of my life.

I think God is a little like that. We are His treasures, and He has set aside a special place for us. Each of us brings forth a feeling of love and affection from God, and He cherishes each one of us. We are each one precious in the good Lord's sight, and He knows our individual stories by heart. It is good to know that God loves us so much that He will keep us for all time in a very special place that He has made especially for us. The future glory that awaits all Christian believers is beyond our wildest imagination, and yet we can rest assured that it will far outshine anything we have yet experienced.

PRAYER: Thank you, Lord, that I am one of your prized possessions. Keep me ever in your care, and cover me with your divine love and affection. I praise you for your love and I will try to be a fond remembrance in your heart. Amen.

January 26

But the wicked shall be cut off from the earth, and the transgressors shall be rooted out of it (2:22).

So often it seems like the evil will inherit the earth, rather than the meek. Bad people with evil intentions appear blessed in many ways that good people are not. It is a hard lesson to learn that the rain falls on the just and the unjust alike. Often it would be so nice to see the unkind, cruel, hateful people get what they deserve. Like God's people throughout history, we cry out for God to bring justice upon the heads of our persecutors.

In due time God will do just that. God's time is not our time, however, and we must learn to be patient and wait. God offers us a helpful suggestion in waiting for justice to come. Jesus says, "Judge not, lest ye be judged. Why beholdest thou the mote that is in thy brother's eye, but considerest not the beam that is in thine own eye?" It is easy to sit back and hope for other people to receive their just desserts, but what God wants us to do is make sure that we are doing everything that we should be doing. Justice is God's responsibility. Ours is to do those things which we know are pleasing to God, and to avoid doing the things which He dislikes — like judging our neighbor.

PRAYER: Help me to be patient, and to turn from bitter feelings toward those who do wrong. Let me love them with your love, and help me to look at my own life to see that it is pleasing in your sight. Amen

January 27

My son, forget not my law; but let thine heart keep my commandments: for length of days, and long life, and peace, shall they add to thee (3:1-2).

It is easy to see the Bible as a book of "don'ts" rather than a book of "do's." The "Thou shalt not's" far exceed the "Thou shalt's." This is not a way for God to control us, for there is nothing farther from His intention than that, but it is merely a show of His great love for us that He offers these instructions to us in order to make our lives better. Our God is a God of order and sense. He knows infinitely more than we can ever hope to, and He shares His knowledge with us to help us through our lives.

If we can learn to be obedient to the will of God we will find that life becomes a little easier to live, and a lot more fulfilling. Life ceases to be such a struggle, and it becomes a joy. God sent Christ to fight the battle for us. He has become the victor, our victor. To His disciples Jesus said, "Peace I leave with you, my peace I give to you." He says the same to us. If we can learn to be more obedient to God, this peace and assurance will be ours throughout our entire lives.

PRAYER: Dear God, help me that I might learn to rest in your peace. Life can be so difficult, and I know I cannot handle everything on my own. Be with me, guiding me, and helping me to follow your commandments always. Amen.

January 28

Let not mercy and truth forsake thee: bind them about thy neck; write them upon the table of thine heart (3:3).

Recent movies and books have presented us with a new kind of hero. This hero, male or female, is tough, violent, strong, and cunning. They use few words, usually carry big guns, and they show no mercy. The reason these kinds of heroes are popular is that they mete out vengeance to any and all who do wrong. They wipe out the oppressors, they defend the meek, and they refuse to let the bad guys win. In other words, they symbolize the ideal that good will always triumph over evil.

The problem is, the good they offer is little better than the evil they destroy. Violence begets violence, and the one who shows no mercy shall receive no mercy. "Vengeance is mine, sayeth the Lord." It is not a good thing when men and women take the law into their own hands. We are guided by a higher law: the law of God. The Beatitudes proclaim the virtues that God most respects. We are called to be loving people, who have faith in a God who will provide perfect justice at the end of time. We, as Christian, should take seriously the qualities that God wants us to have, and truly "write them upon the table of thine heart."

PRAYER: Dear Lord, teach me your love, your forgiveness, your mercy, and your truth. Make Christ my one true hero, and let me follow his ways all the days of my life. Amen.

January 29

Trust in the Lord with all thine heart; and lean not unto thine own understanding. (3:5).

The resurrection of Jesus Christ caused so much difficulty for his disciples. They had finally gotten themselves used to the fact that Christ was gone, then, quite suddenly, he reappeared. Logical, rational thinking told the disciples that what they saw could not be true. According to what they knew to be reality, Christ was dead, and nothing could change that. God, however, defies logic and often transcends what we perceive to be reality.

The reality of the resurrected Christ was there for all to see. It was not until the disciples accepted as fact what they could not fully understand, that they were transformed into the foundation builders of the Christian church.

That same resurrected Christ can transform us today. If we will just learn to accept a God who is greater and more powerful than the limits of our minds can grasp, we will begin to experience God more fully. Faith is not without reason, but it is always beyond reason.

PRAYER: Help me, Father, to accept what I do not understand, to believe that which I cannot see, and to trust that which is beyond my comprehension. Amen.

January 30

In all thy ways acknowledge him, and he shall direct thy paths (3:6).

A young athlete won Olympic acclaim and he was asked to comment on his success. His response was, "I knew I would be my best, because God ran with me every step of the way." The sports commentator incredulously asked, "You don't mean to say that you think God helped you win today, do you?" The young man thought for a minute, then said, "If not for God I would not be here today, I would not have the equipment necessary to run and to train, I would not know the meaning of commitment, and I would not feel any need to be the best person I can be. For that reason I said that God ran with me. I could not have won today without God."

What a wonderful statement of faith. All too often we miss God in our everyday lives. From the simple fact of our existence, to the miracle of the life we have been given, to the talents we each possess, we should always be aware of God's presence in our lives and in our world. When we acknowledge Him in our lives, we can rest assured that he will be with us no matter what we do. What great comfort there is in knowing that God is with us to help make us the best people we can be.

PRAYER: Though I may stumble through my life at times, O Lord, help me to know that you are with me to pick me up and to light my way. Alone, I am nothing. With you, I will never fail. Amen.

January 31

Be not wise in thine own eyes: fear the Lord, and depart from evil. It shall be health to thy navel, and marrow to thy bones (3:7-8).

A law student looked for honors and approval from his professors and his peers. His motivation was to "look good" in all that he did. He pursued unbelievably high standards, and when he eventually failed, he was crushed. All of his work to come out on top provided him with nothing. He left law school feeling cheated, a failure.

It is easy to fall into a trap of trying to live up to society's standards. We try to look good for other people. We play at popularity games and try to impress others with our position and prestige. This is sad, because who we should really be trying to please is God. He has created each of us with special gifts and talents, and it is His will that we do nothing more than live up to the potential He created for us. We don't have to try to be something we're not with God. He knows us better than we know ourselves. What is important for us to do is find out who we really are and try to remain true to that identity. God loves us just as we are, and as long as we believe that God knows what He is doing, then we can be satisfied with ourselves as He created us.

PRAYER: Lord, help me to realize my potential. Make me less a person-pleaser, and more a God-pleaser. Grant that I might discover my gifts and talents, then assist me to use them as you would have them used. Amen.

February 1

Honor the Lord with thy substance, and with the first fruits of all thine increase: so shall thy barns be filled with plenty, and thy presses shall burst out with new wine. (3:9-10).

Two men stood at the gate of a great city. While they waited, a poor woman came to them asking for a few coins with which she could buy bread for her children. The first man scowled at the woman and said, "I work hard for my money. I give of my own time, and my own labor. I earn what I reap. Go and do the same for yourself and your family!" The woman began to walk away, but the other man followed after her and said, "Poor woman, take this money, for it is not really mine. I do work hard for it, but it is by God's grace that I have it at all. He gave me the talents I possess, He gave me my strength and knowledge, and He has given to us all the lives we have to live. If I gave to you, I simply give to God what He has provided."

It is good to remember that without God we would not possess the things we do. All things come to us from God, and it is good that we share them. Jesus told the people that whenever they came to the aid of another person in need, they were in fact aiding Him. True prosperity comes only when we learn to give to others as freely as God gives to us.

PRAYER: Oh Father, soften my heart to those who are less fortunate than I am. Help me to appreciate the blessings I have been given, and to share from my abundance. Fill me with the new wine, which is your Spirit. Amen.

February 2

My son, despise not the chastening of the Lord; neither be weary of his correction: for whom the Lord loveth he correcteth; even as a father the son in whom he delighteth (3:11-12).

A college youth moved to a new town and began attending a large Eastern university. The boy had been an outstanding high school basketball star, and so he anxiously awaited try-outs for the college team. On the first day of try-outs the young man was astounded at how tough and mean the coach was. The young man made the team and experienced the most strenuous training of his career. Hour after hour he was drilled by the coach, and whenever he made an error the coach was right there to make him correct it. The team played exceptionally well, and went to the NCAA championships. Though the young man didn't care much for the way the coach treated the players, he had to admit that the coach got great results.

It is rarely easy to accept criticism and correction, and yet it is important that we heed the word of those wiser than ourselves in order to grow and improve. Often the words we heed may seem harsh or unfair, but if they are offered out of love and concern, then they may turn into the sweetest sounds we ever hear.

PRAYER: Lord, let me hear the instructions you know I should hear. Tell me what I must do to grow, and give me the acceptance to deal with those things I would rather avoid. Spare not the rod, but do what You know is best for me. Amen.

February 3

Happy is the man that findeth wisdom, and the man that getteth understanding: for the merchandise of it is better than the merchandise of silver, and the gain thereof than fine gold (3:13-14).

There was a man who genuinely had a "Midas touch." Everything he ever tried was a great success. He had a wonderful job which gave him fulfillment, and he spent long hours working. He was obsessed by the challenge of taking what he had and turning it into more. He amassed enormous wealth and spent all his free time working on investment schemes and plans for gaining still more. He was perfectly happy living life this way, until one day he found he had a terminal condition, and no amount of money could do anything to save him. The man had never faced adversity in his life and he was unused to failure. His whole world collapsed.

How sad it is when we build our world on material possessions rather than the possessions of the heart. The greatest thing we can ever hope to hold is the love and understanding of God. This is the greatest treasure possible. It is tempting to pursue the glitter of gold and silver, but more importantly we should seek after God. In Him our every need will be met, and should adversity befall us, we will always have what it takes to cope with it.

PRAYER: You are the only true treasure, Almighty God. In your love there is no need, no want. Fill me with the true treasure of your Spirit. Help me to know you in all ways. Amen.

February 4

She is more precious than rubies: and all the things thou canst desire are not to be compared unto her (3:15).

A young woman struggled for years to get a management position with a large corporation. She put out excellent work and finally it paid off. She began to travel and new opportunities opened up for her. Everything seemed to be going the way she always dreamed it might. Her success appeared to be complete.

Then she found out that the corporation was involved in some illegal activities. As time passed she realized that the business was deeply involved in terrible acts of cruelty and unethical practices. The young woman had always been a Christian and she was doubly sensitive to the wrongful acts. Faced with such revelations of the corporation's illegal dealings, she found herself with no alternative but to quit.

It is refreshing to know that some people still take their moral values seriously enough to let them rule their lives. It would have been simple for the woman to look the other way and pretend she didn't know what was happening. Instead, she let her heart, governed by the truth of Christ, be her guide. A right relationship with God will always be worth more than personal gain. No greater treasure can be found.

PRAYER: Lord, I so often pursue selfish goals. Help me to remember that nothing in life has value if I do not have a good relationship with you. Be with me, I pray. Amen.

February 5

Length of days is in her right hand; and in her left hand riches and honor (3:16).

Wisdom — the knowledge of God — is a gift from God. He gives it to all people who come to Him seeking true understanding. He will not deny it to anyone, but He will give it in small enough portions to enable the individual to make sense of it. As a person comes to know God better, he or she will avoid those activities which are self-destructive and unprofitable. The person receives a deeper appreciation of the wonder of God in the world. Life becomes more meaningful and the person gains a new understanding of what it means to be a success.

Life is a privilege which God wants us to value. When we turn from Him and pursue our own selfish desires, we lose sight of the sacredness of His gift. We may think that we can find fulfillment in life on our own, but it is through God and God alone that we can come to know the wonder of life most fully. God is the author of life, and He will bless us with its richness if we will only let Him. A full and happy life, rich in meaning and honorable in all ways, is the prize of any believer who will keep God centered in his or her life.

PRAYER: Help me to see the beauty and wonder of this life you have given to me, O Lord. Open my eyes so that I might come to know the richness and fullness you intend my life to have. Grant me this, I pray. Amen.

February 6

She is a tree of life to them that lay hold upon her: and happy is every one that retaineth her (3:18).

In the Garden of Eden stood two trees: the Tree of the Knowledge of Good and Evil and the Tree of Life. There were other trees, but these were the two most important. God forbade Adam and Eve to eat from the Tree of Knowledge, but they disobeyed and ate from it anyway. The story goes that Adam and Eve were exiled from the Garden due to their disobedience. Was it for punishment that God made Adam and Eve leave the Garden, or was it mercy?

God doesn't want any of us to suffer, especially eternally. His action with Adam and Eve made it impossible for them to eat from the Tree of eternal Life, thus insuring that they could not live forever in their fallen state. In His infinite love, God provided us with another way. He gave us a new Tree of Life, His Son Jesus Christ.

Christ died to undo the harm done by Adam and Eve's disobedience. Once He reconciled us to God, God invited us to once more share in the fruit of the Tree of Life. Through Christ, we have the promise of eternity in God's heavenly home. It is with this promise that we truly attain wisdom.

PRAYER: Thank you, O Lord, for giving me the chance to have eternal life. Through your love in the life, death and resurrection of your Son, Jesus Christ, I have come to know your glory. Amen.

February 7

The Lord by wisdom hath founded the earth; by under-standing hath he established the heavens. By his knowledge the depths are broken up, and the clouds drop down the dew (3:19-20).

The word "miracle" sounds strange in this day and age. We have become too sophisticated to accept miracles anymore. It is sad that we have lost such a wonderful idea. A miracle used to be an event which was beyond simple explanation and understanding. Many people say that miracles don't happen anymore, if they ever did.

If only people would open their hearts and begin looking more deeply than they are able with their eyes alone. When we see a beautiful sunset, it affects more than just our eyes. When we ponder the wonder of human life at birth, we are experiencing much more than a mere sensory event. The nighttime sky, the pounding surf of the ocean, the laughter of a child: all of these are miracles in a sense, and all of them are evidence of the wonder of God. It is a special joy to see the world with eyes open to miracles, and to feel life with a heart attuned to God's love. If we understand God, then we must believe in His miracles.

PRAYER: Make me a believer, Lord. Show me the multitude of miracles you have created and are creating. Let me understand creation the way you intended it. Amen.

February 8

My son, let not them depart from thine eyes: keep sound wisdom and discretion: so shall they be life unto thy soul, and grace to thy neck. Then shalt thou walk in thy way safely, and thy foot shall not stumble (3:21-23).

A businesswoman impressed everyone she met with her poise and confidence. Whenever there was an important decision to be made, she didn't even hesitate. Her co-workers came to her for her advice and counsel. She built a reputation for her calm manner and smooth, level head. She instilled trust in everyone she met.

Once she was asked why she was so sure of herself. Her reply? "I grew up being taught to trust. I trust that God is always with me, and knowing that, I can trust that He will help me make good choices. Even though I might make mistakes, I trust that God will always bring good from them."

This is the kind of faith God wants us all to have. Life is less of a burden when we realize that God will be there to bring good from every situation. God is unchanging. His good works continue today and forever. Trust in the knowledge that God will never leave. He is with us in all things.

PRAYER: Help me to believe, to trust, to know. Cast away my doubts, and reassure me that no matter what might happen, you will always be with me. Stand beside me as I grow in faith, and grant me your peace. Amen.

February 9

My son, let them not depart from thine eyes: keep sound wisdom and discretion: When thou liest down, thou shalt not be afraid: yea, thou shalt lie down, and thy sleep shall be sweet (3:21, 24).

A doctor had been practicing medicine for a number of years, when he found that he couldn't sleep at night. After a long successful career, the doctor suddenly felt that his work was futile and senseless. As hard as he tried, he could not save everyone he treated. Many of the people he treated never got any better. His early dreams of healing those who were in pain and suffered began to fail. Night after night he tossed and turned, struggling to make peace with what he felt was failure.

An understanding of God, and what God wants from us as his children, can help us to have calm nights. No human being can take responsibility for life and death. God gave life, and He is the ruler of all life. For some people, God has chosen to allow them to assist in the healing process. He has given men and women the minds and talents to save and sustain life, yet it is always God who ultimately makes the decision of who will live and who will die. Our responsibility is to use our gifts and talents to the best of our abilities. If we will try to do so, we can count on God's richest blessing.

PRAYER: Help me, Father, to utilize the wonderful gifts and graces that you have seen fit to grant me. Bless me as I attempt to be the best person I can be, the person you made me to be. Amen.

February 10

Be not afraid of sudden fear, neither of the desolation of the wicked, when it cometh. For the Lord shall be thy confidence, and shall keep thy foot from being taken (3:25-26).

A teacher returned to her classroom to find chaos had broken out. Paper, pencils and erasers were flying through the air, pictures were drawn on the blackboards and walls, children were running all around the room, and the noise was deafening. One little girl sat quietly in the back corner, refusing to enter into the mischief. As the teacher began to scold the class, she remembered the little girl who was well-behaved. After class, she pulled the young child aside and told her how much it meant to her that she had remained silent and obedient.

Often we feel as though our good acts are missed. When we don't receive credit and acclaim, we feel cheated. What we need to remember is that none of our actions go unnoticed by God. He sees our every move, and he applauds us when we refuse to do those things that we know we should not, but that our society seems to approve of. Our reward will never come from this life, but from the life that awaits us with our heavenly Father. His blessing is ever with us if we will only be patient and believe.

PRAYER: Father, often I feel as though my good behavior is ignored or forgotten. Forgive me for being prideful, and help me to know that you see me at both my best and worst, and love me all the time. Amen.

February 11

Withhold not good from them to whom it is due, when it is in the power of thine hand to do it. Say not unto thy neighbor, Go, and come again, and tomorrow I will give; when thou hast it by thee (3:27-28).

Recently I had a flat tire while I was on a busy interstate. I tried to flag down passing cars, hoping for some assistance. Hundreds of cars passed without even slowing down. I began to think of all the times I had passed motorists in distress and I didn't have the time or the inclination to help them. I felt a little guilty, and it made me much more understanding of those who whizzed past. It also made me much more appreciative of the help when it came.

We are given so many opportunities to help other people in need in our lives. It is important that we reach out and take hold of those chances. Jesus said that every time we help any person in need, it is as if we have done it for Christ Himself. It is easy to decide whether or not we would help Christ. Should it be any more difficult to decide whether or not we should help other of God's children, especially when Christ equated them to Himself? If we have the means to help those in need, there really is no choice. We are called to serve others as Christ was willing to serve us. We must do this whenever we see the opportunity.

PRAYER: Lord, so often I turn my head from those in need. Open my eyes and my heart that I might reach out to them, to extend the hand of Christ to those who themselves are Christ. Amen.

February 12

Devise not evil against thy neighbor, seeing he dwelleth securely by thee (3:29).

"Who is my neighbor?" It is a question that we ask ourselves all the time. Christ calls us to love our neighbor as we love ourselves. Though this sounds easy, it doesn't take long to discover that it is not. Not all of our "neighbors" are lovable people. Is the man who commits murder our neighbor? Is the man who deals drugs or the youth who takes them? Are the people who persecute us our neighbors? Christ's answer to all of these questions would be, "yes!"

If another person does wrong, then God will ultimately judge that person accordingly. We do not have that right. God is interested in our ability to become like Him. Christ gave us a model to follow, and He loved some of the most unlovable characters of His day. We need to do likewise. If we rely on our own powers to love the unlovable we will fail miserably, but with the love of Christ centered deeply in our hearts, we will be able to love even our enemies.

PRAYER: God, help me to learn love for all people. Let me give of myself and sacrifice my own pride in order to serve other people. Your love is the greatest force on earth. With your help I can come to know unconditional love, and I can come to be able to give it away. Fill me, Father, with a caring that will never end. I pray this in Christ's most holy name. Amen.

February 13

Strive not with a man without cause, if he have done thee no harm (3:30).

There was a man in my church who argued about everything. If something was said from the pulpit that he disagreed with, he could hardly wait until the pastor was at the back door so he could tell him. At committee meetings he would share his view whether it was constructive or not. People began to dread having him around, and many people did everything they could to avoid him. Finally, a woman from the church could stand it no more. She spoke to the man, kindly, and told him that he was alienating other members of the congregation. To his credit, the man tried to stop being so argumentative, and he worked at being more positive.

Senseless argument and criticism is destructive. It makes people uncomfortable. It also divides people so that they cannot communicate with each other. There is never anything to be gained by causing tension with other people without cause. There is enough argument and strife in the world without Christians adding to it senselessly. It is not enough that Christians try to do good. It is also vital that they always strive to do no harm.

PRAYER: O Lord, guide me as I try to live a good and righteous life. Help me to both do good to those around me, and guard me that I do no harm. I want so much to do what I should. With your help I will. Amen.

February 14

Envy thou not the oppressor, and choose none of his ways (3:31).

A young Mexican immigrant worked in a midwestern tomato plantation for meager wages. His foreman was a hard man who drove his workers to the point of exhaustion. The young man worked diligently, saving every cent he made, vowing that he would become successful and powerful. Daily he saw the foreman sit in the shade with a cool drink, and he dreamed of a day when he too could bask in the shade while others labored in the hot sun. After many years his dream came true. He rose in favor with the plantation owners, and he was put in charge of some of the fields. He tried to be hard and stern, and to lounge in the shade drinking cool drinks, but he found he was unhappy. No one liked or respected him, and he felt guilty because he knew how hard the laborers worked. He attained his dream, but found nothing in it but emptiness.

There is nothing to be gained by envying those who are in places of authority over us. We may find that we are mistreated, but it is far better to endure minor suffering rather than do that which is displeasing to God. God wants us to choose not to follow the ways of the oppressor, but in all things to choose Him.

PRAYER: Father, please help me to walk in the way of the humble and meek. Keep me from straying into pride and envy. Help me to see the blessings I have been given, rather than long for the things I must do without. Amen.

February 15

For the froward is abomination to the Lord: but his secret is with the righteous (3:32).

There is something exciting and pleasing about being in on a secret. When we are told secrets, it shows that we are trusted and esteemed. It makes us special. It sets us apart. God has made us privy to a very special secret. We have been given information which can change our lives. That secret is simple, yet powerful. God is love, and with Him all things are possible.

This doesn't seem like much of a secret, but it is amazing how many people act as though they are not in on it. For those people who devote themselves to loving and following God, this secret is the greatest joy of their lives. For those who don't know it, it comes as the greatest disappointment and torment when it is revealed. God offers this secret to all people, and it is the obligation of everyone who knows it to share it with as many other people as they can. The secret that God gives to the righteous is a secret that He wants the whole world to share. The greatest desire of God is a day when the secret the righteous share will no longer be a secret. It will be a truth that is known by all.

PRAYER: Lord grant that I might always and everywhere share the blessed secret of your love with everyone I meet. Make me a true disciple of yours, spreading your love and gospel throughout my world. Amen.

February 16

The curse of the Lord is in the house of the wicked: but he blesseth the habitation of the just (3:33).

I have had the pleasure of knowing one of the most faithful families around. The entire family is an inspiration. The mother and father are two of the most loving, caring, devoted people I know, and their two teenage daughters possess a powerful faith and charming personalities. Their home is a haven of peace and comfort. They are always entertaining company, because all who enter their home feel the special warmth and joy.

The family is quick to acknowledge that their love and unity comes from one source and one source only. They are bound together through the love of Christ. In homes where Christ is king and ruler, it is easy to feel God's blessing. There is no conflict or problem that can upset the blessing that God puts upon a faithful household. There is a special peace which God offers to those people who draw upon His love in order to share it with others. Before we can hope to spread the love of God in our own private worlds, we must first learn to spread it in our own homes, with our own families. It is often harder to keep peace and care with those closest to us, but with God's help it can be the most blessed peace of all.

PRAYER: Come, O Lord, to be the head of my household, and the unifier in my family. Let my home be a haven of comfort and joy. Let my love for those closest to me be the special love that you alone can give. Amen.

February 17

The wise shall inherit glory: but shame shall be the promotion of fools (3:35).

A young minister was involved in a dozen programs in his community. Each one of them was well publicized and brought him honor and acclaim. As his reputation grew within his community, his congregation grew annoyed at the lack of time he spent with church affairs. The church members felt that his first responsibility was with them, and as time passed they lost their faith in him. Before long, they asked him to leave the church. His successor was a faithful man who served well in both the church and the community. He never looked for acclaim or recognition, but his fine work spoke for itself. He was well loved and highly respected all of his days.

The truly faithful person doesn't have to go seeking acclaim. It will come to them simply because of the commitment they exhibit. When we pursue recognition, we open ourselves to failure and disgrace. It is better to focus on the work that we need to do, rather than the credit we will receive for doing it. Christ never looked for personal acclaim, but all He did was for the glory of God. As committed Christians, it is important that we also learn to live our lives not for ourselves, but always to the glory of God.

PRAYER: Destroy in me, O Lord, the desire to do things which make me look good. Rather, let me do things to your glory. Help me to be the person you want me to be, not selfish or vain, but more like Christ in every way. Amen.

February 18

Hear, ye children, the instruction of a father, and attend to know understanding (4:1).

Young people are so anxious to begin making their own decisions. When it comes to staying out late, how to dress, what to eat, who to associate with, teenagers want their independence. Learning to make these choices is a part of growing up and maturing, but it takes time to learn to make wise choices. It also takes help. Though young people often resist the guidance and advice of their parents, there is much to be learned from adults who have lived through many of the situations they will face.

We are often just like children when it comes to the instruction of our heavenly Father. There is no situation that He does not know all about, yet we often resist His instruction or ignore His guidance. It is the wise person who learns to take sound advice. As we grow in our faith in God, we also grow in our ability to accept His instruction. It is only as we grow older that we begin to appreciate the decisions our parents made in our behalf as we were growing up. It is also true that we fully appreciate the rules that God has made for us when we mature spiritually.

PRAYER: Dear God, at times I act like a child in my faith. Help me to receive your instruction with an open heart and mind. Grant me the wisdom to know that you are always trying to help me grow and to keep me on the path that I should follow. Amen.

February 19

He taught me also, and said unto me, Let thine heart retain my words: keep my commandments, and live (4:4).

A little girl was told by her parents, "Stay away from the road." Almost every day, the instructions were the same. The little girl obeyed the command, but occasionally she forgot when her ball rolled onto the street, or when she was running with her friends. One day, while the young girl was playing near the road, she saw a puppy run into the street just as a car went speeding past. The car squealed to a halt, but not before it struck the puppy. The little girl watched in awe, and suddenly her parents' instructions made perfect sense to her.

It is sad that all too often we demand proof before we will believe someone else. We want to know why we should obey rules, rather than follow them simply on faith. God has given us a number of commandments to follow. There is no need to question them, especially if we honestly believe that everything God does is for our good. God gives us commandments to insure that we can live, and live fully and happily. It is through faith in God and trust in His love that we come to enjoy life the way God planned it to be.

PRAYER: You have devised such a wonderful plan for life, Almighty God. Lead me in wisdom so that I might come to understand it better, and remain true to all of your commandments. With your help I will be able to hold fast to your Word, and live. Amen.

February 20

Forsake her not, and she shall preserve thee: love her, and she shall keep thee (4:6).

An older friend of mine always lived by the rule, "Let your conscience be your guide." Whenever he was faced by a tough decision, he said, "I stop thinking and I start feeling." For this wise old gentleman, wisdom came from listening not so much to his mind, but more to his heart. He always told me that he knew deep inside whether or not he was making a good choice. Whenever he tried to do what he knew wasn't right, a feeling crept over him, and he could not rest easily until he did what was right.

Truly, God has given us a conscience, a "still small voice," an inner wisdom which guides us and comforts us when we remain true to its instruction. When we choose to ignore the wisdom of our conscience, we face feelings of guilt and anxiety. When we pay close attention to the wisdom of our heart we find that there is special comfort. Doing what we know to be right offers not only freedom from guilt, but also a joy which comes forth from our soul. Christ rejoices each time we open ourselves to the guidance of the Holy Spirit in our lives. Often God speaks to us through our consciences. If we will listen, God will preserve and keep us.

PRAYER: O heavenly Father, I reach out to your guidance and will. Fill me with a special wisdom so that I might always choose to follow the right path. Shine your light before me so that I will never stray. Amen.

February 21

Wisdom is the principal thing; therefore get wisdom: and with all thy getting get understanding (4:7).

There are a lot of wonderful things on this earth that God has given us to enjoy. We live in a beautiful world full of glorious trees, breath-taking mountains, immense oceans, fabulous sunsets, and on and on. Nature is splendid. Bright, sunny mornings with the birds singing and the dew sparkling on the grass are truly a gift of God. It is when we look at the world through the eyes of God that we come to appreciate just how special it is.

Real wisdom is the knowledge of God and all His handiworks. We have been given life so that we may enjoy it. It is a gift from God. When we pursue God, and a deeper knowledge of His will, we are seeking a deeper understanding of all creation. There is nothing greater that anyone can desire than to see this world of ours through the eyes of the creator. In God's creation we can catch glimpses of God Himself. In prayer we need to remember to ask God to help us become wise as He is wise, and in so doing we will see beauty like we never knew it existed before, and we will appreciate life in a new and full way.

PRAYER: O Lord, I want to learn to enjoy life as fully as I can. Open my eyes to see anew, with the eyes of your divine Love. Through your wisdom I can hope to come to know the fulness of life and beauty of your creation. I praise you in your greatness, O Father. Amen.

February 22

Hear, O my son, and receive my sayings; and the years of thy life shall be many. I have taught thee in the ways of wisdom; I have led thee in right paths (4:10-11).

Many times I have heard parents lament, "What have I done wrong?" Parents are all too willing to take the blame when their children make poor choices or get themselves into trouble. Parents want so much for their children to succeed and have pleasant, carefree lives. That is why there is special joy in seeing children succeed. Mothers and fathers can feel pride and take some credit for their children when they do well. It is an honor to the parents of children who succeed, that they have done a good job of bringing them up. When parents take interest in their children and treat them with respect and care, they are giving them as great a gift as is possible. Those children who come from families where they are supposed to have the greatest chance of living good lives when they are grown.

Our heavenly Father has tried to instruct us in the ways that lead to eternal life. He has allowed us to make our own choices, though, and we must take responsibility for them, bad or good. It is His greatest wish that we follow the wisdom of His will. When we do so, it is to His glory as well as ours, that we have learned well. By listening to our heavenly Father, our lives are enriched and the years of our lives will be multiplied.

PRAYER: O God, you have been such a loving Father. Forgive me that I have often ignored the instructions you have given me for my sake. Help me to follow your will and remain steadfast in my commitment to you. Amen.

February 23

Take fast hold of instruction; let her not go: keep her; for she is the life. (4:13).

A lineman for a power and light company was put in charge of training new employees. He took them out and showed them each procedure; taking time to cover each step carefully. No one got past this trainer without thorough drilling and practice. One day a young man came to the lineman for training. During the instruction the young man got distracted and stopped paying attention. The lineman abruptly stopped talking, grabbed the young man by the collar, and said, "You'd better learn to pay attention now, because if you let your mind wander while you work on a live wire, it will be the last time. You won't get a second chance."

Not all instructions are matters of life and death, but the instructions of God are given in order to keep us safe and happy. By following the rules set down by God, we can rest assured that our well being is in His mind. When we speak of the instruction of God, it truly is a matter of life and death. Our eternal life is dependent on whether or not we learn to follow the guidance of God's spirit and try to follow His will all the days of our life. With His help, we may hope to hold fast to His commandments and His promise of life everlasting.

PRAYER: Father, help me to listen carefully with both my heart and head. Fill me with your spirit, that I might know your will. Once I have received your instruction, help me to keep it in my mind, that I might live life fully. Amen.

February 24

Enter not into the path of the wicked, and go not in the way of evil men. Avoid it, pass not by it, turn from it, and pass away (4:14-15).

There are plants in nature which are lovely to look at, but they are deadly. There are animals which seem harmless and even attractive which are dangerous. In life there are many things which seem appealing, yet they have hidden traps. Sin is a lot like that. Most sins are attractive and tempting. We find ourselves desiring things which could possibly harm us. Often we are lured by things which we know will hurt us, but we want them badly enough to take the risk.

It doesn't make sense that we would do things which we know will harm us. The wages of sin is death, and yet it seems that we pursue sin believing that its wages are the finest reward we could possibly attain. A wise person avoids life threatening situations at any cost. That is what we should do as Christians. We should do everything in our power to avoid sin, which should be as odious to us as death itself. It is not enough to try not to sin, but we should do anything in our power to avoid it, turn from it, move as far away from it as possible and leave it as far behind as can be. It is by a conscious effort that we avoid sin, just as it is by choice that we do good.

PRAYER: May I choose the right path, Almighty God, turning from what I know you would not have me do in order to pursue what is fitting in your sight. Guide me through the power of your Holy Spirit. Amen.

February 25

For they sleep not, except they have done mischief; and their sleep is taken away, unless they cause some to fall. For they eat the bread of wickedness, and drink the wine of violence (4:16-17).

A convicted murderer was interviewed recently. The commentator asked the man whether he was sorry for what he had done. The murderer laughed and said, "Why should I be sorry? I wanted to kill the sucker and I did. I've killed other people before, and I guess I'll do it again if I feel like it." Words like that shock the sensibilities and make you wonder what the world is coming to. As Christians, though, we know that evil is real and that it exists in our world. Jesus said that Satan was the Lord of this world, and all it takes is a quick look around to realize that He was right. There are people who enjoy doing mischief and evil. There are hateful individuals who are not happy unless they cause pain and grief.

There is a wonderful assurance for those who choose to follow Christ, and that is that the wicked of this world who seem to so often have the upper hand will be the big losers in the end times. God honors those who hold fast to His laws and love Him with all their heart, mind and soul. Those who scorn Him now will find no solace later. Their bread and wine of wickedness and violence will sour before the bread and wine of life in the Spirit.

PRAYER: Father, we pray for those who have turned from you and choose to do what is evil in your sight. Let their victories pass away, and the victory of Christ shine forth in all its glory, now and forever. Amen.

February 26

But the path of the just is as the shining light, that shineth more and more unto the perfect day (4:18).

A young woman worked at a factory which was about ten blocks from where she lived. She could walk to work, but to do so she had to cross a railroad bridge which was treacherous going when the sun began to set. During the Winter months it was doubly dangerous due to slippery conditions as well as darkness. The woman would have avoided the crossing altogether had it not been for the crossing guard. Each evening as the woman approached the crossing, the guard waved a lantern to signal that he awaited. Using the powerful light, he would lead the woman by the hand across the bridge. Throughout her life the woman never forgot the kindness and help of the older crossing guard.

The lives of those people who are touched by the love of Christ are like guiding lights to others who have yet to find Christ in their lives. They can provide guidance and help, and they shine forth as bright examples of how good life can be. God's light can shine through us if we will only let it. We have the opportunity to show others the difference that Christ can make. When we live life empowered by the light of God, we live as He wishes we would.

PRAYER: Father, please make me a light for my world. Let me shine forth with your goodness, care and love. Let all who look to me see your grace. Help me to magnify the saving light of Christ which you have lovingly given me. Amen.

February 27

The way of the wicked is as darkness: they know not at what they stumble (4:19).

In the early thirties, a gang of robbers planned to rob a midwestern bank. They laid out a nearly perfect plan, breaking into the bank late at night and laying out a complex escape route through back alleys and darkened lots. The day of the robbery came and the initial phases went perfectly. As the alarms pierced the quiet midwestern night, the three men ran off into the cover of darkness. In the darkness and the confusion that followed, the police lost the robbers and assumed they got away. Early the next morning it was discovered that the three men had gotten sidetracked, fell into a water-filled ravine, and were drowned.

Not all individuals who plot evil come to the same end, at least, not in this life. But we can rely on the word of God that those who do wrong are kidding themselves and that one day they will have to answer for the evil they have been responsible for. What they have done in the dark will be revealed in the light of Christ, and that will be their downfall. Christ will one day judge the unjust, and it will come as a surprise to them when they find that they have turned away from salvation. The darkness they live in will seem doubly dark on that day.

PRAYER: I thank thee, Father, that you have ended the darkness of unending night in my life. You have burst forth in the brightest light, and in that light there is no darkness at all. May your light shine brightly in my life always. Amen.

February 28

Keep thy heart with all diligence; for out of it are the issues of life (4:23).

Jesus said, "Where your treasure is, there will your heart be also. (Matt. 6:21) What we feel and believe are the truly precious and meaningful things in our lives. If we don't commit ourselves to what is good and right, then we are empty. Moral poverty occurs when we place things above relationships. Christ sent his disciples out into the world without possessions, but no one in history has known more wealth than those chosen men who walked with Jesus. It is when we choose to walk with Jesus that we can find out what true riches are.

In today's world, it is easy to get distracted by so many things. Lifestyles are presented in magazines and on television that seem so appealing. The "good life" requires money, good looks, nice clothes, and the right car, the right house, the right mate. At least, that's what we're supposed to believe. But it is only when we can free ourselves from the pursuit of such things that we can begin to enjoy life the way God intended it. Money cannot buy happiness, nor can it bring us life. Christ brings us life, and He brings it most abundantly. He is the real treasure, and as long as our hearts remain with Him, our lives will truly be rich.

PRAYER: Dear Father, forgive me when I lose sight of what is really important in life. Help me to keep my eyes focussed on your truth. Enable me to show others that you are the real treasure in life. Amen.

February 29

Put away from thee a froward mouth, and perverse lips put far from thee (4:24).

A young retarded boy ran away from home, throwing his parents into a panic. When the police finally found him and returned him to his home, his mother asked him why he had run away. Tearfully, he responded that other children on the block continually made fun of him. He was unable to deal with their cruel taunting and so he fled.

Too few people realize the power of words. There is both power to hurt and power to heal. In the same way that cruel words can tear down, kind words can build up. Often we feel powerless to do much to help those around us, but one power we do have is to be kind. It is amazing what a smile and a friendly word can do. There is so much unhappiness in the world, and it often seems like there is very little that we can do to fight it. But it is not the large things which ultimately make the difference. It is the small things. The kind hello. The sincere compliment. Things which cost us nothing, but mean so much. It is the responsibility of every Christian to watch the things they say, avoiding unkind or coarse words, and trying always to choose kind and uplifting words.

PRAYER: Fill my mouth with only words of kindness and love. Bless my lips with praise and singing. Protect me from any unkindness I might inflict on another person. Help me to treat others as you would treat them. Amen.

March 1

Let thine eyes look right on, and let thine eyelids look straight before thee (4:25).

When I was in high school I was quite a runner. Day after day I would train, running seventeen miles in the morning and seventeen miles at night. I ate all of the proper foods, took good care of myself, got plenty of rest, and I followed the instructions of my coaches. One of the most important instructions they ever gave me was: when you're in the race, keep your head straight and look forward. Never turn your head. If you do, you'll break your stride and it could cost you the race. I saw it happen time and time again. Runners would just cast a quick glance over their shoulder to see where the other runners were, and that was all it took. They would stumble, lose concentration, and the other runners would catch up and pass.

The rule is one that we should, as Christians, learn to follow. As long as we keep our eyes on Jesus, we will do fine. It is when we are distracted, when we lose sight of God in our lives that we get ourselves into trouble. The rule is a simple one, but an important one: Let thine eyes look right on ... right on Jesus Christ our Lord.

PRAYER: Keep my sight straight, Almighty God. Let me see only You in my life. Make me aware of your presence every day, and never let me turn my eyes from you. Be the vision of my life. Amen.

March 2

Ponder the path of thy feet, and let all thy ways be established (4:26).

A young sales representative was sent to a new area and found that he had terrible difficulties finding the locations of many of his clients. His home office began to receive complaints that the young man was showing up late, and in some cases not at all. An older, wiser sales representative traveled out to visit the young man. Upon arriving, he was shocked to find that the young man had not even invested in a map. All the time he had spent driving from place to place had been done blindly. The older man purchased maps of the sales area and sat the younger salesman down to chart out the locations of his clients.

Many people go through life without a thought about where they are heading. They live one day at a time, waiting for life to happen to them rather than planning how they might make their lives more meaningful. It is good when we are flexible enough to deal with the curves that we're thrown in life, but it is also prudent for us to make the best use of our time while we are here. God gave us our lives to enjoy and make good with. It is for His sake that we should always strive to live the best way we can.

PRAYER: Dear Heavenly Father, help me to do the best I can as I live my life. Make me watchful that I not waste the precious time that you have given me. Amen.

March 3

Turn not to the right hand nor to the left: remove thy foot from evil (4:27).

When recently traveling to my sister's house, I found myself hopelessly lost. She had given me good directions, telling me to stay on a highway until I came to a certain traffic light. I drove down the highway for what seemed like hours. As the miles passed, I began to doubt whether or not my sister had given me the right directions. The doubts grew and grew, until finally I decided to turn off. I headed in the general direction I thought my sister would be, and that was how I got myself lost. As it turned out, I was only a few minutes from the proper light, but because of my doubts, I was led to make a bad decision.

Many times in our lives we will find ourselves in situations where we grow impatient or doubtful. It is during those times that it is most important to hold fast to the promises of God. God is always there, and He knows what is best for us in every situation. It is vital that we not turn to the right or left, but stay steadfastly on the path that leads to God. If we will learn to do that, then the blessings of God will be ours in all circumstances.

PRAYER: Almighty God, forgive me when I doubt your will and guidance. Help me to always have the faith I need to trust and obey. Make me constant in my belief in you. Amen.

March 4

For the lips of a strange woman drop as a honeycomb, and her mouth is smoother than oil: but her end is bitter as wormwood, sharp as a two-edged sword (5:3-4).

It is interesting that we often think of sin as evil. It makes little sense to believe that something evil would be able to tempt us. Rather, it is the seemingly good things which cause us to sin. The saying goes, "It is easier to attract flies with honey than with vinegar." Often sin has nothing to do with evil things, but merely with too much of a good thing. Still, the end result is the same. Sin is sin, and there is no place for sin in the life of a Christian.

Gluttony is one of the most unattractive traits a person can have. Christians should be sensitive to the need that exists in our world. It should be impossible for the Christian to selfishly hoard possessions when God calls on us to share from our abundance. Those things which entice us by their glamour and glitter are false gods. They cause us to pervert our faith and lead us from the true path of Christ. The wages of sin is death, but the turning from sin is the road which leads to life everlasting. With God's help we are able to resist every temptation, no matter how inviting it might be.

PRAYER: So often I find myself tempted to do those things I know that I should not. Please help me, Father, to resist the temptations that come my way. Let me share what I have and avoid the things I really don't need. Amen.

March 5

Her feet go down to death; her steps take hold on hell. Lest thou shouldst ponder the path of life, her ways are movable, that thou canst not know them (5:5-6).

A young woman found the stresses and strains of day to day life to be too much for her. She sought out a psychiatrist who saw her three times a week. During her therapy, the doctor began to talk to her about her connection with the church. The doctor told her that church was a crutch and that only weak people needed to go there. The young woman was instructed to stay away from the church and give up her dependence on empty religion. The woman took her doctor's advice and quit the church. In the months that followed, the young woman's problems increased until she left even her psychiatrist in deep despair.

The world, which is the stomping ground of the devil, is quick to turn us away from God, offering a hundred other fales gods in His place. When we lose God, we've lost everything. We need to beware of people who try to turn our faith from God to other things. Only God can give us the help and support we need to deal with the regular pressures of life. There is no other way, for it is only with God that all things are possible.

PRAYER: There is no answer apart from you, Almighty God. In every situation, both good and bad, you are the strength and the hope. You are every good thing. Be with me in everything I do. Amen.

March 6

Hear me now therefore, O ye children, and depart not from the words of my mouth. Lest thou give thine honor unto others, and thy years unto the cruel (5:7, 9).

Whether we know it or not, we are being watched. Whenever we claim to be something, people will watch us to see whether or not we live up to our claims. Athletes are judged by their performances. Investors are valued for their ability to make big money. Policemen are judged by their abilities to perform well under fire. What is it that Christians are judged for?

When we call ourselves Christians we are claiming to be mirror images of Christ for all the world to see. We are presenting ourselves as examples of what God had in mind when he put men and women on this earth. It is a presumptuous claim we make, and one that carries with it a great amount of responsibility. One of the greatest sins we can ever commit is to call ourselves Christians, then act in ways which are unacceptable in the sight of the Lord. We must continually study the word of God, and follow all of the instructions that God has given to us. We must devote ourselves to imitating Christ in all ways possible. When we fail to do so, we bring dishonor not only on ourselves, but on the entire Christian church.

PRAYER: I pray that I might learn to walk carefully in the steps of Jesus Christ, Almighty Father. Grant that I might be an honor to your truth in all ways. Be with me to shine your light through my life that others may see your greatness. Amen.

March 7

Hear me now therefore, O ye children, and depart not from the words of my mouth. Lest strangers be filled with thy wealth; and thy labors be in the house of a stranger (5:7,10).

The sign nailed to the tree said "No Trespassing." The red letters stood out for yards in every direction. But that didn't stop the young boys from climbing the fence in order to reach the apples that grew on the trees on the other side. One day, a small boy slipped while he was climbing the apple tree, and he fell onto a pile of sharp branches, cutting himself badly, and breaking his ankle. Alone and afraid, the young boy lay crying for hours amidst the tumble of sticks. Finally, the owner of the property happened by. He came out and lifted the boy from the branches. The child was afraid of the wrath of the farmer who had posted such ominous signs, but the old gentleman merely smiled at the boy and said, "I didn't put the signs up to be mean. I put them there to try to keep things like this from happening. It was kindness which caused me to want to protect little boys just like you."

Our loving heavenly Father gives us rules for the same reason. He is hoping to save us from pain and suffering. When we ignore His guidance, we find ourselves in terrible situations. We can feel confident that God is trying to protect us by His rules. He protects us from strangers who would prey on us, and strangers who might mistreat us.

PRAYER: Dear Father, help me to accept the rules you have given me. Guide me that I might always avoid the snares of strangers, and the dangers in life. Amen.

March 8

and say, How have I hated instruction, and my heart despised reproof; and have not obeyed the voice of my teachers, nor inclined mine ear to them that instructed me (5:12-13).

A young woman desperately desired to be able to play the piano. She went to an instructor and asked him for lessons. After a few lessons, the woman expressed frustration that she couldn't play anything. The instructor told her that fine playing took time and hard work. No one simply sat down and began playing without long hours of practice and concentration. The young woman grew angry at her teacher and stormed out of her lesson. She went to other instructors, always with the same result. Her lack of patience and her inability to follow the instructions she was given blocked her ever learning how to play. Finally she gave up, feeling that she had never received the kind of training she was looking for; never admitting that she had been at fault in the least.

So often we are our own worst enemy. We look to others for help, then when it is offered, we refuse to accept it. This is true of our prayers. Too often we come before God asking His help, but when He doesn't respond to us the way we think He should, then we reject Him. It is through trusting the divine wisdom of God that we come to know wisdom for ourselves. God can only do for us what we will let Him. He never forces us to do what we should.

PRAYER: Please help me to open my heart and soul to your will. Forgive me when I turn from your insight and knowledge. Give me the patience I need to wait on You in all situations. Amen.

March 9

Drink waters out of thine own cistern, and running waters out of thine own well. Let thy fountains be dispersed abroad, and rivers of waters in the streets. Let them be only thine own, and not strangers with thee (5:15-17).

Two young men had been friends since early childhood. They had shared everything. They had gone through the same experiences, and they understood each other perfectly. They were closer than many brothers. No better friends could be found. When they went off to college, they became roommates. Soon after college began, one of the young men fell in love with a beautiful young coed. The other man became jealous of his friend, and so he too began to woo the young woman, but behind his friend's back. When his friend finally caught on to what was happening, that friendship came to a bitter and hurtful end.

Fidelity, honesty, loyalty, kindness; all of these are attributes of God that we should desire in our own lives. When we violate these principles, we must pay a price. It is never good to desire that which belongs to someone else. Greed and covetousness result, and they lead to ruin. It is best to always find contentment with "the waters of our own cisterns," those things which are ours, given us by God. When we learn to be satisfied with what we have, then we avoid the pain and suffering attached to taking from others what is rightfully theirs.

PRAYER: I have been given so much that is good in my life, Almighty God. Make me to appreciate what I have, and to stop longing for things which are not mine to have. Grant that my spirit might be satisfied this day, O Lord. Amen.

March 10

Let thy fountain be blessed: and rejoice with the wife of thy youth. Let her be as the loving and pleasant roe; let her breasts satisfy thee at all times; and be thou ravished always with her love (5:18-19).

While walking along the beach one evening, I saw an elderly couple strolling on the boardwalk. The man was blind, and his wife was lovingly leading him along. Her hands were gnarled with arthritis, and her legs were swollen. Both people looked as though they had lived difficult lives. Despite this, I could see the love with which the woman looked upon her mate. I walked up to the couple and told them that I was struck with how much in love they looked. The woman appeared a little embarrassed, but her husband spoke right up and said, "We've been married fifty-two years. I could never have made it without her. When everything else goes bad, I know I've still got the best little woman in the world to love me."

That old gentleman knew the real secret of happiness. It is never in the things we have or don't have. It's not in what happens to us or doesn't happen. The best thing in life is love. Those who are lucky enough to find someone to share their lives with enjoy a special gift from God. But for every person, the love of God is very real, and very much freely given. We can be happy because we can know we are loved. Praise God.

PRAYER: O Lord, giver of life and giver of love. Though I am unworthy, I thank you for loving me so much. Help me to know your love at all times, and grant that I might be able to always spread that love wherever I might go. Amen.

March 11

And why wilt thou, my son, be ravished with a strange woman, and embrace the bosom of a stranger (5:20).

A young woman sobbed, "I just don't know what to believe anymore! I don't feel God with me like I used to." Her life had gone from bad to worse. She had followed in a long line of bad relationships, and bad decisions. She had taken and lost a dozen jobs. She had moved from place to place and was swept up in every new fad to come along. She had joined a group of young people who gathered to meditate and chant together. It was the only place that she felt accepted, but even there she found little comfort as her life crumbled around her. Throughout her childhood she had been a member of a church, and now she felt that she was every bit as devoted with her new group. Still, it wasn't enough.

There is no substitute for the truth and saving power of Jesus Christ. Other groups and sects may appear to be sincere and good, but they are "strange women" who lure us from what is right and good to things we should avoid. The Lord has said clearly, "I am the way, and the truth, and the life. No one comes to the Father, except by me." (John 14:6) Other paths may seem good, but they are false paths which lead nowhere. Stay close to God, avoid "strangers," and all will be well.

PRAYER: There is so much that looks good to me, Father. Protect me from the things which would lead me far from you. Steer me back to you when I stray. Guide my steps by your loving light, Almighty God. Amen.

March 12

For the ways of man are before the eyes of the Lord, and he pondereth all his goings (5:21).

There was an eight year old boy who, like many other eight year olds, was terrified of the dark. One summer he went to stay with his grandparents. They lived far from the city, and so the nights were dark and quiet, interrupted only by sounds of animals and insects. The little boy would cower as the sun set, staying inside where it was light and safe. One night, the boy's grandfather asked him to come sit on the porch with him. As the boy hesitated, his grandfather moved over to him, and laying his hand on his shoulder said, "I'll keep my hand on your shoulder the whole time. You don't have to go out alone." Under the watchful eye of his grandfather, the boy agreed. When they had stepped into the darkness, the boy asked quietly, "Why aren't you afraid, Grammpa?" The old man looked down and said, "Cause I know that God's hand is on my shoulder just like mine is on yours. Remember, boy, you never go anywhere that God is not right there with you."

It is so good to know that we are never out of the Lord's sight. He watches all of our comings and goings. There is absolutely no place that we can go that God will not be also. His hand is always on our shoulder, and He watches all our steps.

PRAYER: Be with me in every situation, Almighty God. Let me feel your loving touch on my shoulder as I face the challenges of every day life. Be my strength and my courage when I find myself lacking, Father. Amen.

March 13

His own iniquities shall take the wicked himself, and he shall be holden with the cords of his sins. He shall die without instruction; and in the greatness of his folly he shall go astray (5:22-23).

A spider toiled along, crafting an amazing web which stretched forth eighteen inches squared. Once finished, the spider spun new webs connecting itself to the corners, until a labyrinth of gossamer filled the corner in which it stood. While the spider busily worked, a larger spider silently crept up alongside. At the right moment, the large spider entered the web, and the creator of it was trapped with no escape.

Sin is like a web. As we become occupied with the things we should not be doing, we become oblivious to the dangers that surround us. We feel that we are in control, when in fact, we are in a very precarious position. There is no good end that can come from a life of sin. We become "holden with its cords," and we cannot get loose. Ultimately, we must answer for our actions before God. If we do not repent of our misdeeds, they become a noose around our neck, and through our folly, we find ourselves hopelessly separated from God. It is good that we always pay attention to the ways we live our lives. It is when we grow complacent that we stand in the greatest danger of losing that which is most important. With God's help, we will never be ensnared.

PRAYER: Lord, I turn my attention to so many things which I should not. My sight is distracted by so much folly. Forgive me when I stray, and shine forth your great light that I might follow its beam back to the source of all life. Amen.

March 14

My son, if thou be surety for thy friend, if thou has stricken thy hand with a stranger, thou art snared with the words of thy mouth, thou art taken with the words of thy mouth (6:1-2).

The young couple was delighted when the first credit card came. They felt swept up in the power they had to purchase some of the things they'd always wanted, without having to part with a large sum all at once. One credit card followed another, and each one was used to its limit. New clothes, new furniture, appliances, stereos, vacations, gadgets; all swept in with seeming ease.

Then the bills came, and the ability to pay them was sorely lacking. The pressure to pay mounted, and it was followed by the frustration of losing all the nice things, then the same of recrimination and bad credit. What had seemed like a good deal in the beginning was nothing more than a nightmare in the end.

It is often easy to be snared by deals which seem to offer something for nothing. There is no such thing. Jesus told His disciples that they were to work for what they received, and not to take any more than was needed. They were not to "strike deals" but let their "yes be yes, and their no be no." It is never wise to live beyond our means to the point where we become a slave to our transactions. In all ways, we should try to work with what God has given to us, waiting on the time when we may attain good things without going into debt.

PRAYER: Help me to avoid the traps which I find in my path each day, O Lord. Grant me the wisdom to know the difference between need and want, and never sacrifice my integrity in order to obtain objects. Amen.

March 15

Do this now, my son, and deliver thyself, when thou art come into the hand of thy friend: go, humble thyself, and make sure thy friend. Give not sleep to thine eyes, nor slumber to thine eyelids. Deliver thyself as a roe from the hand of the hunter, and as a bird from the hand of the fowler (6:3-5).

A young woman moved away from home and settled in an apartment in a large metropolitan area. Her parents came out to visit her, and they took pleasure in buying things for her new apartment. Before they left, they stopped in to see her landlord and paid him three months rent in advance. This was all done out of love for their daughter, but they wouldn't let their girl hear the end of it. Whenever a disagreement arose they reminded her of all they had done for her. Finally, in desperation, the young woman sent them a check for the rent and for the items her parents had purchased for her. She included a note saying, "Please don't misunderstand, but I want you to take this back. A gift is no good with strings attached to it."

When we look at the "gifts" the world has to offer, we need to be aware of the strings which are attached. There is always some catch. With the gifts of God, however, there are never strings attached. All God's gifts come from the greatest love the world has ever known.

PRAYER: See that I give and take freely, Father, never placing anyone in bondage by my actions, nor being cast into bondage myself. Allow me to use the wisdom needed to stay clear of those who would buy my devotion, I pray. Amen.

March 16

Go to the ant, thou sluggard; consider her ways, and be wise (6:6).

On my way to work one morning, I observed the result of some little child's misfortune. A frosted cookie lay face down in the dirt. Upon closer inspection I was amazed at the number of ants which hastily crawled around on the sweet. At first, I thought they moved randomly, but as I watched I saw that there was great order to their movement. Each ant found a jagged corner, then working diligently, it broke off the piece it was after, usually the piece much larger than the carrier, and moved off the site to a nearby ant hill. This went on endlessly, and the cookie shrank in size. A few hours later, I walked past and the ant crew was just finishing up. The cookie was gone, miraculously pieced out, stored for a coming time of need. I thought of all the projects I faced that seemed too large or impossible. I was ashamed that I couldn't even find in myself the determination and drive of a small ant.

Jesus said that with the faith the size of a mustard seed, we could move mountains. How much could we accomplish if we had the commitment of a small ant? Often it is too easy to say, "I can't," rather than "I'll try!" Know this, God blesses those who will give their best effort just because they try to do what He made them to do.

PRAYER: There are so many creatures, Father, who can inspire me and give me guidance. Let me face the obstacles in my life with the spirit of the lowly ant. With its small faith, all things will be possible for me to do. Amen.

March 17

How long wilt thou sleep, O sluggard? When wilt thou arise out of thy sleep? (6:9).

"I sleep every day till noon!" a young woman proudly exclaimed. "I can't remember the last time I saw the sunrise." What a pity that she was so happy that she missed some of God's greatest beauty. So many people walk though their entire lives as if they are asleep. They miss the wonder and glory of the world around them, and they are not even aware that they are missing anything at all. The person who sleeps all the time misses so much. The same is true of the person who closes their eyes to the beauty of God's world.

God made His creation, and He saw that it was good. He gave dominion over the earth to men and women to share with them how good it was. Our lives are creations of God, and they too are good. It is important that we embrace the goodness of our lives, and thank God daily for what we have been given. It is no good to sleep throughout the bulk of our lives. We should wake up. Wake up to the creation that God has given us. It is good, and it is right in front of us to enjoy and take hold of. It was out of God's love for us that our world was given, and it should be from love that we return thanks to Him.

PRAYER: O Father, what a wonderful world you have made. Let me look at the world through your eyes in order that I might see it in all its freshness and light. I rejoice in your glory, now and always, Almighty God. Amen.

March 18

Yet a little sleep, a little slumber, a little folding of the hands to sleep: so shall thy poverty come as one that travelleth, and thy want as an armed man (6:10-11).

The white lines flashed past hypnotically. The road stretched into an endless ribbon of gray. The sound of the radio faded in and out, and the car seemed to sweep the road with a mind of its own. The tires skidded in the soft gravel of the shoulder, and, had it not been for a sturdy guardrail, the car would have gone over the edge of a deep ravine. By the time the foggy mist had lifted from my mind, I was sitting at an odd angle, counting my blessings for being still alive. I had dozed just briefly, perhaps not even a minute, but that was all the time it took for me to end in the ditch. It could have been all the time needed to end my life.

Sin is like that. It creeps up on us, makes us feel comfortable and lazy, and then it strikes when our defenses are down. The results can be tragic. Moral alertness is as important to our spiritual lives as physical alertness is to making sure we stay safe in an automobile. It is when we "fall asleep at the wheel" that evil can take its toll in our lives. The wise driver avoids the road when he or she is physically tired. Isn't it as wise for us, as Christians, to avoid those situations in our lives when we know we are not strong, or when we are most susceptible?

PRAYER: Almighty God, I often grow drowsy in my spiritual pilgrimage. When I am in need of rest, be my stronghold. Protect me from the wiles of the evil one. Strengthen me that I might resist evil, so that it will flee from me. Amen.

March 19

A naughty person, a wicked man, walked with a froward mouth. He winketh with his eyes, he speaketh with his feet, he teacheth with his fingers; frowardness is in his heart, he deviseth mischief continually; he soweth discord. Therefore shall his calamity come suddenly; suddenly shall he be broken without remedy (6:12-15).

A college student loved to play practical jokes. Whenever he found an opportunity, he pulled a gag on one of his friends. No one was safe from his onslaught. Eventually, the people he associated with avoided him, and hated to be around him. Only when he was alone and lonely did he realize that he had been wrong. He attempted to reconcile with his friends, but they had too often heard his apologies, just to be the butt of another unkind joke. The young man who chose to live by the practical joke had to pay the price.

Our actions affect so greatly how our lives will go. We do things which sometimes seem insignificant to us, but to others they are important. One of our largest responsibilities as Christians is to guard our words and actions carefully, always making sure that what we do to others is what we would want to have done to us. Wickedness can take seemingly harmless forms, but once the seed is planted, no matter how small, it can grow forth into a mighty tree, with roots which reach deep.

PRAYER: Lord, I wish to do no one harm. Would that I could, allow me to spread goodness and light wherever I might go. Save me from the calamity which will befall those who live carelessly or foolishly. Amen.

March 20

These six things doth the Lord hate; yea, seven are an abomination unto him: a proud look (6:16-17a).

The new girl stepped cautiously into the classroom. She flinched as she looked at the people in the room. They were all dressed in the latest fashions, had nice hairstyles, and carried expensive purses and book bags. She looked down at her faded blue jeans and sneakers. A flush came to her cheeks. When she looked up, she saw that many of the girls and boys were looking at her with condescending sneers. She wished she could sink into the floor. Before she could control it, tears came into her eyes, and she turned away to avoid further embarrassment. Out of nowhere a voice came forth, "Hi, my name's Janet. What's yours?" Carefully, the young girl looked up to see a smiling, friendly face.

An attitude can be as damaging as an unkind word or a forceful blow. We wield great power in the way we treat other people. If we think that we are better than other people, it will show in our manner, our looks, our words and our actions. God despises the proud and haughty attitudes that people develop. Our duty as Christians is to look at all individuals as equals; brothers and sisters whom we can reach out to. When we look down on others, we do not just withdraw our reach to them, but to Christ as well.

PRAYER: Dear Jesus, help me to see your spirit in all people I meet. Be sure that I never turn from another person due to pride or haughtiness. Teach me to love those around me as you would love them. Amen.

March 21

These six things doth the Lord hate; yea, seven are an abomination unto him: a lying tongue (6:16-17b).

The plan sounded like a good one. The gentleman had sat down with each of the people at the retirement village and explained their policy to them. The cash changed hands, the policies were signed, receipts were given, but that was the last any of them ever heard from the gentleman. He had taken advantage of their situation and made them separate from their hard-earned money. All that could be done was to feel badly that they had been taken in. It was hard to accept that people like that could get away with it. It was a crime.

So often, the deceivers seem to get away with so much. They lie, cheat and steal, and then live it up. It seems that the only ones who get ahead are those who are willing to hurt others to do so. Nothing is farther from the truth. God loves those who will be honest and trustworthy. Lying is abominable in the sight of God, and no one who lives by deception will have any place in His Kingdom. The liar will have to answer to God for what he has done, but those who have lived in the truth will be blessed of God. Men and women who remain true to God's will can rest in the assurance of God's grace.

PRAYER: Dear Lord, I hope that I keep my tongue from hurting anyone through lies or deceptions. Purify my thoughts and my words that they may reflect your grace and love. Amen.

March 22

These six things doth the Lord hate; yea, seven are an abomination unto him: and hands that shed innocent blood (6:16-17c).

Just one hundred years ago it was common practice in the western part of the United States to settle differences with drawn guns and knives. The law of the land was survival of the fittest. Justice was decided by whoever held the greatest force and talent at the time. Law officers were often men who wanted nothing more than to shoot other men. During those days many innocent people died at the hands of ruthless gunmen. Men, women and children lived in terror, never knowing which day might be their last.

In every age, in every place there are people who live by the rule of violence. Their regard for human life is minimal, and they inflict pain wherever they travel. They are seen as strong, when in fact they are sadly weak. Their power is very temporary, and they will be required to atone for their wrongs one day before God. How much better it is to live a life of peace and love. Peacemakers, the meek, those who mourn, they are blessed in the sight of the Lord. Better to be numbered among the blessed than to fall among the accursed. It may seem that the instigators of violence rule this world, but it is the rule of Christ which is the real power, and it reigns in the hearts of all who believe in Him.

PRAYER: Rule in my heart with peace and love. Let me do only kindness to those around me, never harm. Grant that I might be protected from the people who would do me harm, yet let me always face others with forgiveness. Amen.

March 23

These six things doth the Lord hate; yea, seven are an abomination unto him: a heart that deviseth wicked imaginations (6:16, 18a).

The young teacher crossed the parking lot at the end of a long school day. The week before had been unbelievably difficult. Grades had come out, and that always spelled more pressure for the teachers, especially when there were some who didn't quite make the grade. When the young teacher got to her car, she felt her heart sink. All four of her tires had been slashed. It happened all the time. Living in an urban area and teaching young people who often didn't want to be taught was a constant risk. Every time grades came out, someone decided they were going to "get even." Nothing ever seemed to change. Nothing was ever done to catch the kids who did it. She turned away, disgusted, and went back to the school to call for a ride.

A lot of people live for revenge. They hold grudges, let them burn inside, then explode forth to do whatever damage they can. "Vengeance is mine, saith the Lord." When someone wrongs you, your duty is to forgive, not to punish. If someone has done you an injustice, God will call that person to answer for their actions. Nothing good can come from a spirit of hurt and revenge. It is through forgiveness that God can enter our lives and make everything alright.

PRAYER: Heavenly Father, pride often causes me to plot in my heart against those who have wronged me. Create in my heart a spirit of forgiveness, that I may do everything in my power to heal with your great healing love. Amen.

March 24

These six things doth the Lord hate; yea, seven are an abomination unto him: feet that be swift in running to mischief (6:16, 18b).

"Boys will be boys," said the mother of two mischievous young children. Her boys were into everything, causing calamity wherever they went. The children would terrorize other boys and girls, but the excuse was always the same. If the pair caused injury or pain, they were rarely scolded; their mother merely laughed it off and chalked it up to youthful exuberance.

There is a difference between the energy of youth and destructive, disruptive behavior. The curiosity of young children is wonderful, but unwatched it can turn to disaster. A child with a package of matches can wreak havoc. There is nothing to be gained by letting children rule their own lives. They need guidance to protect them from things which might hurt them or others.

The same is true of God in our lives. We so often need guidance and wisdom in order to avoid disaster. What may seem harmless to us may in fact be the path to mischief and away from God. It is wise to ask God's help as we weigh in our hearts what is good and fruitful to do and what is bad or destructive. With his help, we may hope to walk in paths of righteousness and avoid calamity.

PRAYER: There are times, O Lord, when I feel myself drawn to do things that I know I should not do. I all too often rush into situations which I should avoid. Please guide my steps and protect me from straying, Father. Amen.

March 25

These six things doth the Lord hate; yea, seven are an abomination unto him: a false witness that speaketh lies (6:16, 19a).

The little girl threw herself into a fit, thrashing around on the ground, spitting and ranting. The crowd stood around her in amazement. Wide-eyed the little girl pointed at a woman in the crowd, and immediately the magistrates took hold of her and whisked her off to prison. Thus go many stories of the Salem witch trials in America. The fabrications of a few over-imaginative children took root and grew to monstrous proportions. Men and women lost their lives because of the lies of babes. A lie is the worst form of stealing a person can commit. It robs the victim of credibility and honor. It strikes silently and cruelly, and often it allows no room for defense. When we lie, we display selfishness like no other.

Jesus said that He was the truth. If we want to get close to Christ we must put lies and deceitfulness from our hearts. Our words must be kind and reflect the concern and care of Jesus Christ Himself. When we are honest, we take hold of the truth of Christ and spread it to others that we meet. When we lie, even a little bit, we deny the power of truth and reject the goodness that being honest brings. It is by living honest, straightforward lives that we move closer to God in all His glory.

PRAYER: I wish that I could be the person you want me to be, Almighty God. I find that I am dishonest, both with you and with myself. Empower me with a spirit of truth, that I might always live honestly and openly in your sight. Amen.

March 26

These six things doth the Lord hate; yea, seven are an abomination unto him: and he that soweth discord among brethren (6:16, 19b).

The neighborhood gossip got on the phone and eagerly spread the latest dirt. A new neighbor had moved into the area, and the woman could hardly wait to tell her friends what she had seen. "I saw the movers unpack two very large liquor cabinets. I'll bet they drink a lot. And you should have seen the drums and electric guitar that they own. I just know they will play late at night and keep us all awake. You know, you really can't trust young couples these days. They think they own the world." By the time the gossip had spread the word, no one wanted to reach out to welcome the young couple. Frustrated, the young pair felt excluded from the life of their community, and they never could figure out why people treated them so coolly. A year later, the young couple moved away, and they never looked back.

Wouldn't the world be a wonderful place if people spent as much time trying to make peace as they do trying to tear apart? A few choice words can turn an entire community away, but likewise, just a few words can pave a smooth road. We must guard against doing anything that might hurt another human being. It is through kindness and compassion that we display the special love that God has given us to share.

PRAYER: May the words of my mouth always sound sweet and loving. I want to spread peace, not discord. Show me the way, O Lord, that I might help people and show them the love that I would want for myself if I were in their shoes. Amen.

March 27

For the commandment is a lamp; and the law is light; and reproofs of instruction are the way of life (6:23).

A man worked all his life at a mill which rested at the bottom of a steep mountain. Each evening, after a long, hard day at work, the man would begin his two mile trek up the hill. Many parts of the road were steep and tiring. Sometimes the dirt would soften in the rains to a soft mud, which sucked at the man's shoes and made the climbing all the harder. The man never complained though, for each night, as he neared the house, a warm friendly light shone forth from the window to welcome him home and guide his steps. From far away the light shined; first a pinpoint, but then growing larger into the full glow of a lamplight. For the man, there was no more welcoming sight in all the world. For him, that light was home.

As we grow in our Christian lives, the commandments and laws of God are like that lamplight to our eyes. They guide us and warm us, and fill us with that little something extra which makes our travel easy. God shines His light brightly for all to see. It is within that light that we can truly be at home. There should be no greater feeling in our hearts, than the warmth of God's love shining there.

PRAYER: Just as when I enter the light after being in darkness it stings my eyes, so too I feel the sting when my sinful soul enters into the light of Your presence. It is a cleansing light, Father, and I ask that you clean my soul in the fire of your most holy love. Amen.

March 28

For by means of a whorish woman a man is brought to a piece of bread: and the adulteress will hunt for the precious life (6:26).

A man sat trembling in the back row of a darkened, empty church. Sobs shook his shoulders, and his cries brought a young minister from his office. Seeing the man, the pastor walked up to him and asked if he could be of help. The man looked up, tears streaming down his cheeks, and all he could do was shake his head. Finally, he said, "I've done everything I could do. There's nothing left. I cheated on my wife, and now she's left me. I fought with my daughter and she ran away. My son got busted for drugs. I've lost my job due to absenteeism. No, I think I've done all that can be done. I never spent time with my son, I never said a kind word to my daughter, I betrayed the only woman I've ever loved, and I played around just long enough to lose my job. I did this all to myself."

The man buried his face in his hands and resumed crying. The young pastor stayed with the man, sometimes listening, sometimes talking, sometimes just crying along with the man.

People seem so surprised that the price of sin and selfishness is so high. When we take big risks we must expect big losses. It is through God's grace that we can avoid the pain that sin brings. It is in His will that we find the path which leads to true happiness.

PRAYER: Dear Lord, help me to take responsibility for my own wrongdoings. Let me know that I can be forgiven for the things I do wrong, and that I can start afresh, if I will just focus my eyes and my soul on You. Amen.

March 29

Can a man take fire in his bosom, and his clothes not be burned? (6:27).

The cub scout troup had waited all spring for the big camping trip to come around. The dozen young boys piled out of the van and began to set up their tents while the adults prepared the evening meal. The camp was set, the meal consumed, and the group settled in around the big campfire for stories and roasted marshmallows. One bag wasn't enough for the group, so the scout master went back to his car to fetch a second. Before leaving though, he admonished the boys to stay away from the fire. One small fellow, however, was roasting one last marshmallow, which got too soft and fell into the edge of the flames. Without thinking the boy reached to pick it up, and pulled back his hand, alarmed and in pain. The scoutmaster came running back, saying, "What did I tell you?" The young boy denied that he had disobeyed, but the blisters sprouting on his fingers belied his words.

When we fall into sin, it does not simply stay in our own heart. Sin has resulting implications, and they can stretch out in many ways. We may try to deny that we are sinners, but God in His wisdom, sees all and can uncover the "blisters" that sin leaves on our souls. Our coverings bear the burn marks that rise from the fiery passions which occur in our hearts.

PRAYER: Fire can destroy or purify. Guard me from the fire which consumes, and cover me with the fire which cleanses. Make me pure in the fire of your love, removing from my life the ash and soot of the fires of sin. Amen.

March 30

Can one go upon hot coals, and his feet not be burned? (6:28).

Two cars rocketed at one another from opposite directions. The idea was to see who was going to "chicken out" first by swerving their car out of the way of the other one. Both cars mounted speed, coming closer and closer. Supposedly, this was a test of courage and poise. Theoretically, one driver would come forth a hero, the other a coward. Ideally, there would be another day for racing. But, as the two cars approached, it became clear that something was wrong. Neither driver had the wisdom to turn their wheel. The realization came too late, and both cars met at full speed, their drivers never to test their valor again.

Such is the danger of flirting with disaster. Sin is a trap. We think we can control it, but in fact we are controlled by it. Only after it's too late do we see the error of our ways. The point is simple: When we play with fire, we ultimately will get burned. When we tempt the wages of sin, we receive what we ask for. There is nothing to be gained by seeing how close we can come to sin without feeling its heat. Once we slip over the edge, there is no return. Wisdom comes when we realize that we don't have to prove ourselves to anyone. God knows us completely, and He will give us everything we need.

PRAYER: There is great danger in sin, O Lord, that I do not even see. It looks appealing to me, and yet I know deep inside that if I reach out for it I will be harmed. Protect me from the wages of sin, and fill me with the life that never ends. Amen.

March 31

Men do not despise a thief, if he steal to satisfy his soul when he is hungry (6:30).

A man watched an old woman as she made her way through the town market. As she stood in front of the bread rack, she carefully looked around her, then confident that she was not being watched, she slipped a loaf under the cover of her shawl into a shopping bag. The man rushed to the counter to tell the owner what he had just witnessed. The grocer said to the man, "I know, I know. She's done it for years. She never takes much; only enough to feed herself and her cat. Maybe I shouldn't let her get away with it, but it's the least I can do. She's friendly and kind, and she does nice things for people whenever she can. I would want it done to me if I were in her place. What does it hurt?"

Stealing is never right, but sometimes it makes more sense and we can understand it better when the motive isn't greed. Sometimes we act just like the woman in our spiritual lives. We take only what we need, and we don't pay God anything for what we get. There are many times when we find ourselves so starved spiritually that we take and take and take, but give little back. God understands that, and He knows that by feeding us when we hunger we are being strengthened in a way that will enable us to give to others later on. When we come to a place where we can begin giving what has been given to us, then we are truly pleasing to God.

PRAYER: Forgive me for the times when I take without offering anything in return. Fill me with what I need to give to others who have not been as fortunate as myself. Give to me that kind and special word that will allow another person to know that they are loved. Amen.

April 1

But whoso committeth adultery with a woman lacketh understanding: he that doeth it destroyeth his own soul (6:32).

Adultery is one of the sins that most people look upon as being the worst. It robs the participant of ability to be honest and at peace. It causes guilt and it undermines the ultimate plan of God that men and women will join together in order that the two shall become one, in spirit, mind and body. It is a selfish act which takes its toll in a number of ways. It trades in the promise of eternal bliss for a moment of physical pleasure. It has so much power to drive people apart and away from God. Its destruction just keeps on going, and it often leads to ruin.

Yet, it is a sin, no worse than any other. All sin drives us from God, and builds a wall that God refuses to break down Himself. To reconcile with God we must make the first move. We must acknowledge our wrongdoing and ask forgiveness for it. God will be faithful to answer, but it is so much easier to rely on his might and power to strengthen us in times of temptation and weakness. If we will carry God with us in our hearts, then we can avoid the unpleasantness that sin can bring. Understanding comes from a close relationship with God. Sin blocks that relationship and leaves us in a darkness of confusion and despair.

PRAYER: Lift me up, Father, and raise me high above sin and temptation. Keep my eyes centered on You. No more shall I follow the selfish desires of my heart, but in all things I will try to please you. Amen.

April 2

My son keep my words, and lay up my commandments with thee. Keep my commandments, and live; and my law as the apple of thine eye. Bind them upon thy fingers, write them upon the table of thine heart (7:1-3).

There was a man who spent all his days sitting by an old firehouse, telling stories to the neighborhood children. The youngsters would flock around the man to hear him tell of bygone days. One striking feature of the old gentleman was that around each of his fingers he had tied a different colored string. The children would ask what the strings were there for, and the old man would say that each one was to remind him of something important. This was the way he remembered things. But for everyone who came to him, he had this to share.

"You don't need strings to remember the most important things. God gave us ten fingers and ten commandments, and if you keep one commandment on each finger, then you'll never forget any of them."

The commandments of God should be as much a part of us as the fingers which are part of our hands. If we take care to remind ourselves of the laws of God, then they will be forever inscribed on the very "table" of our heart.

PRAYER: I continue to forget the things I should do. Help me to remember what you would have me do. I cannot hope to be the person you want me to be without your help. Amen.

April 3

*Say unto wisdom, Thou art my sister; and call under-
standing thy kinswoman (7:4).*

There were two sisters, as opposite as night and
day. The older sister was quiet and obedient, never
causing trouble and helping others whenever possible. The younger sister was a bit more wild, attending
loud parties and staying out late. She rarely lifted a
finger to help out. Though the two girls had little in
common, the younger sister always looked to her
sibling for acceptance and advice. The younger girl
knew that her sister loved her and would always do
what she thought was in her best interest.

Wisdom, true wisdom which comes to us directly
from God, is as trustworthy as the older sister. The
truth of God is constant; never changing. When we
learn to trust completely in God's promises to us, we
grasp hold of Him in all His glory, and we find new
meaning in the word wisdom.

Family ties are some of the strongest we will ever
experience. Blood ties cannot be broken, and we
have been tied to God once and for all by the blood of
Christ; blood freely given to make us one with the
Lord for all time.

*PRAYER: I feel the warm acceptance of God, just as I
am. I can be myself with God, just as I can be myself at
home, with my family. Thank you, Father, that you have
made this so. Amen.*

April 4

and beheld among the simple ones, I discerned among the youths, a young man void of understanding (7:7).

A small girl set about preparing a menu for her pretend birthday party. She planned a full meal of cookies, cake, candy, ice cream and potato chips. To drink there would be lemonade and soda. Her choices were made from her own affection for the treats, but no thought was given to what might be nutritious or keep her from getting sick. Children many times fail to use good sense when they make their decisions. They need guidance in order to avoid unnecessary pain and suffering. Sometimes children resist the advice of their parents, but they need it nonetheless.

When we compare our wisdom with God's, we find that we are simple and dull in relation. We have neither the experience of God, nor the insight. His knowledge so far exceeds our own that we seem naive and inept. Luckily, God offers His wisdom and knowledge with no strings attached. He does so out of love for us, and He only wants us to avoid the pitfalls that come our way. Christian maturity comes when we can admit that we need help, and accept the aid God so freely offers.

PRAYER: Break my spirit of resistance. Help me to be obedient to your will, Father, as a loving and faithful child. Amen.

April 5

He goeth after the harlot straightaway, as an ox goeth to the slaughter, or as a fool to the correction of the stocks; till a dart strike through his liver; as a bird hasteth to the snare, and knoweth not that it is for his life (7:22-23).

The teenagers lined the fence outside the schoolyard. They knew that someone would be by with what they called "goodies." Any drug a person could want was available every day of the week. One of the boys had been having terrible reactions to the drugs he had been taking, but he waited anyway. He was hooked. It didn't matter that it was wrong or illegal or dangerous. All he knew was that he had to have it.

Drugs are a tragedy in our world. They destroy so many lives. And for that reason, they are a lot like sin. For some people, sin isn't something they are attracted by, it is something they are addicted to. Just like drugs, though, if it isn't cleaned out of the system it can kill. Often we ignore the ramifications of the sins we easily fall prey to. Before we know it, we pass the point of no return. The time to turn is now; turn to God, and away from the sins which can only lead to death.

PRAYER: Almighty God, sin so readily takes control of my heart and mind. Alone, I cannot begin to battle it, but with You I know that I can break free to follow in Your love. Help me I pray. Amen.

April 6

Hear; for I will speak of excellent things; and the opening of my lips shall be right things (8:6).

There was a woman that everyone dearly loved. She never lacked for company, because so many people flocked to spend time with her. She had the ability to engage anyone, old or young, male or female, black or white, intelligent or simple, in delightful conversation. With a beautiful voice she would tell stories of bygone days, and share dreams and wishes with anyone who would listen. She was full of compliments, but never empty flattery. In every situation, she knew the perfect thing to say. In trouble, she spoke words that soothed, in times of stress she spoke words of comfort, and in good times, she knew the perfect joke or anecdote to share.

The gift of speech is a valuable one. It also carries with it great responsibility. We are commanded to avoid silly or coarse speech, but to always use words to uplift and praise. Our words should reflect the presence of God in our hearts. Only the most excellent and right things should spring forth from our mouths.

PRAYER: Let the words of my mouth always produce what is pleasing in your sight, O Lord. Let me build up, rather than tear down. May my speech reflect my great love for you. Amen.

April 7

For my mouth shall speak truth; and wickedness is an abomination to my lips (8:7).

A young woman went to work at a church where youth ministry had never gone very well. The woman had no previous experience with young people, but her enthusiasm convinced everyone that she was a good choice. Over the first few months of her employment, the group grew slowly. However, the growth was continuous. The pastor of the church stopped in to see what the young woman was doing that was so successful. He saw nothing extraordinary, so he stayed after to talk with the woman.

"I've been around a long time. I've seen some good youth leaders, and I've seen some bad, but I've never seen one who has built the group like you have. What's your secret?"

"The kids know I care. They can trust me. No matter what happens, they know I won't lie to them or about them. That's all."

Truth and honesty are important if we hope to have good, strong relationships. God loves truth, and those who commit themselves to it are blessed in the eyes of God. We can hardly please God more than when we speak truth in love.

PRAYER: Lord of truth and light, be the guiding force of my life. Help me to avoid lies, which destroy relationships and create walls between people. Fill me with your love. Amen.

April 8

All the words of my mouth are in righteousness; there is nothing froward or perverse in them. They are all plain to him that understandeth, and right to them that find knowledge (8:8-9).

The crew of young doctors cowered under the tongue-lashing given to them by the chief-of-surgeons. Each doctor knew that their mentor was right, but it was difficult to receive such harsh criticism. Each doctor also knew that the only reason the chief surgeon was so tough was to make sure they were the best they could be. The man demanded perfection, and he wasn't going to settle for less. Only doctors who wanted to be the best could stand to take the kind of scrutiny the chief surgeon put them under. No matter what else might happen, each new doctor knew that they would receive truth and guidance from the older man. They trusted him because they knew he was doing everything he knew to do to make them the best they could be.

How willing are we to place ourselves in positions to be criticized? It is hard to invite others to tell us what we do wrong and how we can improve. Yet, if we want to grow, we need to have criticism given to us. The Lord offers us guidance as we try to grow, and we can be sure that it will be given to us with the greatest love, even though it is often hard to acknowledge that we are lacking. Thank goodness that God is so patient with us, and that He gives us time to change and grow.

PRAYER: Help me to trust the wise counsel of others. I know that I have so much room to grow. Grant that I might have the wisdom to accept the helpful criticism of others and make me to seek your ways. Amen.

April 9

Receive my instruction, and not silver; and knowledge rather than choice gold. For wisdom is better than rubies; and all the things that may be desired are not to be compared to it (8:10-11).

In the mid-eighteen hundreds, thousands of men and women sold everything they had in order to move westward in the great gold rush. Gold fever took hold and pushed people to extremes. People were willing to kill in order to protect their claims to land in the goldfields. The hale and hearty devoted themselves heart, mind and soul to the pursuit of the golden nuggets. All else was considered loss, and many individuals found themselves in ruin, because they had been blinded by a glitter which led straight to disaster.

The attractive glitter of gold, the enticing appeal of wealth has drawn many people toward it, and away from God. Christ said that no one could be the servant of two masters. When we become enthralled by money and all it can buy, we cannot devote our attention to God. The two are diametrically opposed. If only people would pursue God with the same energy that they pursue the glitter of gold. The result would be Christians who gave themselves completely to the loving will of God, and the world would begin to be more the way God intended it to be from the very beginning. It is a choice each Christian has to make, but it is good to remember that the reward in heaven outshines any that we may ever hope to find on earth.

PRAYER: Father, I pray that I might learn to pursue you with every energy of my heart and soul. Be my strength, that I might be able to give myself completely over to your will. Amen.

April 10

I wisdom dwell with prudence, and find out knowledge of witty inventions (8:12).

A powerful businessman was always looking for ways to cut corners. Any shortcut, and cost cutting methods he could find, he would use. It didn't matter whether or not the cuts hurt quality or endangered employees. All that mattered was making the most money for the least cost. For awhile, things worked well, but as time passed, more and more people lost faith in the products that the man's companies produced, and finally he faced financial ruin. All the shortcuts he took seemed to lead to the reward he desired, but in fact, they destroyed the hope of reaching his dream.

There are no short-cuts to wisdom. The knowledge of the heart comes to us from patience, experience, and prayerful reflection. God wishes this wisdom for all of His children, but it comes only over time. Patience is a difficult virtue to obtain, but its rewards are greater than we can begin to comprehend. Short-cuts may look promising in the near future, but it is the person who learns the benefits of waiting who is on the road to true wisdom. It is so pleasing to God when He sees us grow spiritually, and the best way we can show that growth is to learn to say, with Jesus, "Not my will be done, O Father, but yours be done, now and forever. Amen."

PRAYER: Keep my feet on the right path, O Lord. Keep me from straying onto roads which seem to be easier to travel, but lead nowhere. As long as your light shines forth before me, I know that all will be well. Amen.

April 11

The fear of the Lord is to hate evil: pride, and arrogancy, and the evil way, and the froward mouth, do I hate (8:13).

An extremely competent woman joined a small church, and within a short time was a key figure in the running of programs and events. Everything she turned her hand to came out successfully. For a time, people welcomed her enthusiasm and commitment. After awhile, however, fewer and fewer people supported her in her efforts. The reason for their defection was simple: they couldn't tolerate her attitude. She never let anyone forget all the wonderful things she had done for the church. She rattled on endlessly about how talented she was, and good she was at getting things accomplished better than anyone else. She loved the spotlight, and resisted sharing it with anyone. The other members of the church quite simply didn't want to be around her.

It's a sad thing that some people need attention and acceptance so much that they give it to themselves rather than allowing others to give it to them. If we do things simply for the appreciation they bring, then we are doing them for the wrong reason. We should give of our gifts and talents because it is pleasing to God, not because it will earn us respect or praise. God has given us many fine abilities, and it is important that we remember to use them for His service, not caring whether we receive praise or not.

PRAYER: My pride is too often tender and easily bruised. Make me able to serve without hope of reward. I want to serve you freely and without letting my ego get in the way. Guide me in this pursuit. Amen.

April 12

Counsel is mine, and sound wisdom: I am understanding; I have strength. By me kings reign, and princes decree justice. By me princes rule, and nobles, even all the judges of the earth (8:14-16).

Solomon was considered to be the wisest of all human beings. His judgment was sound and fair. Subjects traveled from all over Israel to seek his counsel. His word was law, because people believed that there was no greater mind in all the world. Whatever Solomon decreed, the people gladly accepted. Solomon did nothing more than use the gifts God had given him in the best way possible. Solomon relied heavily on God's guidance and help. He prayed long and hard for God to inspire him with special wisdom. Solomon listened at length to the scribes who read to him from the Scriptures. He was ever questing after a deeper knowledge of God.

Solomon was able to give great wisdom because he was in touch with the source of wisdom: God. As much as Solomon was willing to give himself to God, God was willing to give Himself right back. God showed that He was willing to do the same for us, by giving Himself in the person of His Son, Jesus Christ. All we need do is accept His gift, and try to the best of our ability to follow His example. Like Solomon, we receive strength and understanding from the God who gives us all good things.

PRAYER: Lord, I wish that I could be one with your Spirit, that I might spread your will in this world. You offer so much, and I take so little. Help me to use what you hold forth, that I might reflect the blessed light of your Son Jesus Christ throughout this world. Amen.

April 13

I love them that love me; and those that seek me early shall find me (8:17).

A young girl disappeared on her way home from school. Her parents were in a panic, and they called the police to help find her. After two days of searching, the police put her in a file, and the parents went away depressed. On their own, they decided that they would do anything necessary to find their little girl. They began a search of their own. For six years they dedicated themselves to the recovery of their only child. After long years of desperately hoping and endlessly searching, the pair found their daughter, living just a few miles away with the woman who had abducted her. Many times in the six years the couple had wanted to give up. Repeatedly, they faced feelings of futility and frustration. In spite of impossible odds, and lack of assistance, the pair found their daughter, and were reunited at long last.

When something is the desire of our heart, it should possess us totally. How many of us pursue God with the same diligence as the young couple pursued their daughter? God wants us to do so. Nothing pleases Him more than knowing that we love Him totally and completely. If we will seek God, with our whole being, His promise is that we will find Him.

PRAYER: Sometimes I lose patience when I wait for you to answer my prayers, O Lord. Give me the patience I so desperately need. Help me to pursue you in all ways at all times. Thank you for your promise to always be there when I seek you. Amen.

April 14

I lead in the way of righteousness, in the midst of the paths of judgement: that I may cause those that love me to inherit substance; and I will fill their treasures (8:20-21).

A poor woman called her children to her soon before her death. She sat them down and told them, "I never had money or nice things, and I'm sorry that I don't have good things to leave you, but I always tried to do what was right by you. If I brought you up right, so that you do what you know is right to do, then I have left you more than any amount of money."

The woman was right. The things money buys are temporal, they wear out, break down, and then they're gone. A good sense of values is worth more than all the money in the world. The greatest gift we can hope to give another human being is that of wise counsel. We often hope that we can leave a legacy, a testament to our life, after we die. There is no more fitting legacy than helping other people learn to love life and enjoy it every day. We can make our lives an example of the truth of Christ, letting others see just how much Christ can change lives for the better. He will "lead us in the paths of righteousness," but only so that we might have something of substance, something that will last long after our material wealth has gone. That is the real treasure, and God gives it freely to all who will take it.

PRAYER: I try to turn my eyes from material gain, to true gain: the gain of eternal life. Help me to follow your instructions that I might have your righteousness. Grant me a small portion of your holy inheritance. Amen.

April 15

The Lord possessed me in the beginning of his way, before his works of old. I was set up from everlasting, from the beginning, or ever the earth was. When there were no depths, I was brought forth; when there were no fountains abounding with water. Before the mountains were settled, before the hills was I brought forth (8:22-25).

When God spoke to the prophet Jeremiah, He said, "Before I formed thee in the belly, I knew thee; and before thou camest forth out of the womb I sanctified thee, and I ordained thee a prophet unto the nations." (Jer. 1:5)

The mind of God is amazing. From the very beginning of time, God has had each and every one of us in His mind. He knows us completely. There is never even one moment when we are out of God's vision.

When we talk of the day we became Christian, what we are really speaking of is the day that we came back to God. It is we who turn from Him and walk down other paths, but we can rest assured that whenever we come back to God's way, He will be right there waiting for us. He rejoices when we walk in the paths of righteousness, and He mourns for us when we fall onto paths which lead from His glory. We can't fool God, because He knows us so well. Thank goodness there's no reason to even try.

PRAYER: O Lord, you know me so much better than I know myself. Help me to know myself as you know me. Assist me to be the best person I can possibly be. Just help me to grow, Father. Amen.

April 16

When he prepared the heavens, I was there: when he set a compass upon the face of the depth: when he established the clouds above: when he strengthened the fountains of the deep (8:27-28).

The three weeks before the trip seemed to drag on, and the little boy counted the days until his uncle came to pick him up. His uncle was going to take him out of the city to drive across the country to California. It was as exciting as a trip to the moon.

The day for the start of the trip came, and the pair set out on their adventure. When the trip was over, the little boy was asked what had been the best part of the trip. Without hesitation, he said, "The Grand Canyon!" When asked why, the boy said, "My uncle said that you could see all the layers of time which have gone by by looking at the stripes in the rock. He told me that the very first layer was put there by God, and that God was there when every other layer was laid on top. But you know what? He also said that before God ever started making the Grand Canyon, He started thinking of me and loving me!"

We may look on our world with wonder and amazement, but nothing is more amazing than the fact that it was all made for us, out of God's infinite love for us. We owe Him thanks and praise every day, for giving so much.

PRAYER: O Lord of majesty and grace, you have indeed created a beautiful world for our comfort and joy. Thank you for sharing this great gift with me. Help me to appreciate it more fully, and to care for it with wisdom. Amen.

April 17

when he gave to the sea his decree, that the waters should not pass his commandment: when he appointed the foundations of the earth: then I was by him, as one brought up with him: and I was daily his delight, rejoicing always before him; rejoicing in the habitable part of his earth; and my delights were with the sons of men (8:29-31).

"Even if there is a God, how do I know I can trust Him?" a skeptical young woman asked. "I mean, we must assume an awful lot to think that He can know everything that is going on."

This poor woman suffers from a very common affliction: doubt. How can we know that God watches everything that goes on? We do so by faith.

Jesus Christ came that we might have a way to remove all doubt that God works all things for good. Christ assured us that God indeed watches over all people and that He reigns wisely and with justice. Christ Himself was present with God in creation. Christ dwelt with God, and when He came He proclaimed the truth of God for all people. The truth of God comes to each person individually through their relationship with Christ. If we will only open our hearts to Christ, we will no more need to doubt and question. We may rest in the knowledge that Christ is Lord, and that God is with us all the time.

PRAYER: O Lord of creation and love, You rise above time and space to dwell everywhere and everytime at once. You hear even my most quiet cry. Help me to trust in your truth and reality. Answer my every doubt with "I am." Amen.

April 18

Blessed is the man that heareth me, watching daily at my gates, waiting at the posts of my doors (8:34).

A security guard worked at the same job, watching the gate of a chemical plant, for fifteen years. For that entire time, no one had ever tried to break into the plant. The guard watched television, read books and magazines, drank sodas, and walked the grounds. Often, he would doze off, passing the long, tedious hours in slumber. It hadn't always been that way. When he was first hired, he had sat alertly at his post, making his rounds promptly and completely. He had spent hours working on ways to improve security at the factory. That hadn't lasted long. The dull routine of the work, and the late hours took their toll. As time passed, so did the guard's enthusiasm.

One night, while the guard slept, three men broke into the plant and made off with thousands of dollars worth of valuable chemicals and drugs. In an instant, the guard lost his position because of his inattention when it mattered most.

Christians need to take heed. Our attention must be on the Lord. We never know what might lie ahead, and so we should consciously try to be the best we can be in all circumstances. If we live each day as if it were the day we would meet our Maker, then we won't be embarrassed on the day it finally comes.

PRAYER: I pray that I might be alert and fully awake to my duties as your loving disciple. As I follow your will, let me not grow weary or tired, but fill me with every energy that I might be ready when my time comes. Amen.

April 19

For whoso findeth me findeth life, and shall obtain favor of the Lord. But he that sinneth against me wrongeth his own soul: all they that hate me love death (8:35-36).

A young man sat, trembling, in the police station. He had been picked up for shoplifting, and now he waited for his parents who were on their way to pick him up. Being arrested was frightening and embarrassing, but it wasn't half as bad as having to face his mother and father. As they burst through the door, the young man saw that his mother had been crying. He bowed his head in shame and awaited the fury to come from his parents.

Instead, he felt his mother's arm wrap around his shoulders, and his father's big, warm hand on top of his head. He looked up through tears and saw that both his parents were watching him with love and concern.

The boy asked, "Aren't you angry with me? Why aren't you yelling at me?"

The mother spoke up, "Honey, when you hurt we only want to help you. You've done wrong, but that doesn't mean we stop loving you. What you did hurts us, but we'll work it out together."

God loves us every bit as much. No matter what happens, if we work to find God, we will find love like we never thought possible.

PRAYER: Dear heavenly Father, I fall prey to so much temptation and sin. I am ashamed that I cannot do what You would like for me to do. Thank you for your forgivenss and love, especially in times when I don't deserve it. Amen.

April 20

Wisdom hath builded her house, she hath hewn out her seven pillars: she hath killed her beasts; she hath mingled her wine; she hath also furnished her table (9:1-2).

When I first began my ministry, I did so as a student in seminary. I had never served people officially before, and it surprised me when I was treated with so much respect and consideration. People showed that they had faith in me and it helped me to be able to minister to them; many of whom were much older than I was. I was treated royally, and was a little embarrassed because I didn't think I deserved it.

When we come into God's presence we may find ourselves surprised at how well God treats us. We come to Him as sinners, ashamed and afraid, and He treats us like kings and queens. We are not strangers who receive the lesser quality, but we are sons and daughters, welcomed home, and treated to only the best. God lays out the finest for His children, and it doesn't matter that we are undeserving. Children rarely deserve the love their parents have for them, but love, true love, cannot be earned. Love is a gift, and God freely gives His love to each and every child who will accept it. All we must do is accept the gift, not earn it. Wisdom comes to those who don't question the giver, but accept the gift with gratitude.

PRAYER: Gracious and giving God, I cannot give you great enough thanks for all you offer to me, a humble child. Help me to give others some of the precious, unconditional love that you have given me. Amen.

April 21

Whoso is simple, let him turn in hither: as for him that wanteth understanding, she saith to him, Come, eat of my bread, and drink of the wine which I have mingled. Forsake the foolish, and live; and go in the way of understanding (9:4-6).

At a youth camp, a young crippled girl found that she did not fit in. Her affliction caused her not only physical deformity, but it also affected her speech. The other children, unwittingly cruel, mocked her and refused to let her participate in their activities. Even the counselors excluded her from many activities and games, thinking that she was incapable of joining in. On the final day of the camp, the young girl sat in the large circle of campers. Each was asked to share something from the week that had passed.

When it came to the girl, she looked around the circle and labored to say, "You haven't been very nice to me. Some of you wouldn't even talk to me. Because I'm weak and talk funny you acted like I was retarded and you made fun of me. That's okay. You know why? Because Jesus loves me, and that's all that really matters. And I'm not mad at you because He wants me to try to love you, because He loves you." The group sat still in a long, awkward silence.

Wisdom is the knowledge that God does love us, and that there is nothing greater in all the world. If only more people were as special as the little girl.

PRAYER: O Father, I am crippled in so many spiritual and emotional ways. Through your love, grant that I might rise above my limitations and become a more loving and caring person. Amen.

April 22

He that reproveth a scorner getteth himself shame: and he that rebuketh a wicked man getteth himself a blot. Reprove not a scorner, lest he hate thee: rebuke a wise man, and he will love thee (9:7-8).

A woman was given a project to do for a large advertising agency. She selected two other woman to work with her on the project. The supervising woman worked closely with the other two for weeks, and finally a finished product was presented to the clients for approval. The project came back with comments, and a list of changes were called for. The supervisor called in the two other women and shared the list. One of the women sat calmly and listened to the proposal, while the other woman flew into a rage. She felt that she was being insulted and she criticized the clients for not knowing good work when they saw it. When the supervisor defended the clients' rights, the woman slammed down her portfolio and stormed from the office saying that she quit.

If we can't take criticism we cannot hope to grow. Growth comes from finding our weaknesses and working to build them into strengths. When we try to help people who aren't willing to admit they can grow, they deal with us in anger. When God calls for us to change, how will we react to His request? Will it be with anger, or will it be with humble obedience?

PRAYER: Often pride gets in the way of my maturing spiritually, O Lord. Help me to receive criticism with grace, and to work always to improve myself. Soften my heart to the comments of others, and let me deal with others in love and care. Amen.

April 23

Give instruction to a wise man, and he will be yet wiser: teach a just man, and he will increase in learning (9:9).

A college professor laid out his philosophy of teaching on the very first day of classes. "If you will let me, I will teach you as much as I can in these few short weeks, but if you resist me, I guarantee that you will learn nothing. You won't like everything I tell you, but if you will follow my instructions, you will leave here much better thinkers than when you came in."

The professor was a task master, who demanded perfection from his students. Many students, too lazy to put forth the proper effort, lost interest and complained about the strict grading and harsh comments. The few truly dedicated students found their professor to be one of the finest they ever had, and they valued his opinion above all others. This man helped them to be better than they thought possible.

God offers us the same kind of deal. If we will be open to His leadership, He will help us to realize our full potential. If we resist His help, then we can never hope to reach that goal. Wise men and women got to be that way by listening and trying to improve themselves. They are never content with who they are today, but they always look forward to what they can become.

PRAYER: May I grow a little bit today, and every day to come, Almighty God. Let me keep my ego in its place, never refusing to hear the things I should hear, in order that I might improve myself. Amen.

April 24

The fear of the Lord is the beginning of wisdom: and the knowledge of the Holy is understanding. For by me thy days shall be multiplied, and the years of thy life shall be increased. If thou be wise, thou shalt be wise for thyself: but if thou scornest, thou alone shalt bear it (9:10-12).

A young woman took a job at a zoo tending animals. Her third week on the job, she was shown how to feed the lions, tigers and other big cats. Large portions of meat were stabbed by long spears, and then they were stuck through the bars of the cages to the animals. While in training, a piece of meat slipped from the end, and lay half in and half out of the cage. The woman moved up and reached to pick up the meat. The lion inside the cage growled and pounced against the bars, reaching through and badly scratching the young woman. Her trainer rushed over and said, "Don't ever do that. Use the stick. If you had been closer and the cat's reach a little longer, you wouldn't be here now. I hope you remember that scratch the rest of your life."

In so many situations we feel that we are in control, that nothing can happen to us. We forget how truly fragile we are. We become complacent and lose our fear, our respect, for things we should remember about. The fear of the Lord is nothing more than knowing who He is and respecting Him. If we learn that fear, all our days will be long, and our lives will be safe and happy.

PRAYER: O Lord, help me to keep from letting down my guard for even one minute. Open my eyes to my limitations and grant that I might acknowledge my shortcomings. Only you are God, and I worship and praise you with all my heart. Amen.

April 25

A foolish woman is clamorous: she is simple, and knoweth nothing. For she sitteth at the door of her house, on a seat in the high places of the city, to call passengers who go right on their ways: Whoso is simple, let him turn in hither: and as for him that wanteth understanding, she saith to him, Stolen waters are sweet, and bread eaten in secret is pleasant (9:13-17).

A flock of ducks flew south in perfect formation. They followed the powerful instincts to fly onward, racing from the shifting weather, faithfully flying after the leader who showed them the way. Occasionally, the lead duck would spot a clearing with other ducks, and resisting the instinct to continue. he would lead his flock down for rest. In the safety of the clearing, they could find food and energy could be restored.

At one point, a clearing appeared, and ducks bobbed freely in the marsh. The lead duck circled, leading the flock closer to the ground. Suddenly, the birds sensed that something wasn't right, but before they could climb higher into the sky, shots rang out and many plunged into the cold water below.

When we allow ourselves to be distracted from our pursuit of God, the results can be disastrous. Sin, which leads us from our pursuit of the Lord, can pull us into situations that we don't want to be in, but before we can change them we are trapped.

PRAYER: Keep my sight on you, O Lord. Clear my vision so that your light is the only thing shining in my eyes. Protect me from the diversions and decoys which can lead me into ruin. Amen.

April 26

Treasures of wickedness profit nothing: but righteousness delivereth from death (10:2).

A man climbed to the top of the business world by shrewd investments and fast talking. One of his favorite ploys was to build low budget housing and then to rent it at rock bottom prices. Renters would then improve the property, the man would raise their rent forcing them to move, then he would rerent at a higher rate. Though it brought in lots of money, it also brought him a reputation that lasted throughout his life. Everyone knew that he would stop at nothing to make more money, and it little mattered that he hurt many people to make it. When he died, he was one of the wealthiest men in the country, but he was also the loneliest.

Nothing could be worse than facing death alone; without the love of God in your life. All the things money can buy pale in comparison to the worth of having God with us. Taking advantage of other people in order to gain things for ourselves is wrong. It is an abomination in the sight of the Lord, and it builds walls which cannot be broken down. However, if we learn to live our lives for others, we will find the true treasure that God has in store for us. Righteousness delivers us from the death that destroys the very root of our soul.

PRAYER: Father, thank you for never leaving me alone. I have everything I need as long as I have you. Stay close by me, and teach me how to give your blessed love to others. Amen.

April 27

The Lord will not suffer the soul of the righteous to famish: but he casteth away the substance of the wicked (10:3).

"I'm used to getting what I set my sights on," said an executive to one of his business partners. "I don't care what it takes, any amount of money, but I want my daughter to get into the best school." After a few phone calls, promises of favors, and expensive gifts and bonuses, the girl was in a fine college, and the business executive got back to his affairs.

A lot of people get accustomed to having their own way. They learn to manipulate other people, and to pay for favors. Money becomes a tool by which they control people and situations. The fatal danger to this kind of thinking is that it will work in every situation.

The problems is that Jesus Christ is no respecter of persons. Money has no influence over God. The wealth of man has no value in the presence of God. True wealth is the love and fear of God. This wealth is available to all people, and no one can take it away. It can't be bought, it can only be freely received, as a gift. But if it is received, it cannot share space with material wealth. We must choose one or the other. The riches of man will be cast away by God, but the wealth of heaven will save all believers from famishing.

PRAYER: Nourish my soul with your greatness, O Lord. Fill me with contempt for the treasure which fades away and crumbles to dust. Set my heart on the true treasure, which never fades, and shines more brightly than the sun. Amen.

April 28

He becometh poor that dealeth with a slack hand: but the hand of the diligent maketh rich. He that gathereth in summer is a wise son: but he that sleepeth in harvest is a son that causeth shame (10:4-5).

Two nurses were in the running for a staff position in a large metropolitan hospital. One was a hard working young woman from the Midwest who had striven her whole life to be the best nurse she could possibly be. She studied long and hard and was at the top in her class. She continued to study and learn new techniques and practices. The other was a young man whose father was the hospital administrator. He did his job, but no more. He did just what had to be done, and that was all. He figured he was the favorite as far as the new position went, so he sat back and awaited the decision. He was shocked when he learned that the young woman had been selected.

There is nothing to be gained by resting on our laurels. Hard work and integrity are important values to possess. If we can learn to be disciplined in our daily work, then we can improve our spiritual discipline as well. It is pleasing to God when we put forth our best efforts. When we refuse to do our best, then we are failing to utilize the talents and gifts that God has given to us all.

PRAYER: I want to be a faithful and devout servant, O Lord, doing all that is required of me, using my talents in the best possible way. Help me to do what is right, keep me diligent, and turn me away from the temptation to avoid my responsibilities. Amen.

April 29

The memory of the just is blessed: but the name of the wicked shall rot (10:7).

A matron of the church donated all of her free time to helping out. She worked in the office, visited the sick, she made phone calls, delivered flowers, formed prayer groups, served the women's clubs, and welcomed new people to the neighborhood. Whenever anyone was sick or in need, she was first to offer help. If anyone was grieving, she was there with a kind word. Everyone felt a special fondness for this wonderful woman. When she died, the sanctuary of the church was packed. Memorials were made in her honor, and tales of her kindness were told for years to come. In time, her reputation became legendary. No one joined the church who didn't hear the stories of this great woman.

The woman of the story never did anything for glory or recognition, yet by virtue of her commitment and love, her name became synonymous with charity. Everyone loved and respected her, and after she was gone, they did everything in their power to help her kindness live on. What more could we ever want than to be loved so much that our lives could still make a difference even after we are dead? The memory of the just is truly blessed, and it is truly a gift from God if we are to be so lucky.

PRAYER: Not that I would seek the acceptance of men and women, Father, but please allow that I might be loved in this life, and after it is done. Bless my life, and make it a testament to your Glory. Amen.

April 30

The wise in heart will receive commandments: but a prating fool shall fall (10:8).

The story is an old one, and one that is happening all too often. A couple prepared to leave a party where they had over-indulged. The woman was drunk, and her husband only slightly less so. As they began to put on their coats, a friend offered to drive them home. Insulted, the husband refused to even consider it. The husband and wife stumbled to their car, amidst the protests of their friends. Despite the warnings and admonitions, the couple sped off in their car. As it rounded a tight curve, it swung out into the oncoming lane and struck another car. Though the husband and wife were only slightly hurt, the other driver and his son were killed.

Foolish people refuse to recognize wisdom, even when it is right in front of them. It doesn't matter who offers the suggestions. Both friends and foes are ignored. When our egos get in the way of clear thinking, we are on a pathway that leads away from God. God glories in the person who will listen to good advice, and do what is right. God doesn't give us instruction in order to ruin our good time. His word is offered only to give everyone the chance to live life to the fullest. It is the wise in heart who receives instruction gladly. The fool stumbles down the road to destruction.

PRAYER: Unplug my ears, O Lord, and let me hear the wisdom of those who care for me. Destroy my foolish pride, and lead me to paths of good sense and smart choices. Keep me from hurting myself and others. Amen.

May 1

He that walketh uprightly walketh surely: but he that perverteth his ways shall be known (10:9).

The stone face of the mountain seemed to stretch upward forever. It had a magnetic effect on the boys who had come to the camp. All of them were anxious to have the chance to climb to the top. The counselors warned them not to try it by themselves, but each year some foolish soul tried it anyway. This year was no different. While part of the group went to the ballfield for softball, two of the youths snuck off to attempt the climb. Before long they gave up, unable to master the tricky cliff.

The next afternoon, the counselors took the boys on the climb, and everyone made it. The older boys who had made the climb hundreds of times before, guided the younger boys, telling them where to hold and where to step.

When we who walk this earthly road get into trouble, we often do not have the good sense to listen to those who have walked our road before us. There is nothing wrong with relying on the help of others to make it through life. God is the author of all life, and it makes sense that we should turn to Him in times of trial or difficulty. When we don't, we cannot be surprised that we don't make it through. Our help is always in the Lord.

PRAYER: I try my best to get through life, O Lord, but often I find myself at a halt. I don't know where to turn, where to step, what to hold onto. In those times, Father, help me to remember that you are there to guide me. Amen.

May 2

He that winketh with the eye causeth sorrow: but a prating fool shall fall (10:10).

Her uncle had been a wonderful story teller. In fact, she had never known when to believe him and when to know he was kidding. She had believed the stories of the Amazon and the war, and even his days as a pro baseball player. She had thought her uncle could do anything. It had been devastating when she had found out that he was alcoholic, and that he would have to be put in an institution. In the years that passed she had found out that her uncle had never been to the Amazon, had never played pro ball, and he had even been turned down by the army. She never really got over her disillusionment, and it made her skeptical of everyone she met. She lost faith in heroes.

Each one of us has had a tall tale to tell at some point in our lives. With tongue in cheek, we have put someone on. There is nothing wrong with pulling someone's leg, so long as it isn't a way of life, and that we don't do damage by our untruth. We need to be able to trust others. We need honesty. And other people need to be able to trust us. Honesty is a valuable virtue. We have the power to change lives when we speak the truth. If we tell people fables, we lose credibility and weaken our power to help them.

PRAYER: Help me that I never undermine the faith that others have in me. Let me be honest and open, so that I might have the opportunity to make a difference in their lives. Amen.

May 3

In the lips of him that hath understanding wisdom is found: for a rod is for the back of him that is void of understanding (10:13).

The old farmer pulled at the leather rein which dangled from the mule's mouth, but the mule dug her hooves into the soft earth and resisted his efforts. The farmer spoke coaxing words to the mule, but she refused to budge. In spite of all the farmer's efforts, the old mule held her ground. In frustration the old man pulled a branch from a hickory tree, stripped off the bark, and fashioned a switch from it. Moving around the mule to her hind quarters, the farmer swung back and laid a stinging stripe along the mule's backside. Without hesitation the mule was up and moving, motivated by the tender memory of the moment before.

Often God tries to gently lead us along the paths of righteousness and goodness, but we resist. Many times the only way our attention can be gotten is through a stinging blow. It is never offered out of anger, but always out of love. No parent who loves his or her child ever strikes them to hurt them. If they strike them at all, it is to help them learn. God never does anything to try to hurt us. Every action of God's is an action of love.

PRAYER: Forgive me that I am often resistant and stubborn. Break my spirit of defiance, no matter what it takes so that I might openly receive every instruction that you give. Amen.

May 4

He is in the way of life that keepeth instruction: but he that refuseth reproof erreth (10:17).

The judge watched carefully to see where his golfing partners were. Confident that he wasn't seen, he gave his ball a hefty kick. The ball traveled forward about twenty-five feet, onto a soft patch of close-cropped grass, in direct line with the green. He saw nothing wrong with it. He had done it as long as he golfed, and he told himself that his partners did it, too. On this occasion a booming voice cried out, "Hey, what are you trying to pull? Your ball was in the trees!" A raucous verbal battle ensued, with both sides accusing the other side of cheating. Regardless of guilt, the judge always defended himself completely.

We really do kid ourselves when we think cheating is a way to get ahead. There is nothing to be gained by cheating. Our victories are empty ones, and we open ourselves to criticism and doubt. We lose our credibility and turn people against us. It is in honesty and truth that we find fulfillment. God dwells in truth, and He loves honesty. This is the way of life, but the way of death is through sin.

PRAYER: I am sorry for the ways that I try to get ahead by dishonesty. I am not honest with myself, and then I am not honest with you. Forgive my deceptions, and lead me in the light of your truth, O God, now and forever. Amen.

May 5

In the multitude of words there wanteth not sin: but he that refraineth his lips is wise (10:19).

The board meeting had dragged on and on. Every person seemed to have an opinion that they wanted to share. The chairperson had aired her views a number of times. She droned on and on about the point she was trying to make. The rest of the staff were no different. A lot of words were spoken, but very little was being said. Then the program coordinator raised his hand and asked to be recognized. He had not said a word throughout the whole long discussion, but now he broke silence. He spoke slowly and deliberately, saying a few simple sentences, but he brought a hush over the entire room. He spoke the truth, and everyone saw the virtue of his argument immediately. That was the way he had always been.

It is a true gift to be able to listen and speak carefully. Too often we speak just to hear our own voices. People rarely get in trouble for saying too little, it is when they say too much that they feel regret. Jesus often sat and listened to the people. He let all sides speak their piece, then He would reply. His answers were direct, short and to the point. People trusted Him because He said nothing more than what was needed. Would that we could learn to do likewise.

PRAYER: Please make me slow to speak, quick to listen and grant me the wisdom to speak as Christ would. Fill my mouth with your Holy Spirit. Amen.

May 6

The lips of the righteous feed many: but fools die for want of wisdom (10:21).

The young woman sat enthralled by the words of the young preacher. She had attended church with her parents when she was young, but she found it boring and stupid. She had managed to avoid church for years, but she began to feel a longing deep inside, and its nagging had led her to this place. The boredom she remembered from her youth was gone. The truth of the preacher's words touched her at the very root of her soul. Tears rolled down her face as she realized all that she had missed over the years. Her heart beat with joy that she at long last felt as though she had come home.

When words of truth are spoken from the heart, they reach out to people to give them a rich blessing. It is important that we ask the Spirit of God for guidance as we speak. When we allow God's words to spring from our mouths we become agents for His glory here on earth. We have in our power the ability to feed those who find themselves spiritually hungry. May we use that power wisely and well.

PRAYER: Lord, I so want to serve you in all ways. Take my words and make them yours. Pour out your grace through my lips, and make my speech a blessing to those who hear. Amen.

May 7

The blessing of the Lord, it maketh rich, and he addeth no sorrow with it (10:22).

"As I grew up, I made a lot of mistakes," his grandmother had told him before he went off to college. "I made foolish choices, and I hurt myself and others. There was one choice, though, which I have never regretted, and it's never paid me a moment of sorrow. That choice was to let the Lord Jesus into my heart. Don't you dare leave for school till you let Him into yours!"

Her words stayed with him, and it helped him a lot through the four years of school. He did make bad choices, and he did feel hurt sometimes, but he never felt alone, and he never regretted that Christ was in complete control of his life.

The love of God is something that no one should be without. It is the only thing we can ever receive that has no strings attached. It is given to us to give our life more meaning, and brighten all of our days. There is nothing in our relationship to the Lord that can possibly cause regret or remorse. A good relationship with God is the path to true wealth, and it is a richness that nothing can destroy.

PRAYER: O Lord, you have made my life so wonderful. I am rich in a way that I never knew possible. I have escaped the worst possible poverty, and I praise you for giving me your love so freely. Amen.

May 8

As the whirlwind passeth, so is the wicked no more: but the righteous is an everlasing foundation (10:25).

The sky turned an ugly black, and the lightning creased the sky. Powerful rolling thunder echoed for miles, and the bottom of the clouds broke downward into a massive funnel. The tail of the cloud whipped downward until it met the ground. As it touched, debris flew high into the air. The cloud cut through the farmland, clearing the land wherever it wandered. One farm completely disappeared from the face of the earth. Fields were stripped of their growth, and trees snapped sideways like twigs. The fury of the storm mounted, then began to subside. The powerful tail of the tornado, whipped once, twice, then shredded, throwing wisps of haze into the air. The tail rose and separated, and then was no more. Nature had claimed victory, and reminded everyone where the real power lay.

The future of the evildoer is similar to that which lies in the path of the tornado. In its time, it will be swept completely away, and after the coming of the Lord, it will be as if it never existed. But, just like a firm foundation, the true believers will remain standing after the storm. When our foundation is the Lord of all creation, there is nothing that can destroy us.

PRAYER: Be my foundation, Lord. Let the winds sweep past me, but let them never carry me away. My hope and trust is ever in your love. Amen.

May 9

The righteous shall never be removed: but the wicked shall not inherit the earth (10:30).

The old apple tree had stood in the corner of the orchard for years. Its trunk was yards wide, and its branches stretched high into the sky. It had weathered many storms, even surviving being struck by lightning twice. It had long since retired from bearing fruit, but it cast shade over the yard and roof of the old farmhouse. Its roots dug deep into the soil, and nothing could move it from its place. The winds of time had long given up hopes of blowing it down, and the leaves thundered in defiance whenever a breeze kicked up.

As we dwell in Christ over the years, we lay roots which form a foundation which makes it impossible for us to be moved. Nothing can sway us if we plant ourselves completely in His love. If our roots are not in the Lord, we are shaken by the slightest thing, and we have no anchor to hold us in place. Christ invites us to take hold in the fertile soil of God's love. When we take root there, we are there eternally, and nothing can affect us. We are nurtured and strengthened by the grace of God, and we can depend on growing strong and secure in His care.

PRAYER: I place the seed of my faith in your soil, O Lord. Nurture and feed it so that it might take root and grow. Help my faith to grow strong and tall in the light of your love. Amen.

May 10

False balance is abomination to the Lord: but a just weight is his delight (11:1).

In times long gone, traders would sell grain by the measure of weight to those who would come to them. Many would place stones in the bottom of the bags in order to increase the weight. By the time their ploy was discovered, the sellers were long gone. Many traders made their fortunes by cheating unsuspecting buyers. This practice was widespread, and nothing was done to protect the innocent.

It is a terrible feeling to be cheated and know that we are helpless to fight it. We hate being on the receiving end of other people's selfishness and cruelty. We long for some way to even the score. Thankfully, God has promised that the score will indeed be settled. Those who live by deception will find themselves outside of the grace of God. No one who makes their living by the blood, sweat and tears of others can be numbered among the children of God. They have turned their backs on the ways of the Lord, and so they will pay the penalty. It is comforting to know that God sees all things, and that He will sit in judgment in the last days. Remain steadfast in the Lord, and He will grant you His favor.

PRAYER: O Lord, soften my heart against those who take advantage of me. Guide my dealings that I never take advantage of another of your children. Let my life be one of fairness and honesty. Amen.

May 11

When pride cometh, then cometh shame: but with the lowly is wisdom. The integrity of the upright shall guide them: but the perverseness of transgressors shall destroy them (11:2-3).

Summer spelled freedom. The five young boys gloried in the unrestricted time they had. On one occasion, the boys found a pair of canoes by the bank of the river. One of them said, "Come on, let's take them out. Nobody'll know." Another boy said, "I can't go out. I'm not that good a swimmer." "Yeah, me neither," said another. "Aw, come on. You guys are chicken."

One of the boys gave in, but the other remained adamant in his protest. "You can call me any name you want to. I'm not a good swimmer, and I'm not taking the risk."

The other four boys pushed off and paddled far out onto the lake. As one of the canoes turned, it was struck by a series of waves, which tossed it over. Both boys were thrown from the boat. Only one resurfaced.

When pride causes us to ignore danger and do what we feel we should not, it can result in terrible trouble. Wise is the person who knows his or her limits and acts accordingly. God wants us to use the talents we have, and the first talent to use is common sense.

PRAYER: O Lord, watch over me as I try to do what is right. I act foolishly so often. Guard my steps. Grant that I might use the mind that you gave me, in the best way possible. Amen.

May 12

Riches profit not in the day of wrath: but righteousness delivereth from death. The righteousness of the perfect shall direct his way: but the wicked shall fall by his own wickedness. The righteousness of the upright shall deliver them: but transgressors shall be taken in their own naughtiness (11:4-6).

A group of children gleefully circled the line of chairs, while music played in the background. When the music abruptly stopped, the children raced to the nearest seat, and plopped themselves down. One lone child stood, then walked off the floor, taking a chair with her. The music resumed, and the game continued. Eventually, one boy stood and one boy sat, and the game came to an end.

It is a little too simple to compare life to a game of musical chairs, but in the end of time there will be winners and there will be losers. Those who pay attention, and play by the rules will find that their reward is in heaven. Those who have been inattentive will find that their future will be loneliness and despair.

We live as though we know what tomorrow will bring, when in fact we have no idea. In musical chairs, the participants anticipate the music's end, and they ready themselves to move quickly. In life, we should be every bit as ready, so that when the music ceases, we won't be caught napping. Regular prayer and reading of the Scriptures can help us to stay ready.

PRAYER: I'm listening for your word, O Lord. Guide me by your love, that I might always be ready to meet you face to face. Keep me attentive, Lord, and make sure that I don't slumber. Amen.

May 13

When it goeth well with the righteous, the city rejoiceth: and when the wicked perish, there is shouting. By the blessing of the upright the city is exalted: but it is overthrown by the mouth of the wicked (11:10-11).

It was extremely difficult coming from a small town to try to break into the big leagues. The boy had played basketball since he could walk. He practiced every day, and everyone in town knew of his love for the game. All through his high school years, the entire town turned out to watch him play. When he was selected to play with a major college, the entire town declared a holiday and celebrated his good fortune. He progressed wonderfully, and was selected in the first round to play pro ball. Each resident took personal pride in the success of the young man, and they rejoiced in his success.

When a Christian behaves in a manner fitting for a child of God, all of heaven rejoices. Our home is where God dwells, and all of its residents take particular pride in the success of the family members who are still on this earth. God's heavenly city rejoices at the righteousness of His followers. By our words and actions, God's heavenly home is exalted, and His glory shines forth for all to see.

PRAYER: Father, I hope you are proud of the way I live my life. I want it to be a testimony to your greatness. I pray my life may be a blessing, causing great rejoicing. Bless my attempts to honor you. Amen.

May 14

He that is void of wisdom despiseth his neighbor: but a man of understanding holdeth his peace (11:12).

As a child, I remember a man who lived down the street who frightened me terribly. He was an older man who was paralyzed on his left side. His face was disfigured, and he limped along on a cane. He had a low, gravelly voice which he used to yell "You brats stay away from me! Come too close and I'll split your head." For years I would race past his house, trying not to look at his face. I felt relieved when the old man died, but later in life I found out how lonely and hurt the old man had been. He had lived a hard life, had no friends, and took his frustrations out in the only way he knew how. The man I had once thought was a monster was actually just a poor, lost soul.

I think often of how I misjudged the old man, and feel foolish that I never tried to get to know him. I made judgments without knowing all the facts. It truly is the person who is without wisdom who despises his or her neighbor. Those who have understanding refrain from jumping to conclusions and they hold their peace. There is so much good we can do, if we will only be patient and find out all the facts first.

PRAYER: I am too quick to judge, Almighty God. Grant me the patience and wisdom I need to live by the rule of gold; that I might treat others as I would like to be treated. Amen.

May 15

A talebearer revealeth secrets: but he that is of a faithful spirit concealeth the matter (11:13).

One junior high school boy confided in another his love for a certain girl. The first boy asked the second one to keep his secret. By the end of the school day, the rumor was all around about the boy and girl. The first boy was mortified as others mocked him and teased the girl he liked. In shame, the boy ran home, and in the weeks ahead he avoided both his friend and the girl of his affections. Through a thoughtless and cruel act, one person was able to shame another and build walls that blocked a relationship from ever starting.

Gossip is one of the most sinful and selfish acts we can engage in. It robs others of their honor, and places them in positions of mockery. Gossip can never build up, but only destroy. It casts doubts, and puts others down.

God favors the woman or man who keeps silence when a friend confides in them. Trust is one of the most powerful forces on earth. Every good relationship has trust as its cornerstone, even our relationship to God. When we learn to trust God, we have the weight of the world lifted from our shoulders. We can live in faith, knowing that God works all things for good, and that He will be with us always.

PRAYER: When a friend speaks to me in confidence, let me be trustworthy and devoted. Seal my lips from ever saying anything which brings another person shame or grief. May the words of my mouth be a blessing. Amen.

May 16

Where no counsel is, the people fall: but in the multitude of counselors there is safety (11:14).

All the young widow left behind was a note, saying, "I could have made it if I just had someone to talk to. I can't stand being all alone. I know my problems aren't so much greater than those of other people, but I need someone to help me solve them. I can't do it by myself anymore."

Out of desperation and loneliness, the woman took her life. This is the tragedy of those who don't know Jesus Christ. With Christ in our hearts we are never alone. God rejoices when we pour out our hearts to Him, confiding our deepest needs and desires. We all need someone to talk to. When there is someone to talk to, we feel happy and fulfilled. The load is taken off our hearts, and we are liberated. God is our savior and protector. He listens to even the smallest of our cries. We can rejoice that we have someone who understands us so completely, and cares for us so totally. When no one else is there for us to talk to, God remains by our side, never leaving, never turning.

PRAYER: My Lord, I need a haven in this stressful world. I need someone who will share my burdens and hear my cries. I need to feel that my cries are being heard. Hear, O Lord, the murmurs from the depths of my heart. Give me peace, that passes understanding. Amen.

May 17

He that is surety for a stranger shall smart for it: and he that hateth suretyship is sure (11:15).

Having landed a quality, high-paying job, it was only natural to want to look good. The clothes, the car, the accessories were all part of the image. It hadn't seemed like such a bad idea to go into a little debt in order to get the things now. He had felt that the job was secure. Now the job was gone, and everything he had still had payments left on it. There was no way he could afford the car. His credit cards were all spent to their limits. He sat looking at the bills shaking his head. There was no way he could hope to pay for the things he had purchased.

Credit is necessary in order to live in this day and age. But credit is a tool. It is to be used, but not abused. To purchase beyond our means is to steal. We are not entitled to something for nothing. It is much better to buy that which we can pay for. Debt is a trap. We can be swept in before we know what is happening.

Only God should control our lives. Certainly, we should not sell ourselves into bondage to material possessions. Being debt free makes us able to follow God, and all His commandments. When we fall into debt, we must turn our attentions from God to the almighty dollar. When we are solvent, we are free to focus our attention solely on God.

PRAYER: Grant me wisdom that I might know my limits. Guard me from entering into debt that I cannot hope to pay. Make me content with what I have, that I might not be tempted by what I do not have. Amen.

May 18

A gracious woman retaineth honor: and strong men retain riches (11:16).

Judas Iscariot possessed qualities that Jesus considered worthy, or he never would have been selected as a disciple. Judas followed faithfully for the better part of three years as he shared in the ministry of Christ. At a time when he should have been most strong, he proved weak. He gave in to the temptation of the sparkle of silver, and he betrayed his friend and Lord. He had lived so very close to the true treasure: the love of Jesus Christ, and he threw it all away due to his weakness.

Everyone sins. That is a sad, but true. Often we are weak when we want to be strong. It is vital that we hold on to the love of God in those times when we are most sorely tempted. God offers us His strength when our own strength is not enough. All we need to do is pray for this strength and it will be given to us. When we fall prey to sin, and we allow it to control us, we join with Judas in betraying the truth of Christ. When we call on God to help us in our weakness, then we have found true wisdom and strength. If we will deal honestly with God, He will shower us with treasure which cannot be taken from us, and honor which testifies to the glory of Christ.

PRAYER: O Lord, I pray that I might make you proud of me. I will try to please you by my actions, and praise you with my words. Be with me, Father. Amen.

May 19

The wicked worketh a deceitful work: but to him that soweth righteousness shall be a sure reward (11:18).

The scribes and Pharisees watched the movements of Jesus very carefully. If at any time, Jesus contradicted His words by His actions, they would have been able to discredit Him, and the Christian movement would have come to a screeching halt. Due to His divine nature, Christ was able to live a life free from sin, and thereby gave us an example of how we should strive to behave. The reward for living the life of Christ is eternal life in God's heavenly home. There is no other way that we can hope to attain heaven than through the love and grace of Jesus Christ. If we earnestly desire to follow Christ with all our heart, mind and soul, then Jesus will be faithful to judge us favorably when we come before Him.

Living the life of Christ seems an impossible task. On our own, it would be, but we have the promise of Christ that He will send a helper into our lives. We have the guidance of the Holy Spirit, and when we find that we have trouble following Christ's example, we can rest in His help. We must be honest with God, and open to His leading through the Holy Spirit. If we will do that, we will indeed sow the seed of righteousness, and God most surely will grant us our eternal reward.

PRAYER: O Lord, I want to follow in your footsteps, but they loom so large before me. I feel unworthy to attempt to live as you did, or to even hope for the reward you promise all who will be faithful. Bless my attempts, Father. Amen.

May 20

They that are of a froward heart are abomination to the Lord: but such as are upright in their way are his delight. Though hand join in hand, the wicked shall not be unpunished: but the seed of the righteous shall be delivered (11:20-21).

In a small midwestern town, a concerned group began a crusade against pornographic materials being sold in public places. Their protest met with resistance, so they hired a firm to investigate the matter for them to see who they were really up against. By the time the investigation was over it came to light that not only were area businessmen involved, but also the mayor of the town, the chief of police, two school administrators, and three powerful lawyers. The group gave up, as they felt the deck was favorably stacked for the opposition.

Evil is a difficult thing to fight, and it seems impossible to defeat when it is made manifest in a large group of people. It is strange that evil forces seem to have no trouble combining their strength, while often the forces of good never manage to get together. It is comforting to know that in the end, God's goodness is stronger than any amount of evil on this earth. Those who are evil in the sight of the Lord are an abomination, and they will have no part in His heavenly kingdom. The upright are a delight to the Lord, and it is those people who will dwell with God in heaven eternally.

PRAYER: Protect me from those who try to do me harm, O Lord. In the face of evil, help me to remember that you are God, and evil has no power over you, or those who choose to follow you. Amen.

May 21

The desire of the righteous is only good: but the expectation of the wicked is wrath (11:23).

A young boy was asked by his father to go out and mow the yard. The boy said he would do it, but then got interested in a television program. The father came back into the house and reminded the boy of his chore. The boy went out to the garage to get the mower, but got distracted when he found his brother repairing his bicycle. Finally, after watching his brother work for awhile, the young boy wheeled the lawn mower out of the garage. As he filled the mower with gasoline, a group of his friends came by to ask him to go to the movies. Hesitantly, the boy said he would go. He pushed the mower back into the garage, and making sure his father was nowhere in sight, he ran off with his friends. When evening came, the boy thought of a number of excuses to give his father to avoid the punishment he knew he would receive.

When we fail to do the things we are supposed to do, we have to pay the price. No one can make a promise to God, then break it, and expect nothing to happen. Thankfully, someone has taken the punishment for our misdeeds. Through Christ's holy sacrifice for our sake, we may approach God, asking forgiveness, and be secure in the knowledge that He will respond.

PRAYER: Hear me, O Lord, as I confess the wrong things I have done. Forgive me when I fail to live up to your expectations. Help me to do what is right to do. Guide me to repentance, that I might follow always in your light. Amen.

May 22

There is that scattereth, and yet increaseth; and there is that withholdeth more than is meet, but it tendeth to poverty (11:24).

During the great depression, two families shared a house in Pennsylvania. One family occupied the upper floor, and the other family lived on the lower. The family which lived downstairs was always inviting people in to share what they had. Whenever there was an opportunity for them to help out, they would do so. No matter how much they gave, they always seemed to have enough. The family on the upper floor, however, scoffed at the way the downstairs family lived. They stored all extras in a locker in the pantry. They gave nothing away. It was not until they found that rats had gotten into their pantry, that they were sorrowful for what they had done. Interestingly, the rats had not disturbed the downstairs pantry.

Selfishness leads to despair. True joy comes to us, not from what we own, but from what we are able to give to others. We were put on this earth to serve one another, and when we fail to do so, there is a price to pay. When we give what we have, God will bless us with more, and the blessing will be double because of the joy that giving brings.

PRAYER: Take what I have, Lord, and use it for your glory. I have nothing except what you have given me. Help me to share from my abundance, and to give all that I can to those who are in need. Amen.

May 23

The liberal soul shall be made fat: and he that watereth shall be watered also himself. He that withholdeth corn, the people shall curse him: but blessing shall be upon the head of him that selleth it (11:25-26).

A terrible drought befell a certain kingdom. It lasted on and on, and the king began to fear that he and his family might begin to suffer. He began to hoard the grain that was grown and he imposed harsh taxes on the people. Each time he took food from the mouths of his subjects, however, he caused them to grow more angry and resentful. At long last, the people rebelled against the selfish king, and they killed not only him, but his family as well.

God wants us to be giving and loving in the bad times as well as in the good. Kindness should not be conditional on whether or not it is convenient. A giving person is well loved, and reflects the kind of love that Christ came to spread upon this earth. Both Old and New Testaments give us the rule we should follow when we are asked to give: Do unto others as you would have them do unto you. If we will begin to share what we have, then we will be rewarded by our Father who sees all things that we do.

PRAYER: Make me a giving person, Almighty God. Keep the example of Christ firmly planted in my mind. Show me ways that I might give to others who are in need, and open my heart to them. Amen.

May 24

He that diligently seeketh good procureth favor: but he that seeketh mischief, it shall come unto him (11:27).

There was a man who took it upon himself to dress up like a clown and go into neighboring hospitals to visit sick children. He was not hired to do so, but he went out of a deep love for children and a desire to bring joy to them during difficult times. He spent his own money on small gifts and balloons, which he gave wherever he went. The children loved to see him come, as did the parents and the hospital staff. He refused to tell anyone who he was. He was a truly happy man, not because of the honor he received, but because of the love he was able to share.

Sometimes it is easy to forget that the good feeling we receive from doing good is the greatest reward. Our egos get in the way, and we long for recognition when we do good things. When we diligently seek to do good, we procure the favor of God, and there is nothing greater we could ever hope to achieve. Jesus Christ came to this earth as a gift freely given from God. It was not deserved, but we are so thankful that it came. It is the same spirit of giving that God looks for in His children. When we have opportunities to give, we should do so with no thought of reward or recognition.

PRAYER: You have given so very much to me, Lord, now help me give of myself to others. I want to serve you with gladness, and reflect the light of your love to all the people I meet. Destroy my selfish spirit, and replace it with your giving grace. Amen.

May 25

He that troubleth his own house shall inherit the wind: and the fool shall be servant to the wise of heart (11:29).

There was a man who ran his offices with an iron hand. He tolerated no levity or lightheartedness. Business was a place for serious minds and committed spirits. Money was the ultimate goal, and every effort had to be put forth in order to obtain it. Any breach of the businessman's rules resulted in quick termination. There were never office parties, no gifts or bonuses given at holidays, and never an offer of financial help to employees in need. After 50 years of business, the man decided to retire, and he found himself quite shocked when there was no farewell celebration in his honor. No one called to check on him, and he retired lonely and friendless.

There is nothing to be gained by mistreating those around you. We receive what we give, and it is important that we learn to show kindness and love early in life. A person who gives freely from the heart is well loved, and his or her days will be filled with joy. It is the foolish person who lives their life selfishly and harshly. For as we live, so do we die, and there can be nothing worse than dying with no one to care. Bless those whom you meet, and blessings will be yours forever.

PRAYER: Treat me as I have treated others, Lord. Keep me mindful that you are watching over my actions, and that I will receive what I have given out. Help me to show kindness, caring and love to everyone I meet, Father. Amen.

May 26

Whoso loveth instruction loveth knowledge: but he that hateth reproof is brutish (12:1).

Law school had seemed like a dream. The young woman had worked many years to get there, and now it was unreal. She never thought there could be so much work to do. She had given it everything she had, and now it was coming down to the last week of her last year. Her efforts paid off. She finished at the very top of her class, and she was lauded with honors. She looked around at many of her classmates. She knew how disappointed some of them had been with their own performances, but she couldn't really feel sorry for them. They all had the same opportunities, and some used them well, others abused them. Each one got what they paid for. She loved to study and learn, and she received the benefits of her labor.

It is true of all of us that we will put forth the most effort to do the things we love most. We will give all we have to some cause or project that we love and believe in. Jesus Christ wants to be that cause in our life. He wants us to pursue Him with everything we've got. If we will do that, we will know God, but if we follow some lesser god, then we will never know Him. It is good to listen to the word of God and to seek Him in scripture. By knowing God, we may have all the blessings that God can bestow, and we will rest in joy, eternally.

PRAYER: I want to seek you with every ounce of my being. Help me to devote myself wholly to you. Grace me with true knowledge, and lead me by your instruction, O Lord. Amen.

May 27

A virtuous woman is a crown to her husband: but she that maketh ashamed is as rottenness in his bones (12:4).

A minister faced his retirement after serving churches for over fifty years. He sat down at his typewriter to collect some thoughts for his farewell message, and his mind swept back over his years in ministry. As he poured through the years, his thoughts kept coming back to his wife, the woman who had supported him and stood beside him through many good and bad times alike. She had been his inspiration and his confidant. She had encouraged and endorsed him. She had stood in the wings, always cheering him on, but rarely receiving the recognition she deserved for her part in his ministry. Without her, there would have been no ministry, for it was from his wife that he received much of his drive and desire. Indeed, God had graced him with a loving wife, knowing that she was what he needed to be a whole person. Without her, he would have been nothing, but with her, he was a king.

Spouses can be a wonderful support to one another. That, in fact, is a large part of their role. Christians are parts of the bridge of Christ, the church. It is our duty to remain faithful to Christ, and to work to bring honor upon Him by our virtue. Our lives can be crowns upon the head of Christ, for all the world to see.

PRAYER: Lord, I want to be a faithful and loving servant. I pray that my actions might be a source of pride in your sight. Help me to remain true to your Spirit, and a shining light in your world. Amen.

May 28

The words of the wicked are to lie in wait for blood: but the mouth of the upright shall deliver them. The wicked are overthrown, and are not: but the house of the righteous shall stand (12:6-7).

When the pencil box disappeared, the little girl saw her chance. Going up to the teacher, she said, "I saw Timmy around the desk. He took the pencil box." The little girl had not liked Tim, and she felt that it would be great fun to get him into trouble. The teacher brought Timmy into the room, and told the little girl to repeat her story. Timmy burst into tears and said, "That's not true. I never took anything!" The teacher sent Timmy home with a note for his parents, and she thanked the little girl for coming to her.

The next day, when the little girl arrived at school, the teacher was waiting with Timmy and another boy. "This boy came to me this morning and admitted taking the box. Why did you say Timmy did it?" Suddenly, the lie didn't seem like so much fun. The little girl never thought she might get caught.

There is only one outcome for people who live by the lie. They will have to answer for their actions before God. It is much better to always speak truth, for the mouth of the upright will indeed deliver them.

PRAYER: May my speech always be truthful and my words always uplift. Forbid that I should ever hurt anyone by careless speech or an unkind word. Grant that I might speak with your grace and your love at all times. Amen.

May 29

He that is despised and hath a servant, is better than he that honoreth himself, and lacketh bread (12:9).

It wasn't so terrible growing old knowing that someone would be with you. All her life she had many friends, some older, some the same age, a few younger. Now she sat surrounded by many people, celebrating ninety years of a wonderful life. She knew of so many people her age who had no one. It upset her sometimes to think of people being that unhappy. Still, many of these people had done nothing in their lives to reach out to others, so it wasn't too surprising that they had no one around them now. Her husband had always told her, "You reap what you sow." She knew he was right. She was just glad that she had sown good seed throughout her lifetime.

No amount of self-love will comfort us in the end. It is through our relationships that we find fulfillment. It is important that Christians keep themselves in right relationship with God. If we pursue God, He will be with us all the days of our lives, and we will never know the pain of loneliness. We may have all of our creature comforts taken care of, but it is the emotional comforts which become so much more important as time goes by.

PRAYER: O Lord, you are my comfort and my support. I am so very glad to call you not only my Savior and Lord, but also my friend. Be with me through the rest of my days, in good times and in bad, so that I am never alone. Amen.

May 30

He that tilleth his land shall be satisfied with bread: but he that followeth vain persons is void of understanding (12:11).

A member of my youth group complained because his father wouldn't let him have the car whenever he wanted it. It's not fair." Actually, the young man had been told that if he was to drive the car, he had to help maintain it and keep it filled with gas. His father had never said that he couldn't use it. So often we take for granted the things which are not ours. We think we deserve things when we have no real claim to them at all. When we are forced to work for something, we appreciate it so much more. When things are just handed to us, and we make no personal sacrifice, then we don't learn the true value of things.

We sometimes complain to God that we have to work too hard, or that we wish we had all the things we want, but if God freely granted all of our wishes, we would lose sight of how blessed we really are. When we have to work for something, then we know its value, and we stop taking things for granted. It is good for us to learn to appreciate what we do have, and to quit dwelling on all the things we wish we could have instead.

PRAYER: O Lord, you have given me so very much. Thank you that it has not come too easily, but that I have had to put forth an effort to obtain it. I have been blessed in so many wonderful ways, and so I offer my thanks and my praise. Amen.

May 31

The wicked is snared by the transgression of his lips: but the just shall come out of trouble. A man shall be satisfied with good by the fruit of his mouth: and the recompense of a man's hands shall be rendered unto him. The way of a fool is right in his own eyes: but he that hearkeneth unto counsel is wise (12:13-15).

The man's hands moved over the wood with great love and care. The sharp tools never gouged or split, but they cut into the wood with precision. Each joint was perfect, and the result was furniture of the highest quality. It made mass produced furniture look pathetic in comparison. Many people were annoyed at the high price tag that much of the furniture carried, but people who recognized the quality of the skilled craftsmanship did not hesitate to pay the price. Each piece of furniture carried with it love and devotion to quality.

In our lives, when we produce that which is good, we will receive good compensation. When we produce inferior results, we cannot expect our reward to be great. We should strive to be perfectionists in our relationship with God. The same love and attention we pay Him will be what we can hope to receive. God is anxious to give His children good things, and we can be pleased with ourselves when we know He is giving us that which we are deserving of because we have tried to be the best we can be.

PRAYER: Almighty God, giver of good things, author of all life, help me to be a craftsman at the trade of life. Let me live a life of quality, giving attention to the finer points of life, and always giving glory and honor to you. Amen.

June 1

A fool's wrath is presently known: but a prudent man covereth shame (12:16).

The man impatiently looked at his watch. He was sure his friend had told him to be on this corner at 5:30 sharp. It was now ten until six, and he still had not shown up. The man grabbed his coat and briefcase and headed for home. All the way home he grew more and more angry. It was his birthday, and it had been tradition for him to meet his friend for an after work drink. They had done so for better than twenty years. He'd never been stood up before.

When he turned the corner and headed toward his driveway, he noticed the car of his friend parked in the driveway. Getting from the car, he slammed the door, and stormed into the house. Seeing his friend, he flew into a rage. "Where were you? Some friend. You promised me that you'd pick me up. You lied to me!" The man's face was red with rage and hurt. So angered was he that he didn't notice the cake or the circle of friends who had waited to surprise him. An embarrassed hush settled over the entire group.

Anger can be a terrible thing. Everyone has the right to get angry, but it should never control us. We should be prudent and learn to hold our tongues, so that we might not embarrass ourselves and others by our uncontrolled wrath.

PRAYER: Help me to think before I react, Father, that I might not cause grief or pain. Let me learn patience and control so that my actions may be a glory to you rather than a shame. Guide my actions and my words, Father. Amen.

June 2

He that speaketh truth showeth forth righteousness: but a false witness deceit (12:17).

I knew that I could always turn to Ed for an accurate appraisal of how I'd done. Each Sunday, after I stepped out of the pulpit I looked forward to my talk with Ed. Other people would offer kind comments about the sermon, but Ed would tell me the good and the bad, and he would do it lovingly and honestly. He wouldn't pull any punches, but every comment he would make would be salted with grace. The Eds of the world were a pastor's best friend. I could learn more from Ed in five minutes than I could in a year of preaching class. Ed was the best thing that ever happened to my sermons.

It is not always easy to hear the truth, but it is always good. The truth can lead us on to be better than we already are. When we walk in the truth, we are walking toward God. God is truth, and the more time we spend in honesty, the more time we spend with God. Not only should we seek out truth in others, but we should let others know that they will receive truth when they come to us. There is very little we could want more than for other people to be able to trust us. Trust is the cornerstone upon which solid and lasting friendships are built. We can do a person no greater service than to deal with them in truth and love.

PRAYER: As David prayed, so I pray. May the words of my mouth and the meditations of my heart be always found acceptable in thy sight, O Lord, my strength and my redeemer. Amen.

June 3

There is that speaketh like the piercings of a sword: but the tongue of the wise is health. The lip of truth shall be established for ever: but a lying tongue is but for a moment (12:18-19).

Words spoken in the heat of anger are spoken so quickly, but their impact goes so deep. Once said, words cannot be taken back. It seems to take many more words to heal than it does to hurt. It takes one unkind word to cut someone to the quick, but it may take a dozen apologies to make everything well again.

The words of our mouths are the reflections of our hearts. Like a fountain, we spring forth either good or foul water, depending on the source. If we keep Jesus Christ enthroned in our hearts, then we can rest assured that all of our words will be gracious, but if we continually take control of our lives back from Christ's loving hands, then we must take responsibility for words that may issue forth in anger or unkindness. Christ is willing to transform our hearts, to clean up the source of our life's fountain. When we give our lives to Christ, we allow Him to make us new. It is good to give our lives to Him daily, that we might always be reminded that He is the Lord and ruler of our hearts. With Christ in control, our words will be established forever, by the truth of Christ within.

PRAYER: Consecrate my life, this day, O Lord. Make me new, inside and out. Please be the ruler of my heart, dear Jesus. I am nothing without your spirit guiding from within. Shine through me, O Lord. Amen.

June 4

Deceit is in the heart of them that imagine evil: but to the counselors of peace is joy (12:20).

There was a boy who had to be better than everyone else. He spent most of his time making fun of others. He would bully anyone who was smaller than he was, he always tried to prove he was smarter than everyone else, and he would spread rumors about nice people to make people think less of them. The only people he was nice to or hung around with were people he could feel superior to. Everything he did was to further his own reputation and to throw dirt on the reputations of others around him.

Often our own egos and insecurities cause us to think more about ourselves than others. We allow pride to interfere with what we know is right and good. Christ, God become man, bowed Himself down to wash the feet of His disciples. He went so far as to die a criminal's death on our behalf. If God could give so much of Himself for us, why should it be difficult for us to sacrifice a little of ourselves for others? When we give our lives to satisfying our own selfish needs rather than the needs of others, then we practice a deceit that God cannot stand. When we learn to live our lives for others, and we work to make peace instead of causing discord, then we know a special joy that only God can give.

PRAYER: Forgive those times when I allow selfish pride to get in the way of showing my love for others. Let me know the joy that comes from following the example of Christ, sowing seeds of love and peace wherever I go. Amen.

June 5

A prudent man concealeth knowledge: but the heart of fools proclaimeth foolishness (12:23).

There was a woman who thought she was the authority on every subject that came up. Whether it was asked for or not, the woman offered her opinion. No one else could finish a thought or sentence without her butting in to present her thoughts. Some people avoided her, but she didn't care. She always told herself that they were closed-minded, and weren't worth her concern. She felt that her opinions were as good as gold, and so she proclaimed them proudly. What she perceived to be great wisdom caused others to feel pity and embarrassment for her.

There are few things worse than a know-it-all. No one likes to have knowledge lorded over them. The person who talks the loudest and longest generally has the least to say. It is much better to watch carefully our words, and learn to use them well and sparingly. We all have important things to say, and we all have a right to be heard, but we should be as interested in what others have to share as we are committed to our own thoughts. There is a saying, "'Tis better to remain silent and appear a fool, than to speak and remove all doubt." Meant as a joke, perhaps, but there is a wisdom there that we all can learn from.

PRAYER: Make my words a blessing rather than a burden, Father. Grace my tongue with the ability to speak wisely and concisely, never being a bore, and help me to be ever mindful of the things other people might wish to share. Amen.

June 6

Heaviness in the heart of man maketh it stoop: but a good word maketh it glad (12:25).

The day had been absolutely terrible. From the moment she had gotten up in the morning things had gone wrong. Her son had dragged his feet just long enough to miss the bus. Then she had gotten caught in traffic and the car over heated. By the time she made it to work she was over an hour late, and her boss had read her out. She had missed some important work the day before, which resulted in another lecture. She had dumped a cup of coffee on her skirt at lunch, then had broken a strap on one of her best pairs of shoes. Her car hadn't been ready when she went to pick it up, and she had to sit for an hour and a half until it was fixed. She thought, "If one more thing goes wrong, I will scream."

She ran up the steps to her house dreading the thought of making supper and cleaning up after the children, but as she opened the door, her heart leaped. The house was spotless, and dinner was waiting on the table. A note at her place read, "For the world's greatest mom. I love you." Suddenly, the weight of the day was lifted and things got much brighter.

It is the small ways that often mean the most. We have great power at our disposal to make other people's lives so much brighter and happier. It is a joy to God when we use our power for good, and use it often.

PRAYER: A kind word can do so much, Lord. Help me to know when to say a kind word or offer a compliment. Let my words be a joy to those around me. Grace my speech with the light of your love. Amen.

June 7

The slothful man roasteth not that which he took in hunting: but the substance of a diligent man is precious (12:27).

The squirrels worked diligently to lay aside stores for the winter. They moved from place to place, burying and storing their precious nuts. They worked from early in the morning until dusk. As they settled into their homes of sticks and leaves, two bright, beady eyes looked out from under the bushes.

A possum poked its head out from the brush and sniffed at the air. It moved from hiding place to hiding place, uprooting and eating all of the squirrels' hard earned stores. After it ransacked the lot, it returned to its home for a rest.

If you are a squirrel, the tactics of the possum are extremely hard to swallow. There are so many people in the world today who feel they should be entitled to something for nothing. They reap profit from the labors of others without a thought of gratitude or thanks. It is good to know that what is done in this earthly life is all seen by our Father in heaven. Nothing occurs which is outside of His knowledge. Those who receive their reward on earth by ill-gotten means will receive no reward in heaven. It is the diligent and devoted here on earth who are pleasing to the Lord and whom He will richly reward in heaven. Our reward lies ahead, and we will enjoy it eternally.

PRAYER: It is hard to work so hard to see so little gain, O God. PLease give me patience and the strength to proceed. Keep my eyes set on the reward that lies ahead, not the riches that this world can offer. Amen.

June 8

A wise son heareth his father's instruction: but a scorner heareth not rebuke (13:1).

It seemed like his father was always picking on him. "Do this." "Do that." There was never a time when he left him alone. Sometimes the boy thought it would be better if he didn't have a father. He couldn't get away with anything., and if he ever got caught doing something he wasn't supposed to, his old man would be on his back in a flash. It wasn't fair.

When he grew up, and had a family of his own, he realized that his father had kept after him to teach him how to live life properly. He hadn't been so tough: in fact, there were times when he wondered how his dad had ever kept from being harder. He wished there were some way to thank his father, but he decided the best way was to be a good father to his own kids.

Often we scorn instruction and rebuke because it isn't what we want to hear. But there comes a time when we are glad that we had the instruction. The words come echoing back to us, and we begin, at long last, to understand why they were offered. Too often we reject the words without actually paying attention to them. We need to listen to instruction no matter how much we don't want to hear it. It takes maturity to realize that others may know what is best for us, and in God's case, no one could ever know anything better than He does.

PRAYER: Break my resistant spirit, O Lord. Help me to open myself to your wise counsel. Lead me in the paths that I need to walk, and be patient as I learn to listen. Guide and protect my steps, Father. Amen.

June 9

Righteousness keepeth him that is upright in the way: but wickedness overthroweth the sinner (13:6).

Old time Western movies had a magical appeal. Good and evil was clearly defined by the color of the hat. The bad guys always got theirs in the end, and the good guys battled unbelievable odds, and always came out on top. There seemed to be something inherently wrong with the bad guys which tripped them up, and led to their downfall. The good guys knew all the right moves, and never made the same kinds of mistakes as the bad guys did. Righteousness would be rewarded and wickedness would be destroyed. People who loved Westerns loved them because there was such a basic sense of justice.

We all want justice. We need to believe that good will ultimately prevail, and that evil will be destroyed once and for all. Christ did just that. Christ slammed the door on evil and ensured that good indeed would prevail. Through Christ's victory over death, sin was overthrown and death lost all power. Virtue and righteousness prevailed, sending forth a light that will never be extinguished. The Westerns had the right idea. The black hats don't stand a chance. The good guys have already won!

PRAYER: Lord, I praise your victory over the grave, and rejoice that death has been destroyed for all time. Sin has no lasting power because you have washed me clean in the blood of Christ. I thank you, and I praise your holy name, for giving me such a precious and lasting gift. Amen.

June 10

There is that maketh himself rich, yet hath nothing: there is that maketh himself poor, yet hath great riches (13:7).

He had worked long and hard, and finally had enough saved for the stereo he'd always wanted. He had dreamed of this set for years. Now it was within his reach. The night before he was to go out and buy it, a knock came at his door. One of his closest friends came in crying and told him that her father had suffered a stroke, and that he was critical. She said she felt helpless because she was so far away, and she didn't have the money to get home. It would cost over four hundred dollars to make it. Hesitantly, he took the money from its resting place and he gave his friend the amount she needed, plus a few extra dollars. He told her not to worry about it. All she had to do was go home and take care of her father. When she left, he found he couldn't be sad. The stereo would wait. It really wasn't that important. What was important was that he felt great inside.

Things lose value quickly when we make them more important than people. When we give what we have out of love for others, we come to know a joy beyond words. Selfishness kills the spirit, but giving sets the soul ablaze. We come in contact with Christ's spirit the more we give to others and the less we think of self.

PRAYER: Take from me the things I have to give for others. All I have is yours, heavenly God. Make me an agent of your giving and love. Let me spread the joy of your light to everyone I meet. Amen.

June 11

The light of the righteous rejoiceth: but the lamp of the wicked shall be put out (13:9).

Two roommates prepared for finals. One had been diligent all through the semester, and had studied every night. The other had floated through classes, doing very little work throughout the semester. As finals approached, the first student was relaxed and reviewed quickly and quietly. The other roommate found that he was lost, buried beneath a mountain of work too high to climb in the small amount of time left. The first student studied normal hours, then got plenty of rest and was fresh for the exams. The other student studied late into the night, burning the midnight oil, and found himself exhausted as the testing began.

When we do the things we know we should, and we face up to our responsibilities, we find that they aren't really such a burden at all. When we shirk our duties, however, we find that they can become too much for us to handle. That light which burns within each one of us, burns most brightly when we do the things we should. When we avoid doing what is right, the light flickers and dims. Righteousness fuels the fire. Wickedness works to snuff it out. The choice is ours. We can burn brightly, shining forth with the light of Christ, or we can shine weakly, in danger of going out at any moment.

PRAYER: Let my light shine forth brightly, Lord. Feed the fire which burns within my breast. Make it a beacon of your love for the entire world to see. Help me to shine without flickering or fading. Amen.

June 12

Only by pride cometh contention: but with the well advised is wisdom (13:10).

A professor hated to be questioned. His word was law, and any student who challenged him was in for a fight. He would argue his side, and would take glee in tearing apart his less-than-well-informed opponent. He prided himself on his knowledge, and he could not tolerate having that knowledge threatened. Few people tried to argue their point, because they knew they couldn't win. The professor greatly hindered his ability to teach because he intimidated students who had legitimate questions so that they would not raise them. Even though he was the best at what he taught, most students avoided him because of his haughty attitude.

When we become too proud of our accomplishments, we lose the ability to communicate with other people. We value our own achievements higher than we value others' rights. Our attitude becomes one of being right or being the best at any cost. But the cost is too high. We are called to show love and caring for other people. We cannot show them appropriate love if we think they are our inferiors. We must learn to bury our pride and begin to sacrifice our egocentricity in the name of love for those around us.

PRAYER: What I know is not nearly as important as who I am. And who I am is not even close to who you created me to be, Father. Help me to grow into a maturity where I can set self aside, and give freely of myself to others. Amen.

June 13

Wealth gotten by vanity shall be diminished: but he that gathereth by labor shall increase (13:11).

A successful actress had made millions just on her looks alone. Her face had graced the pages of a hundred ads, and she appeared on television and in movies regularly. She received as much as $60,000 for an episode of a regular series on television. Everything seemed to be going well, until an accident scarred her, and she was no longer in demand. Though she had made millions, she had spent millions just as fast. She left acting a poor and bitter woman.

We often envy the life of stars. We believe that they have everything a person could want, and that their lives are somehow magical. There is magic to the lives of stars, but it is not all good. Some of the magic is 'here today, gone tomorrow.' Nothing is permanent, and the big money they make is gone with nothing to show for it.

It is good to be satisfied with what we receive for the labors we pursue. What we receive as wages for the work we do is money well received and deserved. We can be proud of the fact that we work hard for our money. It is right that we should receive gain for the effort we put forth. God rewards those who are steadfast in their labors. Those who receive wealth for their vanities have already received their reward.

PRAYER: Make me steadfast in my endeavors, O Lord. Keep my eyes set on my labors, and bless all my efforts. Let me feel the joy and contentment that honest labor brings, Almighty God. Amen.

June 14

Hope deferred maketh the heart sick: but when the desire cometh, it is a tree of life (13:12).

The snow fell furiously. Looking from the picture window, it was impossible even to see to the street. The wind blew the snow into great drifts, and travel had come to a standstill. Their son should have been home hours ago. He was driving in from the north, and they had hoped he would beat the storm. His mother sat transfixed by the blizzard, trying to gaze through it for some sign of her son. The father paced the room, mumbling occasionally about getting his coat and going out after him. The minutes ticked by into hours, and a tear trickled down the woman's cheeck.

As darkness fell, two dim lights cut through the swirling white. A police truck pulled up in front of the house, and a young man jumped out. He ran through the front door and greeted his mother and father. His mother burst into tears, and his father grasped him in a bear-like embrace. The tense period of waiting was over, and the rejoicing began.

Waiting is never easy, but when we are anticipating something hoped for and it doesn't appear, we have to fight the disappointment, and sometimes fear. However, when our desire finally arrives, the joy is even greater. As we Christians await our eternal home, we grow more appreciative of it as time goes by. When it is finally ours, our joy will be overwhelming.

PRAYER: Patience is one thing I could use more of, Lord. As I look toward heaven, and long to be united with you, please fill me with your patience, and allow me to learn all I can during my earthly stay. Amen.

June 15

Whoso despiseth the word shall be destroyed: but he that feareth the commandment shall be rewarded (13:13).

The woman sat at her desk reading the Bible over her lunch hour. One of her associates came up to her and said, "You don't really believe that garbage, do you? That's for weirdos and Jesus freaks." The woman looked up at the young man and said, "Have you ever read it? Do you know what it really says?"

"Hey, I don't have time to waste. You go on and read your fairy tales. I'll stick to reality."

"What happens if this is reality?" she asked, holding up the Bible.

"I'll worry about that when the time comes," he replied.

The time for a decision like that is now. If people reject the opportunity to read the Scriptures, and come to know the truth of Christ, then they will not get a second chance. Anyone who despises the word of God will have no place with God in the final times. It is the person who reads the Bible, and lives their life accordingly, who will receive the reward of life everlasting. There is no greater book in existence, and it behooves each person to take its contents very seriously. Only a foolish person criticizes something that he or she has never read. It is the prudent person who makes time to investigate, then draws a conclusion based on what they have experienced.

PRAYER: You have become real to me through the reading of your word. Assist me as I attempt to spread your word and bring others to the threshold of your truth contained in the Old and New Testaments. Bless this effort. Amen.

June 16

Every prudent man dealeth with knowledge: but a fool layeth open his folly (13:16).

A youth bragged to his friends about an escapade where he had hot-wired a car and gone joy riding with his girl friend. He told and retold the story a number of times, until it came to the attention of the school principal. The principal notified the police, and they arrived on the scene to talk to the boy. They led him out of the school in hand-cuffs, and a permanent blot went on his record. Had he not acted the part of the hot-shot, no one would have known who had done it. As it was, he set a trap for himself from which he could not escape.

Sometimes it is hard to know when to keep our mouths shut. We foolishly talk about things better left unsaid. The wise man or woman learns early when to hold their tongue. There is nothing to be gained by bragging of our misdeeds. Those things should be forgotten quickly, and the good things that we can do should be shared instead. God is not proud of us when we commit sins, and He is doubly displeased when we brag about them. God rejoices at the right that we do, and He respects us more when we learn to speak discretely and wisely.

PRAYER: Father, I ask that you guide my words. Guard that I may never speak proudly of the things I have done wrong, but let me repent totally, and be made clean. Let my words be words of kindness and charity, and help me to know when it is better not to speak at all. Amen.

June 17

Poverty and shame shall be to him that refuseth instruction: but he that regardeth reproof shall be honored (13:18).

A man who was very successful in business was asked what his secret was. He answered, "I never think I know everything. I'm always ready to listen to a new idea, and I always want to know when I'm doing something wrong." For forty years he had been a top financial consultant, and he had a reputation for listening to even the youngest of colleagues. He never defended himself when he was rebuked by his superiors. He merely listened to the comment, then did his best to improve.

This is the kind of spirit God wants in His children. God wants each one of us to grow to our full potential. Jesus tells us that we should be perfect as God Himself is perfect. The only way we can hope to move in that direction is to open ourselves to the constructive comments and criticisms of others. People can see from the outside, things we might miss from the inside. Having the integrity and wisdom to seek out the counsel of others shows a definite desire to grow. We can do little else that is so pleasing to God. Only a fool refuses to listen to the observations of others. That person is too insecure to listen, and too self-centered to want to grow.

PRAYER: Dear heavenly Father, bless me that I might grow to my full potential. Inspire me by your word and by the example of your Son, Jesus Christ. Fill me with your Spirit so that I may more closely resemble you in all that I do. Amen.

June 18

The desire accomplished is sweet to the soul: but it is abomination to fools to depart from evil. He that walketh with wise men shall be wise: but a companion of fools shall be destroyed. Evil pursueth sinners: but to the righteous good shall be repaid (13:19-21).

The young man was basically a good person, but he didn't have too many friends. He didn't seem to fit in with too many groups, so he found himself hanging around with the less desirable crowd. They accepted him just as he was. He knew there were times when he should have refused to go along with them, but it just didn't seem worth the risk. Now, he wasn't so sure. He was sitting in a police station, waiting to see what would happen. They had been picked up for vandalism, and even though he hadn't joined in the destruction, he was being held just the same.

If we choose to follow in the footsteps of fools, we will also have to suffer the consequences. When we walk along blindly, we are in danger of falling into sin. We must watch our steps and turn from that which is evil. It is our obligation to flee from sin and evil. If we keep company with fools we will be destroyed by our own folly. It is much better for us to surround ourselves with those who are committed to what is right and good. Then we will not have to fear the result, for God will see our efforts, and He will reward us richly.

PRAYER: The company I keep influences me greatly, O God. Help me to discern who I should have as friends and who I should avoid. Let my company be a blessing to others, and lead me in all your ways. Amen.

June 19

Much food is in the tillage of the poor: but there is that is destroyed for want of judgement (13:23).

The farmland was rich in minerals, and its produce was bountiful. The farm workers labored long and hard, and through their efforts the yield was high. Unfortunately, the laborers received little recompense for their hard work. The farm was owned by a large corporation, and the residents were all hired by the farm at low wages. Their land was taken from them, and they in turn were made slaves to it. Most of the farm workers were on the verge of starvation, while they worked in plentiful fields each day. The injustice of it all was incredible, but true. Their land was some of the most fertile in the world, but they were among the poorest of people.

Injustice should touch us at the very root of our soul. That part of us which is in God's image should be enraged by the unfairness in our world. And it should be the Christ in us which compels us to try to fight injustice wherever we see it. We may not be rich or powerful, but we do control our actions and our resources. We have the ability to refuse to support others who would take advantage of the poor. We can speak out against injustice, and we can offer comfort to anyone who is persecuted. When we do this, we have the joy of our heavenly Father.

PRAYER: Ours is a world of great injustice and inequality. Please guide me that I might work to change the way things are. Open my eyes to the plight of the poor, and lead me in the ways that I might combat it. Amen.

June 20

He that spareth his rod hateth his son: but he that loveth him chasteneth him betimes (13:24).

Everyone envied Jim. His father allowed him to do anything he wanted. He wasn't expected to do any work, he never had a curfew, and he got just about everything he asked for. His father never yelled at him, and he never got in trouble. He seemed to have everything he could want. That's why it came as such a surprise when he ran away from home.

When they finally found him, he told his friends that he couldn't take it any more. He knew his father didn't love him. His father didn't care at all what happened to him. What had seemed so good to all Jim's friends turned out to be torture for Jim himself.

We need guidance and instruction. There are times when we wish we didn't have to have it, but it is vital for us to grow. God gives us instruction out of love for us. We might think that it would be easier if God didn't give us His law, but eventually we would feel abandoned and unloved. God knows what is best for us in every situation, and we know of His love because He is with us to guide us every step of the way. We would be completely lost if we could not feel God's presence in our lives. Thankfully, we never have to worry about that happening.

PRAYER: O Lord, I thank you for your presence in my life. Though I often do not want to be told what I should do, I know that your word is given out of love and concern for me. Make me open to your instruction. Amen.

June 21

The righteous eateth to the satisfying of his soul: but the belly of the wicked shall want (13:25).

Two men had been friends throughout their lives. One man was extremely wealthy, having accumulated great riches throughout his life. The other man was well off, but he could hardly be considered wealthy. The rich man asked his friend, "Why is it you have so much less than I do, but you appear to be so much happier?"

His friend replied, "I've always been content with what I had. You, on the other hand, have set one goal after another. Once you attain one goal, you set one higher. I've always had everything I wanted and lacked nothing. You've never been satisfied with what you had, but always wanted more."

When we look at what we have and are thankful for it, we find that we are fulfilled, but when we are always longing for the things we do not have, then we find ourselves in want, and we cannot be happy. The wise person looks not at what they do not have, but they concentrate on what is theirs. The fool ignores the blessings he or she has been given, and they focus on the things they wish they could own. So long as we look to the things we do not have, we can never be satisfied, but if we will be content with what we have, then we will never have to know want. God has given graciously to us all. It is right to thank Him for His great gifts.

PRAYER: O Lord, I cannot believe how much I have. I cannot thank you enough for all you have given me. Help me to remember that true wealth is not measured by what I own, but by the joy that you have put into my life. Amen.

June 22

He that walketh in his uprightness feareth the Lord: but he that is perverse in his ways despiseth him (14:2).

A man had a different girlfriend every few months. He would meet someone new, move in with her, grow tired of the relationship and then move on. His life was fraught with loose morals and a lack of commitment. One girl once asked him to go to church with her. His answer to her was, "Look, I don't have much to do with God, and He doesn't have much to do with me. I'm not going out of my way to have some preacher make me feel guilty for living my life the way I want to."

Wrongdoers usually know that what they do is wrong. They sense that they are not living as they should, and they will avoid any situation which points that out to them. Many people who choose to walk in the paths of sin react in anger to the idea of God. They do not want to believe in anyone who would tell them not to do the things they love to do. The person who tries to live a good life, doing what they feel to be right, embraces the idea of a loving God who rejoices in what is right. God will indeed make us feel guilty when we do what is wrong. Guilt is given that we might know when we have strayed from the right path, and it can motivate us to return to the place where we know we should be.

PRAYER: O God, I often hide myself from you in shame at the things I know that I should not be doing. I feel guilt, and it makes me feel alien to you. Bridge that chasm I put between us. Forgive my wrongdoing, and lift me high within your love. Amen.

June 23

A scorner seeketh wisdom, and findeth it not: but knowledge is easy unto him that understandeth (14:6).

A girl sat in the circle of the Bible study and listened to the lesson being taught. When asked what she thought, she replied, "This is stupid." She folded her arms across her chest and leaned back in her chair. She tuned out the rest of the lesson, and afterward she vowed never to return. A friend of her said that she was being closed-minded, but she said, "I don't have time for this junk. I want to know how to live better, just like everybody else, but I don't think this helps at all." The girl never gave the group a second chance.

It is interesting how some people can find the answers they are seeking in churches, while others seem unaffected. Partially, it has to do with the attitude we come with. If we are open to God, and are willing to give Him a chance to disclose Himself, we will find Him. But if we come skeptically, and we scorn His power to change lives, then we block His effectiveness. For every attempt He makes to reach us, we come up with some excuse to explain it away, and we come away as empty as when we arrived. If we come before God unwilling to listen to His word, then we will never find wisdom, but when we are open minded and willing to hear, God will grant us the knowledge we so desire.

PRAYER: I come before you with an open heart and an open mind. Grant that I might have knowledge which passes human understanding. Guard me from doubt and disbelief. Open my eyes to your truth. Amen.

June 24

Fools make a mock at sin: but among the righteous there is favor (14:9).

A fifteen-year-old boy was left alone for the weekend while his parents were away on a trip. The boy had a group of his friends over, and while they were together, he suggested they take his mother's car out for a drive. A few of his friends protested, but he said, "Come on, my dad lets me drive sometimes. It won't hurt anything."

"What if we get caught?" one boy asked.

"We won't get caught. Quit being a chicken."

The boys went out and got in the car. The young man drove out onto country roads, and hit the gas. The car sped along, and all was fine until they came to a curve. The car was going too fast, and skidded from the road into a tree. None of the boys were hurt, but the car was badly damaged. One of the boys said, "We won't get caught, huh? This is all your fault!"

When we mock sin, and pretend that we can't be hurt by it, we are fooling ourselves. Sin has great power to hurt and destroy. Only a fool thinks otherwise. The wise man or woman knows the risk of sin, and they learn to avoid it. When we resist sin, we are walking in the favor of the Lord.

PRAYER: Father, remind me of the danger of sin. Keep me from the things which can destroy me. Set my feet on the path of righteousness, and never let me stray. Be with me as I journey, Lord. Amen.

June 25

The heart knoweth his own bitterness; and a stranger doth not intermeddle with his joy (14:10).

The woman was in shock at the death of her husband. They had been married for fifteen years, and she had settled into the idea that they would be together forever. She couldn't quite believe that it was true. Every once in awhile she would walk through the house just to make sure he wasn't there somewhere.

Her friends had been so kind and helpful, but she was glad they were gone now. She thought if she heard one more person tell her they knew exactly how she felt she would scream. They didn't know. They couldn't. Somehow it was different. She'd said the same thing on a number of occasions, but never again. It didn't do anything to help. Her pain was her own, and there was no way that anyone could share it.

It is good to have friends that care, but we can have no friend greater than Jesus Christ. Christ dwells within our heart, and so He is the only one who can honestly comfort us when our heart is broken. Christ is as close to us as we are to ourselves. He is a part of us, and when we suffer, He suffers, but also when we rejoice, He rejoices with us. We are one with Christ, and it is so good to know that we never have to face life alone. He is with us in good times and bad, and He will never leave us.

PRAYER: Christ Jesus, you know me to the very depth of my being. Dwell within my heart, and grace it with your strength and love. Let me feel your presence within me. Guide me, protect me, stay with me, I pray. Amen.

June 26

There is a way which seemeth right unto a man: but the end thereof are the ways of death (14:12).

The day's work had been so long and hard. The man stood on the road where the train tracks crossed. If he took the road, the walk would take another half hour. If he cut across the train trestle it would take only ten minutes. Looking both ways down the tracks, he decided to chance it. He began to cross the high bridge. About halfway, he heard the familiar whistle of the evening train. Usually it was a sound of comfort, but now it struck terror into his heart. Glancing over his shoulder, he saw that the train was coming on fast. He began to run, but he had little hope he could make it to the other side. He had always told his boys never to try to cross the train trestle because of the danger. He only wished now that he had taken his own advice.

Often we are fooled into believing that something wrong is right. We make excuses to ourselves, and then we proceed to do something we know to be wrong. When we do that we must be prepared to pay the consequences. It is much better to avoid risk and do those things that we know we should. If we will walk only on the path of righteousness, then we will come to know a life free from dread and fear. It is through a life well lived that we come to know true happiness and joy.

PRAYER: Jesus Christ, my Lord, you have saved me from myself. You guide me in the paths of righteousness for your name's sake. Keep my feet firmly planted on the path which leads to life eternal. Amen.

June 27

Even in laughter the heart is sorrowful: and the end of that mirth is heaviness (14:13).

She hated closing time at the bar. The crowds had thinned and the lights were unplugged, and everything quieted down. It got too quiet. She had to face the thought of going back to her lonely apartment. She came to the bar to melt into the noise and laughter. She could be charming in the right setting. She could at least have a good time for a few hours, but it always came to an abrupt end and she had to face her desperate unhappiness. She sometimes wished she could find a party which never ended, but that was senseless. Eventually she would have to come back to reality, and her problems would all be waiting for her when she did.

So many of our attempts to find happiness end in futility. We look in all the wrong places for fulfillment and happiness. We exert such energy pursuing good things, and we never attain them. The deep loneliness that we sometimes feel inside is a homesickness for our creator and heavenly home. When we take Christ into our hearts, we never have to face the loneliness which destroys. We stop looking for artificial answers, and we focus our attention on the one real answer: God. In Him, we find fulfillment and life.

PRAYER: O God, you have given my life such meaning. I no longer seek other answers, for I have found the one true answer. In Christ I have found everything I could ever desire. Thank you, O Lord. Amen.

June 28

The simple believeth every word: but the prudent man looketh well to his going (14:15).

The TV preacher had sounded so sincere. For years, the woman had faithfully sent in money whenever she could. The work he did was so important, and he had brought her so much comfort through the years. She had given a lot, even when she really didn't have extra to spare, but it had all been for the glory of God. She was a part of a growing ministry which spread God's word throughout the world, via satellite. She had been proud of her efforts, until now.

The headlines read that the minister was being indicted for fraud and illegal use of funds. He lived in a palatial estate, and drove big fancy cars, but she always had believed that they had been gifts. Now it appeared that he had used money from people like her to fund these luxuries. She felt so used and silly. It was enough to make her lose faith. Now what would she do?

As stewards of God's world, we are charged to look wisely before we enter into new areas. God gave us our minds to use to His glory. We must think carefully before we commit ourselves to any proposal. It is the wise person who walks carefully, but the fool rushes ahead, asking no questions, and taking no precautions. Faith is admirable, but only when it is founded upon wise action and thought.

PRAYER: Allow me to deal with prudence and good sense, Father. Help me to discern truth from that which is false. Make me a good steward of the gifts I have been given. Help me to do what is right, keeping me from foolish ways which might destroy. Amen.

June 29

A wise man feareth, and departeth from evil: but the fool rageth, and is confident. He that is soon angry dealeth foolishly: and a man of wicked devises is hated (14:16-7).

The two players sat transfixed, their entire concentration on the chess board in front of them. The match had gone on for over an hour, and the heat was rising. Both players were looking for blood. They had played masterfully. Then, as quickly as it had started, it was over. A single wrong move resulted in defeat. The loser stood up abruptly and wiped out the table. He stormed to the side of the room, and slammed his hand into the wall, breaking bones and tearing the skin. He cried out in pain and rage, and yelled for the room to be cleared. When the storm subsided, he sat alone in pain and shame, not only from his defeat, but from his childish display.

Self-control is an important part of the Christian's life. Christ had many occasions where He could have lost control and wreaked havoc on His enemies. That would have destroyed His mission on earth; to teach love and provide an example for how we should live our lives. Anger is a natural reaction, but it cannot be allowed to take control of us. When we live by our passions, we live on the danger line, and eventually we will fall prey to sin. The wise person learns to respect the power of his or her emotions, and they depart from situations where they might lose control.

PRAYER: O Almighty God, save me from myself. When anger rises within my heart, help me to control it and channel it in constructive ways. Do not let me be a captive to my passions. Amen.

June 30

The evil bow before the good: and the wicked at the gates of the righteous (14:19).

During the Second World War a group of German soldiers moved through a small town, burning and looting as they went. They destroyed many buildings, including a part of an old church. Then they moved on. During the night, they met up with an enemy troop, and they retreated into the town. They ran to the door of the church which had been partially destroyed. They pounded on the door, begging for sanctuary. As the Allies marched ever closer, their begging turned to desperate cries. When the priest opened the gate, he found the soldiers lying face down in the dirt, sobbing.

This picture is a good example of the evil-doer before the judgment seat of God. Those who have traveled through life doing wrong deeds without a care will find themselves on the verge of destruction. They will have no recourse but to throw themselves on the mercy of God. The wicked will be laid low, and they will bow before goodness. They will cast themselves down before the gate of heaven, but for many it will be too late.

The time to choose right over wrong is now. There is no time to wait. God will number the good among Him, but the sinner will find himself outside of God's presence. He has given each of us the same choice. Whoever is not for Him is against Him. Where we will end up is completely up to us. How will we choose?

PRAYER: Lord, be with me. Do not cast me away from your presence, but keep me ever protected by your love. Amen.

July 1

The poor is hated even of his own neighbor: but the rich hath many friends (14:20).

I had a friend who got along wonderfully with me when we were alone, but when his other friends were with us, he treated me as if I were beneath him. He was wealthy, and so were many of his friends. They had their own language, and they judged people by what they owned, what they wore, and what they drove. One day, in frustration, I told my friend that either he could treat me the same way no matter who we were with, or he could forget having me as a friend. To my surprise, he chose to end the friendship.

It is amazing how we find ways to judge one another. We set standards for acceptability and draw lines defining what is good enough and what isn't. We categorize people, and force them into molds. This is wrong. We do our neighbor an injustice when we judge him. We are all children of God, and it is our purpose to see the face of Christ in all our brothers and sisters. When we treat another person as an inferior, it is as if we were doing it to Christ. Jesus taught us to love all people, regardless of their status. We are to accept everyone just as they are. When we learn to do that, we begin to love our neighbors as God loves us.

PRAYER: Make me love everyone equally, O Lord. Help me to accept everyone just as they are. Help me to see my brothers and sisters as you see them, through eyes of unconditional love. Amen.

July 2

He that despiseth his neighbor sinneth: but he that hath mercy on the poor, happy is he (14:21).

The yard had become a junk heap. There were rusty automobile parts, mattresses, pots and pans, bottles, and old magazines, not to mention the general rubbish that had accumulated. The neighborhood was in an uproar. Maybe the police would shake them up. If something didn't happen soon, there were certain members of the neighborhood who were ready to take things into their own hands.

When the police came, they found an old couple who spoke very little English, and the husband suffered from many ailments. They wanted to keep their property nice, but they just weren't able to. When neighbors had complained they had tried to ask for help, but no one would pitch in. They felt totally helpless, and they were frightened by what might happen.

We can be so mean to each other without ever meaning to be. If more people would offer to help rather than threatening or bullying, our world would be a much more pleasant place. When we reach out to help others in need, we are displaying the love of Christ which is at home within our hearts. When we refuse to show kindness to our neighbors, we are showing that Christ has no part in us.

PRAYER: *Almighty God, may my actions always prove my love and devotion for you. Help me to share the love you have given to me with those who need it most. Make me a loving disciple, following Christ's example, and learning to love my neighbor as myself. Amen.*

July 3

In all labor there is profit: but the talk of the lips tendeth only to penury (14:23).

The politician promised so many wonderful things. His constituents wanted to put their faith in him. They kept hoping someone would come along who cared about their plight. Every time new promises were made, the hopes of the people soared. Each time, though, their hopes were dashed to the ground, as the great talk dissolved into just so much wind. This time they hoped it would be different. They had to hold onto something. Promises were the best they could find. If even half the talk resulted in action they would be a great deal better off than they were now.

Talk without action can be destructive. If we make a promise we must be committed to following through. Jesus told the people of His day that they should not swear, because when they didn't do what they said, it was a sin. It is good for us to commit ourselves to helping other people, but when we make empty promises, we are being cruel and unloving. It is through action that we show how much we care, not through mere words. Actions speak louder than words, and actions done in love speak the truth of Christ in our lives. Let us always strive to follow the example of Christ, saving our words until we are ready to act.

PRAYER: You have given me so much, O Lord, let me now share it with those who need it. Let not my words be a trap for me, but let me act in a way pleasing to you. There is nothing that needs to be said, only love needs to be shown. Amen.

July 4

A true witness delivereth souls: but a deceitful witness speaketh lies (14:25).

There is a grand lady who stands in the New York harbor. Her name is Liberty. She holds aloft a torch which has been a guiding beacon to a land of freedom and democracy. Her witness is to a very special kind of truth. It is a truth that many people from many different lands never have the opportunity to know. It says that every person has the right to a full and happy life. True, it is an ideal, and there are many people in America who don't realize their rights, but it is a dream that is readily available to everyone who wants it.

God's people have ever been in search of a Promised Land. As Christians, we know that our Promised Land awaits us in heaven. It is the responsibility of every believer to bring about God's kingdom on this earth. We should walk in the truth of God. If we will devote our lives to His truth, then we can become the Christian nation that our founding fathers envisioned. The promise of truth in our land has attracted many, many people. However, when we turn from the truth, then the promise offered is just a lie. God blesses those who dwell in His truth. When we wrap ourselves in God's truth, we shine brightly, a beacon for the world to see.

PRAYER: Thank you for the dream of truth and righteousness. Let me be a part of that dream. Help me to shine forth the light of your truth for others to see. Establish your kingdom within our hearts that we might know your truth here and now. Amen.

July 5

In the fear of the Lord is strong confidence: and his children shall have a place of refuge. The fear of the Lord is a fountain of life, to depart from the snares of death (14:26-27).

A young Russian was arrested for smuggling Bibles into area prisons. He stood before a tribunal for sentencing, and they shipped him off to a high security prison. Each day, he was taken to a warden who asked him if he was sorry for what he had done. His answer was always the same. Each time he said no, he was beaten, then returned to his cell. Years went by, and the daily routine continued. The Russian prison hoped to break the spirit of the young man, but instead, an interesting thing happened. The prison held thousands of prisoners, and over time, many of them were converted. Within the prison a great revival took place, all because the young man refused to renounce his faith in Christ.

The story is a familiar one. Christians have been persecuted over the centuries. When they withstood the torture and torment, they proved to be powerful witnesses to the truth of Christ. A good knowledge of God gives us confidence so strong that nothing can shake it. The truth of God is a fountain of life, and by dwelling within it, we depart from sin and all its ramifications. When we stand fast in the truth of God, He will give us everything we need to hold on.

PRAYER: Be with me, God, to guide me, to support me, to strengthen and love me. Never depart from me, Lord, that I might stand fast in the face of every trial and persecution. Allow me to be an example for others. Amen.

July 6

A sound heart is the life of the flesh: but envy the rottenness of the bones (14:30).

A college woman was always comparing herself to other people. She watched the way other women dressed and acted, and she was intensely jealous of women she considered prettier or more intelligent than she was. Whenever she went out on a date, she spent time talking about how she wished she was like other women she saw. She was dissatisfied with herself, and she could talk of nothing else. Men quickly tired of her incessant complaining and comparing. Her envy caused her to become bitter, and she began venting her anger on her friends and classmates.

Envy is like a cancer. It starts small, but it spreads quickly, and it is extremely destructive. It causes us to be dissatisfied with ourselves the way God created us to be. It says that we think we deserve more than we really have. It is a form of selfishness which causes us to be less than we should be. When we conquer envy in our own lives, then we grow strong and sound, and we have God's favor. It is good for us to learn to be happy with ourselves and the things we have. It is better to thank the Lord for our many blessings than to curse Him for the things we feel cheated without.

PRAYER: There are many things I wish that I could have, Father, which others possess. Please help me to be content with the things I have now, and help me to rejoice that others have been blessed with special abundance. Let me begrudge nothing to other people. Amen.

July 7

He that oppresseth the poor reproacheth his Maker; but he that honoreth him hath mercy on the poor (14:31).

A couple walked along a darkened street and came upon a young woman sitting with a baby in her arms. As they passed, the young woman held forth a hand and asked for some small gift to help her feed her baby. The couple recoiled from the girl's hand, and they hurried on their way. As they strolled along, they realized that they were not alone. Another person followed them. They quickened their pace, but the figure stayed right behind them. Finally, in frustration and fear, the man turned to the stranger and asked him what he wanted. The stranger replied, "You have had the chance to feed the Son of God and you have turned away. Therefore, if you would hope to come into God's glory do not be surprised if He turns from you." With that the stranger walked away, leaving the couple to stare in disbelief.

Christ said that when we help others who are in need, it is the same as doing it for Him. All of God's children were created in His image. When we reject any one of God's children it is as if we are rejecting Him. He wants us to give from our abundance to make life more comfortable for one another. When we see the world through the eyes of God, we have compassion on the poor and suffering, and it becomes our heart's desire to help them.

PRAYER: You have put me here with a purpose, O Lord, and it is to learn to serve you. I can best serve you by meeting the needs of those I see in need around me. Grant that I might never turn away from someone in need. Amen.

July 8

A soft answer turneth away wrath: but grievous words stir up anger (15:1).

The man had always lived by the adage, "Fight fire with fire." He was truly a fighter. No one ever got the best of him. He'd seen his share of scuffles, but he did alright. His brother had always been a namby-pamby kind heart, who thought peace should be kept at any cost. He hated how his brother would swallow his pride in order to keep the peace. He knew that he would never do that. That was the coward's way out. It was much better to let everybody know you weren't going to be pushed around. Let people know who's boss, and they won't give you any trouble.

One of the big problems in the world today is that everyone wants to show the rest of the world who the boss is. No one wants to back off or work for peace. Each party wants to prove to the other that they are the most right. As long as we refuse to negotiate or compromise, we will have fighting. The desire of God is that we will learn to use kindness and love in order to solve our problems. A wisely spoken word could save much unpleasantness if only we will take the time to think before we act. Nothing good comes from stirring up the anger of our opponents, but there is much to be gained through kindness and common sense.

PRAYER: Soften my heart and the words of my mouth, dear God. Let me be a peacemaker, rather than an agitator. Let my words spread comfort and calm, and make my actions a testimony to your great love. Amen.

July 9

The eyes of the Lord are in every place, beholding the evil and the good (15:3).

The corporate offices of a large company had a wonderful record for security. In its twenty-five year history, there had never been a break-in. There had been attempts, but the intruders were always apprehended before they could make a move. The secret to the fine security record was a high-technology video center which allowed a watchman to keep tabs on all key entry points to the building. By sitting in a chair surrounded by monitors, the watchman could see the entire plant. Nothing could happen without the guard being immediately notified.

God is like that watchman. There is nothing which occurs that God is not immediately aware of. No matter how insignificant an act may seem, it does not escape the notice of the Lord. His eye watches everyone: the good, the evil, the young, the old, male, female, black, white, red, yellow, every person who lives upon this earth is in God's loving sight. It is comforting to know that He sees us in the good times and the bad, and that He knows exactly what is going on. He can share in the innermost thoughts we have, and he knows our desires before we even express them. God knows us, and He loves us, totally.

PRAYER: Keep your eye upon me, Lord. Watch my comings and goings, and be with me in everything I do. Bless my actions, and keep me protected by your loving care. Help me to do the things which are most pleasing in your sight. Amen.

July 10

The sacrifice of the wicked is an abomination to the Lord: but the prayer of the upright is his delight (15:8).

There was a man who came out to church only on Easter. He felt that it "looked good" to put in an occasional appearance. He wanted people to think well of him, and to know that he supported his church. Each year he made a big gift to the church, making sure that many key people were aware of the large amount. He bragged of his support, and how much it meant to the church. Whenever he was asked to serve the church in any way, however, he couldn't find the time. Only when it was advantageous for him to be associated with the church would he consider it. His connection with the church was purely public relations.

Scripture says that God loves the cheerful giver, but He wants the giver to be sincere also. Financial contributions are always important, but they are not nearly as important as the gift of self which each person should give. We are to give ourselves body, mind, and spirit to the work of Christ's church. Anything less is not good enough. The gift given for the wrong reasons is an abomination to the Lord. The gift of the upright, rightly given, is a true joy to the Lord, and it is His delight.

PRAYER: O Lord, take my life and consecrate it to your service. Take not only my gifts, but also my talents and resources as instruments for your ministry. Guide me in the ways that I can best serve you, and grant me the wisdom to know where you want me to go. Amen.

July 11

Hell and destruction are before the Lord: how much more then the hearts of the children of men (15:11).

A light plane crashed in the desert. The pilot survived the crash and began a long, hot trek toward civilization. He wandered for hours without seeing anything remotely man made. As day turned to night he began to think he had survived the crash just to die a slow, painful death. With morning light, he set out once more in search of rescue. When his last ounce of strength gave out, he sat down and began to cry. His sobs grew in intensity, and they merged with another sound. Controlling his emotions, he looked up to see a jeep approaching in the distance. He bowed his head to say a quick thank you, then waved to the driver of the vehicle.

There are times when we feel that we must surely be out of God's sight, or at least out of His favor. It is comforting to know that God sees everything that goes on no matter where it is. God can see into the very depths of hell, so it is no great wonder that He can see into our hearts to know what we are feeling and thinking. Our lives are open to our creator, and at the time when we think we have no hope, the grace of the Lord will reach down to us and let us know that we are saved. God will never leave us, no matter how far we may go.

PRAYER: Be with me, Father, as I walk along the many paths which make up my life. When I lose my way, and turn from the one true path, wait patiently for me to return, and keep me ever in your watchful eye. Amen.

July 12

A scorner loveth not the one that reproveth him: neither will he go unto the wise (15:12).

There was a woman who was terribly overweight and in failing health. She knew that the best prescription for her was to diet, but she really didn't want to. Her daughter urged her to see a doctor, and she kept promising that she would. Each time she made an appointment, something came up and she canceled it. When confronted by her daughter, she said, "I don't need to go to the doctor to have him tell me I'm fat. I already know that he'll tell me I need to lose weight." The poor woman died due to a kidney malfunction which was totally unrelated to her weight problem. Her fear of the chastisement of the doctor had kept her from getting the help she needed.

When we are afraid to be criticized or advised, we seriously restrict our ability to receive help. Often the words of a critic may be the words that save us from ourselves. When someone's only intention is to help us, it is wise for us to seek their counsel and then heed it. When we run and stick our heads in the sand we stop growing and developing. If we feel guilty or inferior, we might try to avoid those people who would give us advice, but it is always better to deal with problems head on, than to let them balloon out of control.

PRAYER: I am often afraid to hear what others think of me, Lord. I am insecure, and I often wish that I could run and hide. Give me the strength and courage I need to grow and change for the better. Amen.

July 13

A merry heart maketh a cheerful countenance: but by sorrow of the heart the spirit is broken (15:13).

"You never get mad. You always seem to be happy and having a good time. I don't understand it. I wish I could be like you." The two walked along the beach, together. "It's really not that hard. You just have to decide that you're going to be happy, then do it. I got tired of being unhappy about everything, so I decided to quit," the other answered.

"It can't be that easy. There has to be more to it."

"It was that easy for me. I just thought about which I liked better; being happy or being sad. I don't like being sad, so I fight it."

We can decide to be happy. It takes work, but it is a conscious effort that anyone can make. God is the giver of the greatest joy a person can ever know. When we make Him the Lord of our life, He can work within us to fill us with this unspeakable joy. All we need to do is ask Him in. When we are filled with sorrow, we break the spirit and we undercut the effectiveness of Christ in our lives. The Lord dwells in joy, and He is well at home in a heart that is happy. When we are truly filled with joy, the whole world can see it. They will notice that we are not like everyone else, and there is no more powerful testimony to the power of God than a smile which cannot be taken away.

PRAYER: Fill my heart with your joy, O Lord. Change the light of my countenance to happiness so that everyone will know the effect you have had on my life. Wherever I go, help me to spread joy and love. I praise you for your gracious gift. Amen.

July 14

All the days of the afflicted are evil: but he that is of a merry heart hath a continual feast (15:15).

"Stop that singing. You drive me crazy, sometimes," the old woman shouted across the hall.

The other woman stopped singing, looked up, and smiled. "Why, I'm just singing because I'm happy. What's wrong with that?"

"I'm not happy, and you shouldn't be either. We're old, sick, nobody comes to visit us, and we live in this dingy little hole in the wall."

"Well, why should I dwell on all that? I've got a sound mind, the sun is shining brightly, and I am not in want of anything I need. I think I'm pretty lucky, don't you?"

"I just think you're nuts!"

When Christ reigns in our hearts, we can see the beauty and goodness of our lives, but when He is absent, then every day is an affliction. The person who is unhappy is doubly resentful of the person who knows true joy. The joy-filled person is a reminder that happiness does not belong to everyone. How sad that every person doesn't come to know the joy that God offers so freely. We can work to spread happiness if we will. Through our actions and attitudes we can convey a lot of what God has done in our lives. People notice the difference, and when we give credit to God, we spread His gospel in a very powerful way.

PRAYER: Lord, make me a beacon of joy to shine forth to everyone I see. Let them see the difference in my life that comes solely from you. Amen.

July 15

Better is little with the fear of the Lord, than great treasure and trouble therewith (15:16).

She had always dreamed of what it would be like to be rich. She had never really been poor, but the idea of having a lot of money had always been exciting. Now it was reality. Her father had died, and all of his wealth was hers. She didn't understand half of what the lawyers had said about taxes and trusts, but she knew she was rich. Already people were calling her and sending her literature about boats and cars and homes. People she hadn't seen in years were showing up from everywhere. She was a little afraid of strangers who came around. Her friend told her that people would be more likely to break into her home to steal from her now. She wondered if she would ever get out from under all the red tape so that she could start living it up.

The minute we begin turning our attention to wealth and possessions, we turn it from the Lord. The less we own, the less we are distracted. The poor person can deal with God continually, but the rich person has to attend to other things. God wants to be the sole possessor of our hearts. He will not share our hearts with any other god. We all must make the choice of what we will pursue. The wise person chooses to pursue the Lord.

PRAYER: Almighty God, there are so many things which pull at my attention. I am blinded by the glitter of wealth and glamour. Shade my eyes in the shadow of your divine Spirit. Guard me from the traps of the world. Amen.

July 16

A wrathful man stirreth up strife: but he that is slow to anger appeaseth strife (15:18).

The first pitch had been an accident. It had slipped from the pitcher's grip and had sailed at the head of the batter. Angry stares were exchanged, but nothing more. The very next inning, the opposing pitcher threw at the batter. The batter tossed aside his bat and he charged the pitcher. Both benches emptied and a brawl broke out. Players and coaches were ejected from the game, and tempers were allowed to cool before the umpires allowed play to resume.

It's a common occurence, and a sad one. Grown men trying to start fights is silly, and it destroys the integrity of the sport. But once a person's pride is damaged, they will stop at nothing to get revenge. Spiteful people live to stir up strife. It is the prudent person, one who holds his or her anger, and stifles his or her pride, who brings forth peace. If we could learn to care less about ourselves and more about others, there would be fewer occasions when we would cause discord. It is the person who loves God who also loves peace. The peacemakers are the true disciples of Christ. To the person who refuses to stir up strife, there will come a great reward.

PRAYER: You have blessed the peacemakers, Almighty God. Please number me among them. Wherever I can be used, let me be an agent of your love and peace. Send me where you would have me to go, O Lord. Amen.

July 17

The way of the slothful man is as a hedge of thorns: but the way of the righteous is made plain (15:19).

It was maddening to try to get the children to do their work. Whenever there was a game or an activity they were ready, willing, and able. But at those times when the chores needed to be done, they were nowhere to be found. They were getting lazy, and it was annoying. It was also troubling to have to punish and threaten in order to get them motivated. They should want to pitch in. They lived in the same house, and everyone had to pull their weight or it just wasn't fair.

The same is true in the body of Christ. In the body there are many parts, and each one must do what it was created for or the body cannot function as well. It is important that we always give our best effort. Anything less is an insult to our creator. We shine a negative light onto God when we are lazy or slothful. Christians should be proud to do their best in all things, as a sign to others that being a Christian is something special and good. Our actions are generally what we are most often judged by. If our actions are positive, then our testimony to God is a positive one, but if our actions are unbecoming, then we shame God, and we give people a bad impression of what it means to be Christian.

PRAYER: During the times when I get lazy, help me remember that my actions reflect not only upon myself, but also upon you, O Lord, and upon all others who call themselves Christian. Help me to always put forth the best image possible. Amen.

July 18

Without counsel purposes are disappointed: but in the multitude of counselors they are established (15:22).

Always before, the department had worked as a team, working out strategies together, and delegating responsibilities to different members of the group. Now, a new chairperson had come in, and she wanted things done her way. She had no desire to hear about how things had been done before. She had been hired to direct operations, and she was going to do it the way she saw fit. Unfortunately, she didn't know the department, and her ways weren't always the best. Effectiveness dropped sharply, and finally the department was disbanded.

When a person thinks they have all the answers, and they refuse to listen to the comments of others, there will usually be trouble. We cannot come into a new situation and know all the things we need to. It is the wise person who seeks counsel from the group who is established there. Without counsel, plans go awry. But when counselors are sought and the opinions are incorporated, then plans can run smoothly and effectively. The best counsel we can hope to seek is the Lord's. He will guide us if we will ask Him to. When we shut the Lord out of our decisions, then we are destined for failure.

PRAYER: Be my guide, dear Lord, and open my mind to new ideas, and my heart to your prompting. Do not let me act unadvisedly, but always lead me to seek the help of those more competent than myself. Amen.

July 19

A man hath joy by the answer of his mouth: and a word spoken in due season how good is it (15:23).

The algebra problem was a tough one. No one had given the right answer yet, and the teacher had gone through half the class. Andrea hoped that the teacher wouldn't get to her. She wasn't sure her answer was even close. Smarter people than she had missed it. The most she could hope for was that someone else would get the answer before the teacher got to her. Her heart sunk and she felt her cheeks flush as the teacher called her name. Timidly, she ofered her answer. To her delight, the teacher praised her for getting the right answer. Andrea felt a surge of pride at her accomplishment.

It is a joy when we know we have done a job and that we have done it well. When we say or do the right thing, it makes us feel good. That is why God wants us to always do what is right. When we live a life of righteousness, then that good feeling never leaves us. We experience not only the joy of a job well done, but we provide a good example for other people to see. God is proud of us when we do what is right and good. We can feel great peace knowing that we are doing what God hopes we will do. His favor is worth more than all the riches of the earth.

PRAYER: I pray that my words may always be full of grace and pleasing to you. When I proclaim your greatness and spread your word, I do what is pleasing in your sight. Help me that I might forever do what you want me to. Amen.

July 20

The heart of the righteous studieth to answer: but the mouth of the wicked poureth out evil things (15:28).

She knew her brother had put so much of himself into his writing. She wanted to be kind, but she didn't know exactly how to tell him it wasn't very good. She wanted to break it to him gently, to save his feelings if it was possible. She loved him dearly, and didn't want anything to come between them. Still, he had asked her opinion, and she had to be honest with him. While she was waiting for her brother to return, her own daughter entered the room and seeing what her mother read, said, "Isn't that trash awful?"

"Honey, be careful what you say. Your uncle might come back any minute."

"So? He's a terrible writer, and the sooner he knows it, the better."

"But there are ways to say it without hurting him. Just saying he stinks won't do anybody any good. You have a lot to learn about kindness, young lady."

A kind person will think before speaking. The power of a word to destroy is unbelievable. An unkind word carelessly spoken can build walls that can never be torn down again. It is much better to think of how we should respond than to blindly and tactlessly spout our opinions. Honesty is not a virtue unless it is spoken with compassion and love.

PRAYER: Salt my words with your loving kindness, dear Father. Help me to know the right words to say in difficult situations. Let me convey only love and caring, no matter what I might have to say. Amen.

July 21

The light of the eyes rejoiceth the heart: and a good report maketh the bones fat (15:30).

Their grandfather had looked so bad, so frail, the last time they had seen him. They remembered their grandpa as a happy man who had loved to spend his time with his family. He gave so much of himself and they loved him. He had always been so much fun to be with. It was terribly painful to see him lying in a hospital bed so pathetically. If he had to die, it would be better for him to go quickly. The thought of seeing him waste away was too painful to deal with.

When they arrived at the hospital, they went right to his room. When they opened the door, he was sitting up in bed. He turned to look at them, and joy came into his face. A sparkle gleamed in his eye, and his granddaughter realized that that gleam was what had been missing before. Just seeing that sparkle gave her a feeling of peace. Seeing him this way she knew he would be alright.

There is something about truly good people which shines forth from within. When we are in the presence of goodness, we feel it. Something deep inside of us responds to that spirit which emanates outward, and we feel wonderful. That something special is God's love, and it cannot be contained once it fills a human heart.

PRAYER: May the joy and peace of my relationship with you show from my face and shine forth from my body. I want everyone to know that I am yours, and that you make all the difference in the world. Amen.

July 22

The ear that heareth the reproof of life abideth among the wise. He that refuseth instruction despiseth his own soul: but he that heareth reproof getteth understanding (15:31-32).

A young dancer wanted to be the best she could be. She auditioned for a number of dance companies, many of whom were interested in her. She chose to go with the one who told her they saw great potential, but she needed to work hard to become better. She worked diligently with the instructors, and she gained knowledge from their expertise. She listened carefully to everything they had to say, and she tried to do everything they told her. Her desire to be a great dancer guided her actions, and she did everything in her power to attain that dream.

If the young woman had allowed her ego to get in her way, she would not have been willing to listen to the people who were best able to help her. If she had been satisfied with where she was, she could have settled for less than was her potential. But when we place quality above all else, then we are able to humble ourselves and listen to the teachings of those who can help us. When we commit our lives to Christ, then we free ourselves to follow the commandments of God, knowing in our hearts that His commandments will lead us to our heart's desire; eternal union with Him in heaven. It is possible to all who will place self aside and open their lives to God.

PRAYER: Lord, I am a selfish person, and I rebel against those who would help me to improve. Break this rebellious spirit within me and lead me in the ways which lead to improvement. Amen.

July 23

The fear of the Lord is the instruction of wisdom; and before honor is humility (15:33).

There was an actor who was fond of telling everyone how wonderful he was. His house was a museum of memorabilia from his career. His rave reviews were framed and hung in every room. Awards graced shelves and tables, and copies of his movies were played on video tape machines on large screens whenever visitors came by. He took such delight in rattling off his achievements that no one else ever felt compelled to praise him.

Too often people seek after honors, when they should be striving after humility. Honors are not something that we deserve. They are gifts, and should be given by others, not by ourselves. Conceit is a sin, and when we praise our own efforts we slip into it. God is most pleased when we commit ourselves to doing what is right. Even if no honors come to us in this life, God will honor us richly in the life to come. It is the humble man or woman who is able to keep their sight set on God and doing His will. If we will use our time doing the things that God has asked of us, we will not have time to brag about our accomplishments. God has given us plenty to keep us busy all the days of our lives. If we stay committed to doing what is pleasing in His sight, He will bless us all of our days.

PRAYER: Keep me humble, Lord. Help me to remember that I am nothing without you. You have given me everything I have and everthing I am. You have blessed me with so many wonderful things, and I praise you. Amen.

July 24

The preparations of the heart in man, and the answer of the tongue, is from the Lord. All the ways of a man are clean in his own eyes; but the Lord weigheth the spirits. Commit thy works unto the Lord, and thy thoughts shall be established (16:1-3).

We have an excuse for everything. When something goes wrong, we can always explain it away. When we forget to do something, we can usually come up with a good reason. If we are lazy or irresponsible we somehow rationalize it. Most of the time, we can satisfy ourselves and others that our actions are pure. This practice will work in almost every case, except in the case of God.

God has given us commandments and rules as guidelines for living a Christian life. He has given us standards by which we can be measured. He has allowed us every possible help, and so when we come before Him, He expects us to deal openly and honestly with Him. If we try to make excuses or convince Him of things that aren't completely true, He will know it, and He will reject our reasons. God sees us as we really are. He knows not only our words, but the intentions of our words. He sees not only the things we do, but He knows why we do them. Unless we commit our lives to God, we will try to live as we want to, not as He wants us to. We will be called to account for our lives, and it is only those who have truly sought to follow God's will who will see heaven.

PRAYER: Lord, you see into my very soul. Please help me to be honest with you, with others, and with myself. Cleanse my spirit, so that I might turn from those things which are an abomination in your sight. Make me the person you want me to be. Amen.

July 25

The Lord hath made all things for himself: yea, even the wicked for the day of evil (16:4).

She had to be the most forgiving woman in the world. Three young hoodlums had broken into her house, had tied her up, stolen all her valuables and she didn't even have a harsh word to say about them. She said, "I'm fine, and that's all that really matters. Those boys are God's children just like everyone else. They have just gone bad. God will take care of them, so I don't have to worry about it one bit."

It is difficult to let go of bad feelings that we hold against other people. When we have been wronged, we want justice done, we want to see the persecutors be punished. Often, we forget that they are children of God, and that we must love even those who do not love us. Jesus said that if we love only those who are good and kind, that we do not know the real meaning of love. It is when we can learn to love those who hate us and try to harm us that we understand what love is all about. If God loved only those who were worthy of His love, then he would never love anyone. Love isn't something earned. It is something freely given, and God expects us to love everyone at least as much as we love ourselves. God created everything on this earth, and it is our duty to respect and honor His whole creation.

PRAYER: Most holy God, it is not easy to love those people who seem evil and try to hurt me. I get angry when people try to take advantage of me. Help me to love with your love, and to see life through your eyes. Amen.

July 26

By mercy and truth iniquity is purged: and by the fear of the Lord men depart from evil (16:6).

She felt so much better. She hadn't meant to hurt anyone and she'd carried the guilt around with her long enough. The minute she heard about the fire, she remembered having left the coffee pot plugged in. Two people were injured and she had been frightened to speak up. Then her supervisor had been blamed and she felt so guilty. She tried to ignore it, but it kept nagging at her. She finally had to say something, not only to clear her supervisor, but also to clear her conscience.

Confession is good for the soul. We cannot hope to improve our lives when we walk around burdened by guilt and shame. When we admit our wrongdoing, we are able to begin anew with a clean slate. We can be so thankful that God forgives us the things we do wrong. Without that forgiveness, there would be no way for us to be united with Him. When we receive God's blessed forgiveness, it is as though we never sinned at all. God forgives and forgets, and once God has wiped our sin away, it is gone for good. Only when we are wise enough to admit our sin can we hope to be cleansed of it. God will not force us to come to Him. Only when we seek Him out and confess our sins to Him will he forgive us and make us new.

PRAYER: Heavenly Father, forgive me for the many things that I have done wrong. Help me to begin anew, starting fresh, and committed to doing what is right and good. Lead me in the paths of righteousness, Lord. Amen.

July 27

Better is a little with righteousness, than great revenues without right (16:8).

It hadn't always been like this. When he had first started in business, he could sleep like a baby. He didn't have a care in the world. Now, it was different. He tossed and turned every night because of the guilt he felt. He was short-tempered and angry all the time. He felt like a heel every time he foreclosed a mortgage. He had worked so long to get where he was, but there was no satisfaction to it, only turmoil. All the money and prestige in the world wouldn't make up for what he was feeling inside. He decided that the only way to deal with it was to quit his job. It was the best decision he ever made.

Sometimes we feel like money will make everything alright. We think that it can cure all our ills and make us whole. There are some things that money cannot do. It cannot give us peace of mind, and it cannot replace human relationships. We need other people, and we must love them more than money. When we serve money instead of people, we lose our sense of all that is right and good. It is much better to have little money and great happiness, than to have mountains of money and no peace of mind.

PRAYER: Lord, I have what I need. Please make me content with that so that I don't go running off, pursuing things I do not need. Make me content with my life as it is, keeping me from dreaming of things that are really unimportant. Amen.

July 28

A just weight and balance are the Lord's: all the weights of the bag are his work (16:11).

The woman was enraged. She had worked at her job for about five months, and she found out that the man who had been hired a month after her had just received a promotion and a raise. She had done as much work as he had, and she had done it at least as well. It wasn't fair. Men got all the breaks, while women were treated like slaves. She went to her boss and laid out her complaint. He gave her an excuse which she didn't believe and she turned in her resignation.

There is much in our world that is not fair. However, we must be willing to pay the price for making our points. Many people will complain about injustice, but they won't risk anything to see changes made. They are unwilling to sacrifice anything in order to take a stand.

We are agents of God's will on earth. God loves justice, and He loves to see His children stand up for what is right. The Lord rejoices whenever one of His believers takes a stand for what they think is right. When we disagree with something, we need to voice our objection. When we see injustice, we need to speak out. Nothing comes of merely complaining in the comfort of our own homes. If we will risk a little bit to take a stand for justice, then God will bless our efforts and He will provide everything we need to persevere.

PRAYER: Help me to be a part of your righteousness, O Lord. Help me to see what is wrong and what is right, and let me speak out when things are not as they should be. Grant me the power to work for change. Amen.

July 29

In the light of the king's countenance is life; and his favor is as a cloud of the latter rain (16:15).

The planting was all done. The soil had been prepared, the seed had been laid, the fertilizer spread. Now all that was left to do was wait. If the rains came soon, everything would be alright, but if they held off just a week or two, it could greatly hurt the crop. The early spring rain was vital. A soft, steady rain could mean the difference between solvency and bankruptcy. The sky was full of deep gray clouds, rolling overhead. With the sound of distant thunder, the farmers breathed a deep sigh of relief.

It is hard to accept that our ultimate fate is in the hands of another. Even as great as God is, it is frightening to know that He holds our destiny in His hands. But just as the farmers feel relief at the first sign of rain, we can feel relieved that our fate has already been sealed by the blood of the Lamb, Jesus Christ. Through His sacrifice we have been bonded to God. When we accept Christ into our lives, we accept the promise of eternal bliss with our Father in heaven. There can be no greater joy than knowing that God's love has saved us, and that our future has been decided by His grace.

PRAYER: I look to you for my salvation, Lord, and I feel joy at the assurance of your great love for me. I have done nothing which is deserving of your favor, but I praise you from the very depths of my soul that you have looked upon me with compassion. Be with me now, and each day to come. Amen.

July 30

How much better is it to get wisdom than gold! and to get understanding rather to be chosen than silver (16:16).

For years, the American government sent food down to the people in Central America. They would set an allotment, then ship it to distribution centers. This provided the people with food for a short period of time, but once it ran out, there was no more, and the people were little better off than before the food arrived. Then, in the sixties, army engineers were sent to teach farming and irrigation methods. The know-how was shared by which Central American citizens could raise their own food. No more would they depend on the limited supplies sent to them from outside. Now they were able to produce for themselves, and no one need go hungry again.

It is better to give people the knowledge they need to do for themselves, than it is to give people things which are here for a short time and then gone. Money, equipment, resources, all fade away over time, but knowledge lasts forever. God could do everything we ask Him to, but then we would not be motivated to grow and mature. It is through doing for ourselves that we learn responsibility and what abilities we have. Caring for ourselves is more precious than gold or silver, and it makes us even more thankful to God in heaven for the blessings He bestows on us.

PRAYER: Teach me to use the gifts and talents you have given me. Help me to do for myself and others rather than wait for things to be done for me. Give me the wisdom to know what to do and when. Amen.

July 31

He that handleth a matter wisely shall find good: and whoso trusteth in the Lord, happy is he (16:20).

A teacher was highly respected for her ability to handle tough situations. Children never seemed to give her a hard time, and if they got out of line, she handled the matter quickly and decisively. Most of the children loved her, and their parents thought she was great. Her classes received good marks, and her pupils displayed much promise. The woman knew how to draw out the best from every student she taught. When asked about her ability to deal with children, she replied, "I pray for each one of them. I may not always know the best way to handle a situation, but God does, and the two of us working together can't miss. I know that He will lead me to do what is best for the kids. I know that with all my heart."

It is wonderful to be able to put all our trust in God. If we will let Him in on all the concerns of our lives, He will share in them and guide us through them. There is great power in prayer. When we pray to God we make our concerns His concerns. We may be able to handle situations well, but we can handle much better if we will ask God's help when we face them. True happiness comes to us when we can be confident that our decisions are sound, and that conviction can be ours if we will only turn to the Lord.

PRAYER: I want to put all of my trust in you, Father. Your wisdom is beyond my comprehension, and I know that you will always do what is best. Be with me when I make decisions and guide my actions. Amen.

August 1

The wise in heart shall be called prudent: and the sweetness of the lips increaseth learning (16:21).

There was a small boy who always looked out for the feelings of others. Whenever the children would begin to tease or taunt another child, the small boy would defend the victim and offer comforting words. If a child fell or was hurt, the small boy ran to help. Whenever one of the children was in need of cheering up, the boy was right there with a kind word. All the adults said that he had the soul of an older man, and they claimed he was wise beyond his years.

Kindness is such a small thing, and yet too few people practice it. When a person is kind it causes others to sit up and take notice. The person who is kind and loving provides an example of what Christ wants for all of us. We enjoy being with kind people. They make us feel good and they cheer us up. They are special people indeed, and it is well for us to join their ranks. God loves to see His children offer kindness to each other. Kindness is contagious, and we should always strive to cause an epidemic of loving and giving. Christians should be the first to be kind, to show the power of God in their lives to make a difference. Wisdom of the heart is the love of God, and it is the greatest gift we can hope to share with others.

PRAYER: I want to sow the seeds of your love wherever I go, dear Father. Make me an agent of kindness and consideration. Help me to lift the spirits of other people and to make sure that they know joy all their lives. Amen.

August 2

Understanding is a wellspring unto him that hath it: but the instruction of fools is folly (16:22).

The little girl had been told a thousand times not to play too near the street. She had never known why her parents were so firm about it, but she tried always to remember that it was forbidden. Once she had played too close, and her father had given her a spanking. She remembered that for a long time. It crossed her mind every once in awhile that she should try to find out what was so bad about the road, but she knew that she would have to go to the road to do it, and she wasn't ready to risk it. While she was thinking about the road, the neighbor's dog bolted out after a car. The driver hit his brakes and screeched to a halt, but it was too late. The dog had been hit and was dead. The little girl watched wide-eyed, and suddenly she understood what she had been told all of her life.

Many times we question the things we have been told. We don't understand why they are important. But when we understand the request and we see the logic of it, then it isn't so hard to follow the instructions. Through understanding comes life. When we refuse to listen to the instructions of God in our lives, we are flirting with disaster. All He has commanded is for our safety and well-being. If we will listen to the word of God, a long and happy life will be ours.

PRAYER: O Lord, I do not understand everything you tell me, but I am trying, and I trust that you know what is best. Help me to be an obedient child, and help me to understand the ways you ask me to live. Amen.

August 3

Pleasant words are as a honeycomb, sweet to the soul, and health to the bones (16:24).

The golden liquid dripped from the combs into the collecting trays. It was amazing to watch the process and to think that this wonderful sweet was the product of a swarm of bees. Processing the honey and cleaning the combs had always been fascinating, and he loved watching it. It had been a part of his growing up. He would help his father and his grandfather, and lick the sweet sticky residue off of his hands. That was good, but what was better was taking the first jar into the house to spread on grandma's homemade cornbread. Nothing was better in the whole wide world.

Christians have within their power the ability to sweeten the lives of the people they meet. Kind words and sincere compliments are like the purest honey, sweet and good. The memory of a word rightly spoken can be a strength and a support to a person in time of trial. A compliment can boost a sagging self-image or make a person feel they are appreciated. We need to feel that others care about us and respect us. Our words are precious gifts to give, if we will use them to build up and praise. When we use our words to heal, we are serving God in a very special way, and His favor is upon us.

PRAYER: When I see the opportunity to offer kind words, help me to say the right thing. Let my speech be a reflection of your grace. Let me serve other people in word as well as deed, Father. Amen.

August 4

An ungodly man diggeth up evil: and in his lips there is a burning fire (16:27).

He knew he would find it if he looked long enough. His opponent could not be the saint he painted himself to be. Every man had a skeleton in his closet. They were unavoidable in politics. Once the public knew he had been treated for drug abuse in college, his pure reputation would be tarnished, and he would be brought back to earth. It didn't matter that it had happened thirty years in the past. All that mattered was that it had happened. It was all he needed to drag his opponent's name through the dirt.

It is sad that so many people take pleasure in the pain they can cause. God wants us to devote as much of ourselves as possible to loving other people, not destroying them. There is nothing good which comes from spreading rumors and trying to discredit those around us. When we live in the past, and in the sins gone by, we are chained to this existence, and we cannot move forward. Thankfully, God forgives us for the things we have done, and we can carry on with a clean slate. It is our duty to do the same for other people. If we hold the past against them, then we judge them unfairly. It is better to see each person for who they are now, and to realize that they too have been created in the image of God.

PRAYER: It takes so little to make others feel good, Father, and yet I don't try nearly enough. Make sure that I not only avoid doing harm, but also make me to do good whenever and wherever possible. Amen.

August 5

The hoary head is a crown of glory, if it be found in the way of righteousness (16:31).

There was a time when the elder members of a society were held in high esteem. Their opinion was sought whenever difficult decisions were made. They were visited by the younger members of society who wanted to be taught the skills that the older people possessed. The aged were the keepers of traditions, and the stories of history and heritage. They were revered and praised. They were taken care of by their children, and they were considered a very valuable resource indeed.

It is a shame that has changed. The older people of our day are hidden away in homes and institutions, or communities of people their own age. Their opinion is rarely sought out, and their skills and traditions are ignored. They have become a burden rather than a treasure. This is sad, because they are a wellspring of wisdom and experience.

Wisdom comes over time. As we live and experience the trials and tribulations of this world, we gain a new perspective on the way things really are. A person who lives for a good long time has seen things that we will never hope to understand. A life well lived is a shining example for others to follow. When we hide it away, we cheat ourselves of the light that is waiting to shine forth. God wants our light to shine brightly, and no one should ever ignore a light no matter what the source.

PRAYER: Help me never to ignore the counsel of those who have lived longer than I have. My elders have much to share and teach. Give me the wisdom to hear their words and follow their instructions. Amen.

August 6

He that is slow to anger is better than the mighty; and he that ruleth his spirit than he that taketh a city (16:32).

The choice came down to two salesmen. The first got great results, but he was a little bit wild, and he couldn't always be counted on. The second man got average results, but he could be counted on every time. The account was important, and they really wanted the best person to go after it. The first man figured he would be selected, while the other man only hoped. It came as a surprise to them both when the second man was selected. It was decided that dependability was more important than a smooth come-on.

If we learn to practice self-control we are well on the road to wisdom. God requires His followers to be disciplined. It is not always easy to be a Christian, but we are expected to hold fast to the faith through bad times as well as good. The disciplined person learns to deal with hardship, and through discipline gains endurance. God loves the person who is steadfast and unyielding in faith. The person who gives up easily and forgets their trust has no place with God. We need to pray for strength in our faith, and trust that God will grant it. Discipline is greater than strength or intelligence or charm. It gives us the foundation we need to build a faith which cannot be shaken.

PRAYER: Give me a faith that will never fail, O Lord. I put my trust in you, because there is nothing on earth which is more powerful than your might. Be with me to strengthen me and give me peace. Amen.

August 7

The fining pot is for silver, and the furnace for gold: but the Lord trieth the hearts (17:3).

The fire glowed white hot. The metal ore was dropped into an oven and it melted like butter. As it liquefied, the impurities and dirt floated to the top. It was skimmed, and then reheated. Once again, any impurity rose to the surface. This was done time and again until nothing made its way to the top. Then it was poured into molds which fashioned the ingots it was distributed in. The intense heat would have destroyed most things, but with gold it simply made it better. No purer gold could be found in existence.

The fire of the Holy Spirit works in our lives in much the same way. God's purging love burns through us, chasing out the impurities and dirt. We are purified each time we ask the Lord into our hearts. He is faithful to take away all our sins and make us pure. Often, it is not easy or pleasant. The fire burns, and it can make us uncomfortable. But the result is worth the discomfort. Being purified in the love of the Lord is an experience which is great beyond words. He sees into the darkest resources of our hearts, and nothing is safe from His healing fire. We are made new and clean in Christ, and we are purified totally. There is no other way. Water may wash us clean outside, but fire is the only way to be purged within.

PRAYER: Make me clean, Father. Send your cleansing Spirit of fire into my heart. Destroy every impurity in my life and remove the dirt which keeps me from being clean. Refine my heart and make it more precious than gold or silver. Amen.

August 8

Whoso mocketh the poor reproacheth his Maker: and he that is glad at calamities shall not be unpunished (17:5).

The girls walked up the sidewalk to the next house. They had been collecting for hunger relief all afternoon, and they had done pretty well. They knocked at the door, and a man answered.

"We're collecting for the starving children in Calcutta. Could you give something?" one of the girls asked.

"No, I won't give anything. I don't care about the poor in Calcutta. If they want to eat, let them work like I do. If they can't get off their tails and earn a living then they can go right ahead and starve."

With that, the man slammed the door in the stunned faces of the girls.

Whether we realize it or not, poor people are our responsibility. God has given us all the same charge: to love our neighbor as we love ourselves. When we know that someone is in need and we turn our heads so as not to be bothered, we take responsibility for the suffering of others. Those who intentionally cause another grief shall be punished by God Himself. God's people care for each other, and if we call ourselves children of God, yet we ignore those who are in need, then we are liars, and God will have no part in us. The choice is always ours.

PRAYER: Do not let me ignore my responsibility to other people who are in need. Help me to learn to be compassionate and caring. Let me use the excess from the abundance you have given me to ease the plight of the poor. Amen.

August 9

A gift is as precious stone in the eyes of him that hath it: withersoever it turneth, it prospereth (17:8).

The rain was coming down in sheets now, and she had no idea how to change a flat. As long as it was raining so hard she held out little hope of getting someone to stop and help her. Suddenly, a rapping came at her window, and she rolled it down slightly.

"Need some help?"

"I've got a flat and I don't know how to fix it."

"You go wait with my wife in my car, and I'll have it changed in a jiffy."

Her savior was a young man with a beard and a kind face. He worked quickly in the pouring rain, and when he was finished he was drenched to the bone. She thanked him and began to pull a twenty dollar bill out of her wallet, but he refused to take it.

"Listen, all I ask is that you remember this the next time you see someone in need whom you could help. Do something nice for someone else, and we'll call it square," he said.

True kindness doesn't look for any rewards. It is done from the heart, and there is no payment great enough to cover it. It is only when we learn from it, and turn around and give it to someone else that kindness is repaid. Giving of ourselves to others is a precious gift, and when we give it, it just keeps on going.

PRAYER: Help me to give kindness, love and care, Father. Bless my efforts, that my gift may grow and spread. Amen.

August 10

He that covereth a transgression seeketh love; but he that repeateth a matter separateth very friends (17:9).

"You never let me forget, do you? Look, I said I was sorry a hundred times. I lied, I was wrong. It won't ever happen again!"

It happened every time they got into an argument. He knew he had done wrong, but he had asked forgiveness a dozen times. It would cool down, but then somehow it would come up and start another argument. If only he would let go of it, but no, he always held it over his head. It hurt to know that he wasn't forgiven. He had blown it and was truly sorry, but to be reminded of it over and over made him feel like a heel. He didn't know how much longer he could hear about it before it would begin to affect their friendship.

True forgiveness only occurs when we treat the subject as a closed matter. If we bring up old hurts whenever feelings fly, then we have never really forgiven. To hold a grudge is to build a wall between yourself and another person. Forgiveness breaks down walls. Christ came to break down walls and lead people to reconciliation. Before true healing can occur, though, we must let loose of all old hurts and start fresh. Forgiveness gives us the clean start we need to heal all wounds. With God's help, we can grow closer than ever before.

PRAYER: Teach me how to drop old hurts into the sea of forgetfulness, and truly forgive those who have harmed me. Fill me with your grace, that I might learn how to be graceful to others. Amen.

August 11

A reproof entereth more into a wise man than a hundred stripes into a fool (17:10).

He'd seen what happened to people who couldn't follow instructions. He'd been in prison a short time, but it didn't take long to learn what to do and what not to do. Some of the inmates were so stupid. They would intentionally disobey, and then get sent off to do hard labor. They never learned. It just wasn't worth it. Well, they didn't have to tell him twice. He was going to toe the line and do just what he was told. There wasn't going to be any hard labor in his future. Prison was hard enough without doing anything to make it worse.

The wise person learns that there is nothing to be gained by sin. With sin comes punishment, and it is better to avoid sin altogether than to try to find some way out of the result. Some people never learn. They do the same things again and again and cannot see their folly. When we sin, it is vital that we turn from sin, rather than head right back into it. When something bad happens, we should avoid it rather than set ourselves up for more pain and suffering. Children learn to do the things they should, and to avoid the things they shouldn't do because they will be punished if they don't. Our punishment comes only once, but it is severe. It is the wise man or woman who decides now not to tempt fate. The wise person follows the rules, and enjoys the rewards it brings.

PRAYER: Keep me on the paths of righteousness, and never let me stray. Give me the wisdom to know what I should do. Amen.

August 12

Whoso rewardeth evil for good, evil shall not depart from his house (17:13).

She had tried everything she knew. She had been kind, she had gone out of her way to be friendly, she had offered her rides home, she had bent over backwards to help her out, and she still was rotten to her. She couldn't understand why anybody would want to be so mean. Her best friend had told her that the girl was spreading terrible rumors about her. This very night she had tried to be friendly, and the girl had called her names. Some of her friends said that the girl was just jealous of her, but still, that didn't give her the right to be so nasty.

It is hard to understand why people have to be so unkind. We can try everything we know to be nice, and still there are some who will not respond in kind. Those people are to be pitied, for they will never know happiness or peace. There is something which causes them to be terribly unhappy, and they vent their sadness on those around them. Christ enables us to return good for good, and even good for evil, but He never likes to see us return evil for good. Happy and content is the person who spreads happiness, but sad will be the person who spreads evil, for the wrong done will never be escaped.

PRAYER: O Lord, make me a doer of good works, and help me to avoid doing things which are wrong or hurtful. Help me to understand the people who do me evil, and guide me to try to help them whenever I can. Amen.

August 13

He that justifieth the wicked, and he that condemneth the just, even they both are abomination to the Lord (17:15).

It had seemed like an open and shut case. All the evidence seemed to point to the innocence of the man. Then there had been rumor of organized crime being involved, and suddenly the case shifted dramatically. Despite huge holes in the argument of the prosecution, the judge had decided in their favor and an innocent man was going to prison. The lawyer had always suspected the judge of some dishonesty, but now he was sure that somebody had the judge in their pocket. There was no doubt about it, the judge had sold out an innocent person, and let the real criminals go free.

Justice is miscarried as often as it is served. Not just in the courtroom, but in everyday life. Good people get persecuted, and evil men and women are applauded as stars and heroes. Somehow our priorities have been badly shaken up. Christ came to change all that. Good people can rest assured that evildoers will be judged according to their actions. What seems so unjust now, will be turned aright when God passes His final judgment. Then, as Scripture says, the last will be first, and those who seem to be first will be last. Evil will be put in its place, and good will rise to reign supreme.

PRAYER: Give me patience, Lord. Everywhere I look, evil seems to be doing better than good. Help me to remember that you are still in charge, and that everything will turn out well in the end. Grant me peace through trial, Father. Amen.

August 14

A friend loveth at all times, and a brother is born for adversity (17:17).

He couldn't believe it. He had worked for the same company for almost thirty years, and suddenly they pulled the rug out from under him. He had never known anything else. It seemed like all his hard work had been for nothing. He had been a good employee, and he had never made trouble. Now he felt ashamed for no good reason. He didn't know what he would do.

A knock at the door brought him out of his deep thought, and he got up to answer it. Outside, his brother waited for him. When he saw his brother standing there, tears came into his eyes. Whenever anything had ever gone wrong his older brother had been there to make him feel better. Just seeing him stand there made him feel like there was nothing to worry about. No matter what happened, he knew he could always count on his brother. He had yet to face any bad situation without his brother to support him, and as long as he could lean on him, he knew everything would be just fine.

As children of God, we can be thankful that we have Christ to call a brother. He will be with us in every situation, both good and bad. He will be our support and our counselor. He will listen without judging, and He will never leave us. He is as true as any brother could be, and we can count on Him to be there for us no matter what.

PRAYER: Thank you for being there when I need you. You are my strength and my shield. I am so grateful for your love. Amen.

August 15

He that hath a froward heart findeth no good: and he that hath a perverse tongue falleth into mischief (17:20).

He had told all his friends he could jump from the bridge to the train as it passed by. He had said he'd done it hundreds of times. They had called him a liar, and double dared him to prove he could do it. They'd even bet him money, so he'd taken them up on it. Now he was standing on the bridge, and his knees felt like jelly. He could hear the train whistle in the distance, and he knew that there was no turning back. He didn't want his friends to think he was a liar, or worse, that he was chicken. The train came into view, and he braced himself. When it got to the underpass he counted ten and then jumped. He was off just a bit, and he slid from the car top and fell to the rocks below. He was badly hurt, but alive. At least he hadn't been chicken.

Lies can only lead us into trouble. Sometimes our words cause us to get ourselves into situations which are dangerous or stupid. We are made prisoners of our lies. It is so much better to live honestly and uprightly rather than in deception. God will reward the honest woman or man, but the liar will have to answer for every falsehood. The upright individual can rest knowing that everything that he or she said is true. The liar has to continually worry that his or her lie will be discovered.

PRAYER: Lord, I want to be truthful in the way I speak. It is easy to slide into lies, and I need your help to avoid the snare. Protect me from my own weak desires which cause me to lie. Fill me with your truth. Amen.

August 16

A merry heart doeth good like a medicine: but a broken spirit drieth the bones (17:22).

Two men went into the hospital at about the same time, having suffered similar heart attacks. One of the men grew depressed and irritable. He felt betrayed by his own body and saw his affliction as a sign of weakness. His attitude was sour and he cursed his fate. The other man took it in stride. He kidded with everyone who came to visit him, and he laughed long and hard. He refused to be brought down by his plight. Instead, he occupied his time cheering up other patients and chatting with the staff. The first man grew weak and frail. The other man left the hospital in good health, and resumed his old life quickly.

The way we face life has a lot to do with how good we will feel about it. If we are negative, then life will be a burden, but if we are positive, life will seem like the greatest gift we've ever known. Happiness is contagious. When we are happy it spreads. However, sadness is contagious, too, and when we are gloomy, we spread a gray cloud over all the people we meet. A positive spirit is like a powerful medicine. It has a great deal of power to heal. It is so much better to face life with joy than to let life get you down. The person who feels that life is bad will wither and fail. God gave us life to enjoy, and He blesses us when we embrace it with happiness and contentment.

PRAYER: Fill my heart with joy that never ends. Let it overflow from my life to touch the lives of those around me. Make me a source of happiness for everyone I meet. Grace my countenance with a smile, bathed in the light of your love. Amen.

August 17

Wisdom is before him that hath understanding; but the eyes of a fool are in the ends of the earth (17:24).

It was boring, that was all there was to it. He tried to pay attention, but no matter how hard he tried, his mind just started wandering. Who cared about English anyway? He could read, he could write his name, that was better than a lot of people these days. He just could care less. It was much more interesting to gaze out the window and dream about the future. He planned on making lots of money and having lots of fun. He'd go to a good college and get a good job. Yeah, he knew everybody said his grades weren't good enough, but he'd find some way. High school was dumb. College was a different thing. He'd really apply himself then, but for now, it was boring.

Too many people live for the future instead of for today. We dream of how things might be, and we ignore how things really are. We focus our eyes far up along the road, and we miss all the sights around us now. The wise person lives today to the best of their ability in order to create a better tomorrow. The fool continually dreams of things he or she wants to do without making any of the necessary preparations. It is good and right to hope for things in the future, but we are responsible to do everything we can to make them come true. Tomorrow doesn't mean a thing unless we have lived well today.

PRAYER: Lord, bless this day, which is a precious gift from you. I thank you for every day that I live. Life is a wonderful gift, and one that I can never hope to repay. Take my life, and consecrate it to your love. Amen.

August 18

Even a fool, when he holdeth his peace, is counted wise: and he that shuteth his lips is esteemed a man of understanding (17:28).

It took every ounce of courage he had to say anything. He had always been shy, and he was terribly afraid of being made fun of. He knew that if he ever opened his mouth, he would say the wrong thing and be ridiculed. He had been that way all his life. People probably thought he didn't know anything, and that wasn't far from the truth. He wasn't overly bright, and that just added to his fear. It came as quite a shock to him, then, when one of the girls in his class came to him for help with her assignments. She told him that she had always thought that he was smart because he wasn't always talking and trying to impress everyone. What he feared most was that his silence would be taken as ignorance, while instead it was being perceived as maturity and intelligence.

We don't have to be brilliant, but it is important that we learn to keep our mouths shut when the situation warrants it. No one likes a know-it-all, and it is much better to say too little, than to always say too much. The wise person doesn't always have to be talking. They find comfort in silence rather than awkwardness. A fool speaks to cover silence, and ends up saying silly and senseless things. The saying goes, "Silence is golden," and in many cases a truer word was never spoken.

PRAYER: *I think that I have so much that is worth saying. Help me to remember that I learn more when I listen than when I speak. Help me to hold my peace, and to give others time to share their thoughts and feelings. Amen.*

August 19

Through desire a man, having separated himself, seeketh and intermeddleth with all wisdom. A fool hath no delight in understanding, but that his heart may discover itself (18:1-2).

I have always had the problem of turning a situation over to God, and then pulling it back and trying to handle it myself. As much as I trust God, I find myself holding back and trying to do things by myself. I know in my heart that God is in complete control, and that there is no place better for my problem than in His care. That never stops me from meddling. I foolishly think that I can do every bit as well on my own. Then, when things fall apart, I chastise myself for my stupidity.

Wisdom comes to the man or woman who can trust God totally, and give up their problems to Him. Peace of mind and heart is a rare and valuable quality, and the person who truly trusts God will find it. There is absolutely nothing we can do better than God, except mess up a situation. If we will learn to let go of our trials, and let God work them out, then we will come to know the real meaning of faith. Faith is the confidence of things not seen, the assurance of things hoped for. When we trust God, He will do everything we ask, and our faith will be made rock solid. Foolish people think they know best, but the person who admits limitations is well on the road to wisdom.

PRAYER: I am so confident of my ability to control my life, and yet there are times when I have just had enough. Let me learn to turn to you for strength and wisdom. You know the way, and you wait to lead me through every trial. Amen.

August 20

It is not good to accept the person of the wicked, to overthrow the righteous in judgment (18:5).

A renter allowed a woman to take a room, knowing that she was a prostitute. He told her that he wasn't concerned with what she did, so long as she kept her business away from his property. He found out that she had begun to bring her customers to her room nights, and he went to have a talk with her. She defended her right to have anyone she wanted come to her room since she paid a good rent. He replied, "Look, I never passed judgment on you as a person, but I don't like what you do. You are always welcome on my property, but I don't have to allow you to do anything you please. It's nothing personal, it's just the way it is."

God feels much the same way. God loves every person completely. It is the things we often do that God does not like. God wants no one to suffer or be punished, but there are certain things we do that He will not tolerate. God welcomes us all to heaven, but He will not allow us to carry our sins with us into His house. If we want to dwell there, we must follow His rules, and not try to make rules of our own. There is nothing any of us can ever do to make God stop loving us, but there are many things we can do which will cause Him to turn us away from heaven's gate.

PRAYER: Lord, make my behavior good and acceptable. Help me to see the errors in my thinking and acting. Lead me away from the things which offend you, and bring me to an understanding of behavior which will make me fit for heaven. Amen.

August 21

The name of the Lord is a strong tower: the righteous runneth into it, and is safe (18:10).

The fort was just a mile ahead. The troops knew that if things got bad, they could retreat to its safe walls. Battle could be frightening, even to the point of despair, but there was special comfort in being so close to a fort. It made you feel almost invincible. At the sound of the trumpet, the doors would open, and there would be comfort and refuge. Let the enemy come. It wouldn't do them any good. The tower of the sentry rose up above the hills, and it was a symbol of strength to every man on the field.

God is that fortress which is always close by. In times of struggle or chaos, we can turn and run to our strength and safety, which is the Lord. He will always be there, waiting with open arms, to receive His children who run to Him from the storm of battle. He is quick to comfort, and will ever defend His own. In His arms we are invincible. There is no force on earth which can touch us. The devil may fling his fiery darts, but they cannot penetrate the walls of God's great love. The world may batter at the door, but it will exhaust itself in the face of such a solid obstacle. Nothing can intrude upon the fortress of the Lord. Once inside His powerful protection, we are safe and sound for all time.

PRAYER: I come to you from the field of battle. I am weary and weak. I need your protection and care. In your love I can rest secure and know that everything will be alright. Open the gate of your love to me now, O Lord, and grant me the safety I so long for. Amen.

August 22

Before destruction the heart of man is haughty; and before honor is humility (18:12).

The opposing team came strutting out onto the court in brand new matching uniforms. The girls warmed up, and they acted cocky. They had been champions two years running, and you could tell that they thought they would have no trouble with the rag-tag band which was there to face them. The other girls looked a little lost on the volleyball court, and they wore whatever shorts and tee-shirts they could throw together. The other team was intimidating, just by their appearance, never mind their attitude.

The games were close, but when the smoke cleared, David had once again knocked off Goliath. The former champs were not quite so haughty now. They looked down at their feet and offered insincere and unconvincing congratulations. Their spirit broken, they headed out of the gymnasium, while the giant killers reveled in their victory.

Sinners kid themselves into believing that they are above the silly faith of Christians. They think that they are too good, too smart for God. When they find out they are wrong, they act as if they had never been told. Humility is a wonderful virtue. It assures the person that they can never be knocked down, because they were never too high in the first place. God blesses the person who realizes they are no better than anyone else.

PRAYER: You have created so many different kinds of people, dear Lord. Help me to love them all equally, never thinking that I am better than any of them. Grant that I might see your image in every human being. Amen.

August 23

He that answereth a matter before he heareth it, it is folly and shame unto him (18:13).

"That's it. I don't want to hear another word about it. I don't care what you have to say, the answer will still be no!" With that, her mother started the car and drove away. She knew that it was a school night, and that her mother wouldn't be thrilled with the idea, but her best friend's grandmother had just died, and her friend's parents had to go away immediately, so she'd asked her mother if her friend could spend the night. Her mother hadn't even let her explain why she wanted her to. All she could say was, "Ask her over on the weekend, then we'll see." Sometimes her mother could be such a pain. She never let her explain anything. Her mother always got the last word, and then slammed the issue shut before she could say her side. It made her so mad.

We are often too quick to speak. When we think we know everything we need to know, and we make a decision without looking at all sides, we are asking for trouble. A wise answer takes time. It takes thought, and it should be based on a good knowledge of the facts. God hopes that we will learn this kind of wisdom. It grows from a respect for others and what they have to say, and it is a sure way that we can show a person that we think they are worthwhile.

PRAYER: Shut my lips from making hasty replies, O Lord. Grant me the wisdom to hear what people are saying, taking time to let the words sink in. Keep me from being a know-it-all, always reminding me that I have a lot to learn. Amen.

August 24

A man's gift maketh room for him, and bringeth him before great men (18:16).

He had worked for this interview for months. He was about to interview one of the most popular actresses of all time, and he was very nervous. He knew little about her, really, except that she loved animals. He had picked up a stuffed dog on the way up to her apartment, just as a token of esteem, hoping that it would break the ice. She received it warmly, and he felt that he had made exactly the right move. She was truly appreciative of the small gift, and it made the atmosphere so much more comfortable for the interview. Afterwards, the reporter became great friends with the actress, and he frequently dropped in with more "pets" to add to her collection.

Gifts given from a pure heart are a real blessing. They let another person know that you care, and they pave the way for a deeper relationship. Often a well-timed gift can heal a wound or cement a relationship. It blesses both gift and giver, and it spreads a feeling that God loves. Giving is a powerful way to show what kind of person you are. Gifts freely given build bridges that last a lifetime. Nothing is finer than a gift given in love, as is evidenced by the divine gift of God's only Son, Jesus Christ our Lord.

PRAYER: Make me a giver, Lord. A giver of time, of talent, of love, of commitment, of peace, of gifts, of all the things that make life worth living. Help me to reflect your giving spirit in every way possible. Amen.

August 25

A brother offended is harder to be won than a strong city: and their contentions are like the bars of a castle (18:19).

He knew exactly what to say. He could get his brother so mad without any effort at all. He'd always been able to do it. He knew the right things to say, the right things to do, everything that annoyed, bothered or hurt him. Whenever they fought he pulled off the gloves and let him have it with everything he had. Nobody could get to him any faster than his brother could. It made him so mad thinking about it. Sometimes he hated him.

The old saying goes, "You only hurt the ones you love." If we didn't love people so much, they couldn't get to us. Members of our own families know us better than just about anyone. They know what makes us tick. They know what makes us happy, and they also know what makes us sad. There is great power within families to cause pain and suffering, but there is also power which can be used to build up and strengthen. If we will use our knowledge of those closest to us to love them, then we begin to understand how wonderful God's love is for us. He knows us completely, and yet, everything He does for us is good and loving. He is our example. Those closest to us should be the easiest to love, not the easiest to hurt. With God ruling in our lives, our closest relationships will be of love and care rather than pain and conflict.

PRAYER: As I come to know people's weaknesses, Father, help me to do everything in my power to protect them, not attack them. Do not let me take advantage of anyone because I know them so well. Amen.

August 26

Death and life are in the power of the tongue: and they that love it shall eat the fruit thereof (18:21).

Pilate looked out over the crowds of people. So, it had come to this. People who usually had no use for him were now coming to him, looking for him to pass judgment on one of their own. It was exhilarating to have such power. With a word, he could bestow life or death. The Nazarene seemed totally unimpressed by his power, but the crowd knew better. They knew that his word was law! No matter how many times he was called upon to pronounce sentence, he still grew tense with excitement. This was power, and he loved it.

There is power in our words. Our tongues are like two edged swords. Our tongues are like two-edged swords. They can protect and defend or they can cut down and destroy. We are in control of them. Sadly, many people act as if it was the other way around; that their tongues controlled their minds. As Christians, it is vital that we learn to control our tongues. James compares the tongue to a rudder. When a rudder is left untended, the ship flounders. Likewise, when our tongues move uncontrolled, the result is disaster. A wise person keeps a firm control over his or her words. Only words of life and light should be spoken, and with God's help we can hope to always have such graceful speech.

PRAYER: O Lord, take control of the rudder and steer this humble vessel. Use the words of my mouth to minister to the needs of others. Let the will of my heart always precede the words of my mouth. Amen.

August 27

Whoso findeth a wife findeth a good thing, and obtaineth favor of the Lord (18:22).

When he'd been single, he had always thought he was doing just fine. After he got married, he was amazed by all the things he had missed before. Having a wife to share his life with had made life so much more exciting. He felt a stronger purpose to the things he did. His work meant more. His free time meant more. And home had a meaning that he had never known before. When he had been single he had always tried to deny the void which was inside him, but after he was married, he gladly admitted that the void had been filled. Being single had been good, but married life was wonderful.

It is good to find a soul mate to spend our earthly life with. We need others to share our experiences and dreams with. A spouse gives us a good outlet for the things which are most important to us. We obtain balance; a second voice and opinion to help us see things in perspective.

A spouse helps us to understand God better. We find on earth a very special relationship which is a mirror image of a relationship God longs to have with each one of us. When we marry, the two become one. When we accept Christ into our hearts, a similar thing happens. He gives us new perspective, and we never have to face any aspect of our lives alone.

PRAYER: Be with me, Lord Jesus. Become one with me, and help me to grow beyond my current limitations. Make me the best person I can possibly be. Recreate me in your holy image. Amen.

August 28

A man that hath friends must show himself friendly: and there is a friend that sticketh closer than a brother (18:24).

A man moved into an apartment and held an open house in order to meet new people. Many people showed up, and they seemed to enjoy themselves enormously. He invited them to come back, and frequently held parties that were the hit of the apartment complex. When he lost his job, and the funds became scarce, he cut back on his entertaining. Many of his "new friends" stopped coming around. A few stuck with him, though, and they kept coming back regardless of what he had to offer them. They were most concerned with how he was doing. The others were merely concerned with what they could get from him.

Fair-weather friends are easy to come by. The real friend, one who will stand by you no matter what, is rare. It is devastating to think that we have good friends, just to find out that they could care less about us when we hit hard times. We need to have friends we know will stick with us in bad times as well as good. God is one such friend.

No matter what happens, God will be there when we need Him. He will never turn us away, and He loves it when we come to Him with our problems. There is no better friend that we can ever hope to have than God Himself. His love never fails.

PRAYER: Teach me what being a friend is all about, Lord. Let me see how you intended friends to act by being my friend. Make me over to do for others what you do for me. Help me to deal with people, always in love. Amen.

August 29

Also, that the soul be without knowledge, it is not good; and he that hasteth with his feet sinneth (19:2).

He looked at his watch again. Ten minutes more and he would be late. He looked both ways, then crept through the red light. He turned the corner and gunned the car along the road. The building was at least ten minutes away, and that was only if there was no traffic and he could park right in front. He pushed a little harder on the accelerator, and the car picked up speed. The light ahead turned yellow, so he gave the gas a shove and sped through it. His destination came into view, but the flashing red and blue lights in his rear view mirror tore his attention away. The police car flagged him down, and the officer was not buying any of his excuses. By the time the ticketing was done, ten minutes had passed, and he was hopelessly late. Mentally, he kicked himself. If he had obeyed all the laws, he would have arrived much earlier than he was sure to now.

When we race through life, we are bound to make mistakes and get caught. Rules are given that we might live safely and happily. They are there for the protection of the masses. God's rules were given for the same reason. When we break them, for any reason, we are being selfish and ultimately we will have to pay the penalty.

PRAYER: Dear God, slow me down. I race through this life as if I was being chased. I need to take time to enjoy life, and to pay attention to your presence in the world. When I run along blindly, I see neither the good which is there, nor the bad which is in my path. Amen.

August 30

Wealth maketh many friends; but the poor is separated from his neighbor (19:4).

It was hard. All through college they had been the best of friends. They had gone everywhere together and done everything together. They had been inseparable. Since they had left college, though, things had changed. Her friend had married into money, and taken a high paying job herself. Meanwhile, she was working with poor families, and her salary was barely enough to feed her and pay the rent. Her friend didn't seem to have any time for her anymore. They had so little in common. Really, the only thing that had changed was their financial status, but that was enough to drive a wedge between them. Her best friend acted like she wasn't good enough anymore.

Money can change many things. It can cause us to act strangely, and it can turn our priorities upside down. The interests of the wealthy are usually not the interests of the poor. The poor cannot hope to reach up to the level of the rich, but those with money have a great opportunity to reach out to the poor. God calls us to give what we can to ease the burden of those who are less fortunate. Money should never close us off from anyone else, but it should ever open new doors for us to enter into God's ministry.

PRAYER: Lord, all that I have has come from you, and to you I commit it. Let me use my wealth to build bridges, rather than to dig chasms. Help me to befriend others not on the basis of economics, but on their worth as children of yours. Amen.

August 31

Many will entreat the favor of the prince: and every man is a friend to him that giveth gifts. All the brethren of the poor do hate him: how much more do his friends go far from him? He pursueth them with words, yet they are wanting to him (19:6-7).

He loved to string people along. He had saved all his money to purchase a fine suit of clothes. He had a thick wad of bills, all ones except for a $100 which he kept on the outside. He'd walk into a restaurant or hotel and flash his wad, and you should have seen the people jump. When he dressed normally, in jeans and a sweatshirt, no one moved to do him any favors, but when he was suited and well set moneywise, people fell all over him. He did it to prove a point, but few people seemed to get it. The regular people got treated like dirt, and the wealthy were treated royally. It was sad, but true.

When we allow ourselves to be blinded by the accessories and the frills, we lose sight of the face of Christ which is in each person. Wealthy people are treated so well in hopes that they will throw some of their fortune our way. A poor person who is treated well is treated so because he or she is respected as a person. God wants us to treat everyone the same way, looking not at what a person has, but at what a person is: a child of the most high God. When we see people as they are, then we can love them equally and purely.

PRAYER: Lord, you do not judge us based on what we own or how much money we have. Teach me to see others just that way. Keep me from being blinded by the glitter of gold, and let me instead be impressed by the light of Christ which shines forth from every human being. Amen.

September 1

The discretion of a man deferreth his anger; and it is his glory to pass over a transgression (19:11).

This was the third home she had been placed in, but it was by far the best. The first place she went, they tried to lock her in her room after dark. They punished her severely, and even hit her. She had run away so many times that they put her back in the orphanage. The second home was like a hurricane. Everybody was fighting all the time. She had called the director of the home for girls in tears, and they had come to get her. This new place was different, though. The people acted like they cared. The fact that she had run away so much, and that she had been sent to reformatory two times didn't seem to make a difference to her new folks. They acted like they trusted her, and when she had asked them why, they had told her that all the other stuff was in the past. They would trust her until she gave them reason not to. She decided right then and there that she was going to try never to give them any reason.

It is so important for us to forgive people their past sins. When we mistrust someone because of their past, we apply a stigma to them that they fight all of their lives. It is better to learn to forgive, and to keep forgiving, so that the person can know that there is no judgment which will come from us. Judgment will come from the Lord. What should come from us is open and honest love, and the gift of a second chance.

PRAYER: Lord, let me forgive those whom I meet, and grant that I might learn to forgive others as you have forgiven me. Amen.

September 2

The king's wrath is as the roaring of a lion; but his favor is as dew upon the grass (19:12).

He had almost forgotten about it. Not two weeks before he had borrowed his father's power drill without asking him, and somehow he had broken the bit. He had been too scared to tell his dad right then, so he kept putting it off. Finally, he forgot it completely. Forgot it until his dad came to his room, holding the broken bit in his hand. He expected to be really lectured. His dad had told him a thousand times not to use his tools without permission. He hung his head and admitted what had happened, but instead of a lecture, his father just laughed and shook his head. He clapped his son on the back and asked him to go to the hardware store with him to get a new bit.

When we do something wrong, we live in a fear of the wrath that is to come. As a person hears the growl before the lion springs, a wrongdoer feels guilt before the punishment comes. If we will heed the feeling of guilt and confess our wrongs before God, His wrath will turn to favor, and we will know forgiveness. That forgiveness, that reprieve from punishment is as sweet and refreshing as the morning dew, and it is a precious and lasting gift. Nothing is better than coming to know the grace of the Lord Jesus Christ, especially in the face of punishment for sin.

PRAYER: How many things do I try to hide from you, O Lord? Forgive my foolish attempts to avoid your wrath and displeasure. Lead me to your forgiveness, Father, and let me know that your love is greater than any wrong I might commit. Amen.

September 3

A foolish son is the calamity of his father: and the contentions of a wife are a continual dropping (19:13).

He had just about had enough. It was bad enough that his son had been expelled from school for fighting ... the third time, and that his wife kept defending their son, but then for them to get into a fight over the whole affair in public, it was just too much. All of his friends knew of the problems he had. They all knew that his son was no student, and that he carried a chip on his shoulder continually. They also knew that his wife argued with him all the time. He couldn't stand all the pitying stares and the comments made supposedly behind his back. It hurt him deeply, and he felt helpless to do anything to change it.

It would be wonderful if all of our actions brought honor to our families. Unfortunately, that's an unrealistic hope. No one is perfect. We have to accept each other, flaws and all. Still, we should try to do everything we can to make our families proud of us. We should especially do everything in our power to make our heavenly Father proud of us. Christians are to be examples for others to follow, and when we dishonor God we do a very serious thing. Through our actions we discredit the power of God to make us new people. Our foolishness causes calamity, and our resistance to His will makes other people doubt the power of our faith.

PRAYER: Lord, guide the steps of my feet. Help me to remember that the eyes of other people are on me, seeing the difference you have made in my life. When I dishonor you, I dishonor the entire faith. Forgive me. Amen.

September 4

*He that keepeth the commandment keepeth his own soul;
but he that despiseth his ways shall die (19:16).*

One mistake could be fatal. The cars moved around
the track at speeds close to 200 miles per hour. A
momentary lapse could prove fatal. Everything that
had ever been learned about racing was called into
practice each time a driver sat behind the wheel. Experience was the best resource, but even that was no
guarantee. One bad move was all it took. You had to
pay attention, and you had to know what was expected of you. You only hoped everybody else did
what they were supposed to, too.

Sadly, we don't look at God's commandments as a
matter of life and death. We break an occasional commandment, and nothing much seems to happen. We
don't realize that sin builds a wall between us and God.
Asking His forgiveness breaks down that wall, but we
have to be faithful to do that. Sin is a matter of life or
death. The wages of sin is death. There are no two
ways about it. It is good to know that God is quick to
forgive, and that He will do everything in His power
to make sure that we will come back to Him. We
must pay attention to God's will and do what is expected of us, and we must also try to take every opportunity to help others do what is expected.

*PRAYER: Lord, your word is always with me. Help me
to heed its instructions and follow it closely. Let me not depart
from it, even for a moment, for in the wink of an eye, many
things can happen. Amen.*

September 5

He that hath pity upon the poor lendeth unto the Lord; and that which he hath given will he pay him again (19:17).

A poor woman came to a rich young ruler and asked him for a few coins. The ruler turned her away, telling her to work for her food. A sick man came asking help, and he, too, was turned away. A friend who had come on hard times stopped and asked for assistance, but the young ruler told him to work for his wage. Then the Lord came to him, asking for a small loan. The rich young man said, "Lord, all that I have is yours. Take what you will, and more." The Lord took from the ruler and gave to the woman, and to the man, and to the friend. He said to the ruler, "I come to you in many forms. When you give to any of these, then you give also to me. Hold back nothing from those who ask, and your reward will be great in heaven."

It is hard to see sometimes, but when we give to a child of God, we give also to the Father. God loves to see us care for one another, and he abhors it when we turn away from others in need. The wise man or woman shares all they have, and asks nothing in return. God showed us this way when He gave His Son to be our Savior, requiring nothing more than that we believe. This is the seed of true believing, and it is within reach of all who will take it.

PRAYER: I sometimes turn my back to the poor. Help me to remember that I am really turning my back on you. Forgive me for my unkindness. Let me learn to be unselfish, and take from me what is really yours, Father. Amen.

September 6

There are many devices in a man's heart; nevertheless the counsel of the Lord, that shall stand (19:21).

A woman asked a question of her pastor. "What if Moses had refused to face Pharoah? Or if Abraham had refused to obey God's command to slay Isaac? Or if Christ had decided to follow His will in the Garden of Gethsemane rather than God's?" The pastor reflected on the question for a moment, then said, "I suppose God would have found someone else. If God wants something done, it will be done. His way will be established, not the way of man."

It is important to realize that God will work in spite of us when He cannot work through us. We need to heed His call carefully, for if we are indecisive or resistant, He might just go elsewhere, looking for someone who will follow Him. God's will is supreme, and it is a privilege to be a part of it. We may think of millions of directions for our lives to go, but if we put our trust in God, He will be faithful to set us upon the best path, and He will walk beside us every step of the way. It is a great comfort to know that God is in control, and that in the end, everything will be just as He intended it to be.

PRAYER: God, I do not presume to pretend that I understand everything that you do. Your will is far beyond my comprehension. Thank you for loving me enough to make me a part of your great creation. Walk with me, and be with me this day, and all the days to come. Amen.

September 7

The desire of a man is his kindness: and a poor man is better than a liar (19:23).

Early in their marriage she had loved her husband's gentle spirit and giving nature. He had spent time with the children, and he had loved the free time he could devote to his family. As the years passed, things changed. He devoted more and more of himself to his job. He became obsessed with getting ahead. The pressures he felt at work he brought home with him, and he vented his frustrations on his family. His once-gentle spirit had turned hard, and it appeared that he had forgotten how to give. She was very sad over the change, and realized that part of it was her fault. She had grown accustomed to living well, and the only way their lifestyle could be maintained was through her husband's hard work. Deep inside, she wished that things would be different.

What we want inside will be apparent by the way we live our lives. Whatever we make our god, that we will pursue with all our heart, mind, and spirit. If the Lord is the desire of our hearts, kindness and love will show forth, but if we pursue material gain, or fame, or prestige, then we will be devoid of kindness and warmth. It is much better to forsake all wealth in order to live purely and righteously. God smiles upon us when we remain true to His ways. When we live a life of kindness and caring, He rejoices.

PRAYER: Help me not to be swept up in the ways of the world. They lead down a false path to a poor reward. The path to heaven is a true path, and the reward is greater than anything this world has to offer. Amen.

September 8

Cease, my son, to hear the instruction that causeth to err from the words of knowledge (19:27).

He had a magical ability. Everyone who heard him speak was hypnotized. He seemed to have all the answers and he knew each person completely. People came from all over everywhere to join his little group. They had been labeled a cult, but that was by people who didn't know what they were talking about. The group had received so much. He helped them to understand life, to strip themselves of all worldly constraints, and to find true peace. They would be able to do anything they wanted, just by worshipping him. It was a small price to pay for the truth he was giving them.

It's interesting how many people will follow a false, human, god, when they would never think of devoting themselves to God. God asks us to do things for our own good, while would-be messiahs are self-serving and egocentric. The way of the Lord is the only true way. We kid ourselves when we try to find alternatives. We need to stay steadfast in our pursuit of His will and purpose. We must cease listening to the temptations of those who would pull us away. It is good for us to wrap ourselves in the word of God, the instructions which lead only to true knowledge, and nowhere else.

PRAYER: I am looking for answers, Lord, but I am afraid that sometimes I am too impatient. I search for solutions in places other than your word. Forgive me when I stray. Keep my eyes and my heart focused on you. Amen.

September 9

Wine is a mocker, strong drink is raging: and whosoever is deceived thereby is not wise (20:1).

It always started the same way. A voice in his head said, "One more won't hurt anything." But one more turned into five, and before he knew it he was over the edge. This time it had caused him to miss work. Before, it had made him wreck his car. Once it had put him in the hospital. Where was it going to end? He refused to believe he was an alcoholic. He only drank once every few months or so, but when he did, the results were disastrous. He was a moderately intelligent young man, but when he got to drinking, all reason flew right out the window.

God disapproves anytime we become prisoner to some substance. If we find that we cannot live without something, or that we cannot control our behavior, then that thing must be removed from our lives. There are no two ways about it. Christians are to be disciplined people, and it is vital that we learn to control our actions and our thoughts. Strong drink removes the ability to do that. Christians are constantly being examples of the truth of Christ. If we are controlled by other things, then we dishonor God. We must rise above the things which try to trap us, to show the liberating power of Christ in our lives. If we will ask Him, He will be faithful to give us the strength we need to kick any bad habit.

PRAYER: If there is anything in my life which you are ashamed of, Father, please help me to destroy it completely. I want to be a fine example of your love and power. Make me over to be as good a person as I can be. Amen.

September 10

It is an honor for a man to cease from strife: but every fool will be meddling (20:3).

She wished she could be like her husband. Nothing ever seemed to get to him. He took everything in stride, and he acted as though he hadn't a care in the world. She, on the other hand, worried about everything. She was positive that if there was something that could possibly go wrong, it would. She didn't mean to be negative, but she couldn't help it. She wanted to be able to let go of her doubts and fears, but so far she hadn't been able to.

It's sometimes hard to realize that God gave us life as a gift. Many times it feels like such a burden. God never wants us to suffer unnecessarily. Part of the message that Christ brought to this world was that no one had to face problems alone. God is with us always. Another part of His message was that nothing on this earth is important other than our relationship to God and to our neighbor. Job, finances, illness, and a hundred other things create stress in our lives, but when compared with the bigger picture of eternal life, they are totally insignificant. As Christians, we need to learn to look at the world through eternity-eyes, rather than temporal-eyes. Our home is in heaven, and everything that happens to us now means nothing, so long as we have our relationships in order.

PRAYER: Lord, I get sidetracked so easily. I let the silliest things bring me down. Help me to see everything in its proper perspective. Grant me peace of mind which never ends. Amen.

September 11

The sluggard will not plow by reason of the cold; therefore shall he beg in harvest, and have nothing (20:4).

There is a famous children's story about a little red hen who searched for other barnyard residents to help her bake bread. No matter where she went, all the other animals had some reason why they couldn't pitch in and help. Finally, she decided to bake the bread by herself, and soon the entire barnyard was filled with the enticing aroma of her coop-baked bread. When the other animals smelled the fine bread, they flocked around the chicken coop with their mouths watering. The hen peeked her head out and announced, "Everyone who helped make the bread gets a big slice with butter!" Whereupon, she proceeded to eat hers in front of a group of regretful loafers.

How sorry a day it will be when we are called to stand before the judgment throne of God if we have not chosen to follow His commandments. He has asked us to do what we know we should, and often we disobey, not through an evil spirit, but because of laziness. Just as the animals in the story, though, we can hope to receive no more than we were willing to give in this life. If we give nothing, then nothing will we receive. If we give much, our Father in heaven will heap an unending supply of good things upon us.

PRAYER: When a call comes for obedience or service, let me be the first to raise my hand to volunteer, O Lord. I do not want to be left outside in the last days. Welcome me into your holy presence, Father. Amen.

September 12

A king that sitteth in the throne of judgment scattereth away all evil with his eyes (20:8).

In a certain mythical kingdom, the throne room of the castle was exposed so that all the subjects could see their king. He would rule from his elevated throne, and nothing happened in the kingdom which escaped his notice. Whenever a misdeed was committed, he would summon the perpetrator and have him brought to the throne. There, in front of all his subjects, he would give sentencing. He was always fair and just, and people learned to respect his decree. They felt protected under his watchful gaze, and the evildoers found no comfort in his land. In time, the evil fled the city, and only the good remained, to be watched and cared for by the wise king.

We are subjects to a king who watches everything we do. He sees us at our best and at our worst, and He is fair with us in His judgment and commands. We have nothing to fear from our King, so long as we obey His rules. In the end, we will all stand before His throne, and He will allow us a place in His Kingdom, or He will have us removed. The choice is ours, but it is good to remember that nothing we do escapes His careful gaze. He sees the good and is pleased, and He sees the evil which He scatters with His eyes.

PRAYER: I thank you that I am never out of your sight. I apologize for the things I do which are not pleasing to you, and I ask your forgiveness. Let me know when I please you, Lord, that I might always walk in those ways. Amen.

September 13

Divers weights, and divers measures, both of them are like abomination to the Lord (20:10).

She stormed into the classroom with her paper clenched in her fist. She marched up to the professor's desk and tossed her paper in front of him. A "C+" was scrawled across the head of the paper.

"Why was I given this grade? This is a good paper."

"Good for anybody else maybe, but not for you. You put forth average effort, and you got an average grade."

"That's not fair. My paper is better than most in the class, but a lot of people got 'A's."

"Look, I can give you any grade I please. I think you can do better, so I gave you a 'C+.' That's it!"

"I'll fight it. It's not fair for you to judge some people one way, and other people differently."

It is frustrating to feel like we are being taken advantage of. When we deal with other people, we like to think that we will be treated fairly. By the same token, we should be very careful in our dealings with other people to be sure that we always treat them fairly. God looks kindly on His children who deal with equality and fairness. Partiality is an abomination in the sight of God. We must always strive to do what we know is right.

PRAYER: Lord, let me look upon every person I meet as an equal. Help me to remember to treat them as I would like to have them treat me. Guard that I do nothing to offend or cause suffering. Amen.

September 14

Even a child is known by his doings, whether his work be pure, and whether it be right (20:11).

The class was a mixture. Half the children sat quietly, paying attention and doing the work they were asked to do. The other half ran wild. They were noisy and uncooperative, and it was a battle to get them to pay any attention at all. They refused to stay in their seats, and if you turned your back on one of them, they were out the door, causing a disturbance in another classroom. None of the children were really bad kids, but some of them had not learned any manners or self-control. Their misbehavior made it terribly difficult to teach the children who were cooperative and willing to learn.

Even with children, it is easy to tell what they are like by the things they do. We should not always judge a person by their actions, but it is true that a person gives forth that which is inside. If we are nice, kind, gentle people, our actions will reflect that. If in turmoil, we have anger, or jealousy, or lust inside, then our actions will most likely reflect that, too. That is why it is so important to put Jesus in control of our lives, and to spend time with Him daily. With Him in command, we are assured of living a life which is an honor to God. People watch the way we live. When our lives are right, it proves to people that God has the power to change lives.

PRAYER: O Lord, make me new. Take the storms which rage in my heart, and calm them with a single word. From the peace which you alone can give, help me to spread it to everyone I meet. Amen.

September 15

The hearing ear, and the seeing eye, the Lord hath made even both of them (20:12).

He stood looking on in awe. His son, his firstborn, was coming into the world, and he was a part of it. He stood by his wife's head, and together they shared the wonder of the experience. He had often doubted whether God existed, but now all of his doubts were gone. He looked on at the perfect little creation. Each finger and toe was a testament to God's loving existence. The miracle of life was overwhelming. It was inconceivable that something like this could happen by chance. Only a master artist of incomprehensible power and glory could come up with something so fine as human life.

When we look at God's creation, it is difficult to question anything about Him. There is so much to wonder at in the world. As we learn more and more, it should not make us skeptical of God. Quite the contrary, it should convince us that there is a grand author to all creation, and that His power is far beyond our wildest imagination. Only a foolish person would deny God's existence in the face of such remarkable evidence. To see God, all we must do is open our eyes and look around. His signature is on each one of his creations. He is right there for the person who has eyes to see, and ears to hear. God is all around us.

PRAYER: O Lord, you are indeed everywhere. I look to the sky, and your beauty and wonder meets my eye. I look around, and I see you in the faces of those I meet. I look inward, and thankfully, I see you in my heart. Amen.

September 16

Bread of deceit is sweet to a man; but afterward his mouth shall be filled with gravel (20:17).

His boss had told him that he had to make contact with all twelve of the outlet stores. He struggled through ten, then decided he'd had enough. He never did get back to the other two, but when his boss asked him, he said he'd completely finished. All went well until his boss asked him for detailed reports on all twelve of the outlets. He had no idea what he could say about the two outlets, and he didn't have time to get to them before the reports were due. He falsified the reports he turned in, but afterwards he felt uneasy. He continually wondered if his boss knew what he had done, and it put unusual pressure on their relationship.

When we live a lie, it takes control of us, and it usually leads to more lies. We get caught in a tangled web, and we are continually afraid that we might be discovered. It takes so much more energy to tell a lie than it does to tell the truth. We may not like the consequences of telling the truth all the time, but it is much better than facing the consequences of being caught in a lie. Our God is the God of Truth, and those who live in lies will have no part in Him. The truth is a much better companion, and it will lead us straight to the gates of heaven.

PRAYER: I gain nothing through deception and lies. Lead me in the paths of truth and righteousness. Help me to see that a single grain of truth is preferable to a mountain of lies. Teach me your ways, O Lord. Amen.

September 17

He that goeth about as a talebearer revealeth secrets: therefore meddle not with him that flattereth with his lips (20:19).

A man was seen coming and going from a married woman's house. Her neighbor watched with fascination, and concocted elaborate tales which she shared with her friends as truth. There was no evidence any more incriminating than the fact that the young man came regularly, but the rumor was that the woman was having an affair. The "news" spread like wildfire, and wind of it eventually got back to the woman's husband. He confronted her in anger and hurt. The woman defended herself well. The young man she was seeing was her own brother, who came to the house to study in between his classes. The senseless words of a gossip caused unnecessary pain to other people, and planted a seed of doubt which caused great trouble.

There is no such thing as harmless gossip. Gossip is wrong. It is talking about someone in a negative way who has no chance to defend himself. It is usually based on half-truths and sparse information. It isn't done to build someone up. It is only done to tear someone down. When we tell false stories about another person, we are stealing from them in the worst way. We take away dignity and honor, and we throw dirt on their reputation. It is an evil that God despises because of its basic cruelty. Lovers of the Lord are lovers of all His children. Therefore, we should speak of our sisters and brothers only as we would speak of the Lord, Himself.

PRAYER: May my words be ever praiseworthy. Let no foulness or gossip pass from my lips, O Lord. Amen.

September 18

The spirit of man is the candle of the Lord, Searching all the inward parts of the belly (20:27).

The cave was dark. There was no light coming from within it at all. They felt their way along for a moment, but decided it was much too dangerous. They had no idea how deep it was, where it led, or what they might find as they went. The group went back to find lanterns which they could carry into the new cave. Once lit, the cave was breathtaking. Rock formations caught the light and reflected it in a million little stars. Crystals hung from the ceiling, and each reflected the light of the lanterns to brighten the entire cave. The band of explorers covered every inch, and left no crevice unchecked.

God is like a deep, dark cavern which we cannot see into. One's spirit is like a lantern. It may burn brightly or it may shine forth strongly. As we grow in our faith, the light increases, and we can begin to see God more clearly and understand Him better. As we grow closer to Him, and our inner light increases, we are better able to explore His depth and majesty, and we come to an even closer relationship to Him. He feeds the light of our spirit and then reveals Himself to us in its light. In this way, we come to truly know God.

PRAYER: Reveal yourself to me, Lord. I so want to know you. Fuel the flame of my light that it may shine brightly, illuminating your will for my life. Build my spirit and guide me in the ways that lead to you. Amen.

September 19

The glory of young men is their strength: and the beauty of old men is the gray head (20:29).

A famous ball player reflected over a highly successful career. He had been a feared hitter, and no one challenged his throwing arm from the field. He was well-muscled and a fine athlete. He quit playing while he was still doing well, and it was a decision he felt good about the rest of his life. When he had gotten old, he still had fine memories of his glory days, but that wasn't all he had. He had seen too many players who lived in their own pasts, and that was sad. He had used his time well, had made good investments, developed other interests, and he enjoyed a full and active life as a senior citizen. His strength had faded, his athletic days were behind him, but he had his mind, and no one could take that away from him.

Often we judge younger men by their physical abilities, while we judge older men by their wisdom. Age brings with it certain limitations, but it also gives certain strengths. Experience gives us a perspective on life that we can obtain no other way than by growing older. The aged in our world have a wonderful legacy to offer us in the form of their experience and observations. They have walked a road that we are only beginning. Through their words, we may come to know the traps which lie along the way, and they can help us over them, if we will only let them.

PRAYER: Lord, let me respect those who have lived longer than I have. Open my heart to their instruction, and let me revere them the same way that I revere you. Amen.

September 20

The blueness of a wound cleanseth away evil: so do stripes the inward parts of the belly (20:30).

A woman noticed a large red patch on her leg where she had been stung by a bee. Thinking little of it, she ignored the sting, until two days later her leg had swelled to twice its normal size and the red patch had begun to spread. She went to the hospital, and they rushed her into an operating room, where the leg was pierced and the infection was drained from her leg. The afflicted area was cut away, and the leg returned to normal within a few days, the wound healing within a few weeks.

Often, the only way to heal is to hurt. Operations shock the body, but the corruption must be cut from the sore or no healing will occur at all. The same is true of human beings in their relationship with God. God demands purity, and all corruption will be cut away to insure wholeness. There is no place for evil in the body of Christ. If evil is found, drastic measures will be taken, and like a cancer, it will be removed. God will act as a skillful surgeon, cutting and putting back together again. What will be left will be better than new, and the body of Christ will be healthy for all eternity. Healing can occur no other way, but the Lord will be faithful to save as much as He possibly can.

PRAYER: Father, cut away all that is wrong in me. Though it might hurt, I would rather be able to heal than to sit and die in my corruption. Excise evil from my heart, and heal me in your tender love. Amen.

September 21

Every way of a man is right in his own eyes: but the Lord pondereth the hearts (21:2).

Timidly, the man walked up to the pearly gates and cleared his throat. St. Peter peered at him from a high stool. Without a word, he pointed the man through a huge door, and inside was a throne. The man walked to the throne and said, "I'm ready for heaven, sir."

"What makes you think so?" a voice asked.

"Well, sir, I gave to the poor, I went to church, I never cheated on my wife, I didn't drink, and I prayed twice a day."

"You mean, you got tax deductions, you wanted people to think highly of you, you were afraid you'd get caught, you were allergic to alcohol, and you said grace before meals, don't you?"

"I was hoping you wouldn't know the difference," said the man.

Not only are our actions important, but our reasons for them are important too. God sees us not as we appear to be, but as we really are. He knows every motivation for every move we make. We can't kid God, and we shouldn't try to. We may think we are doing alright if we do the things God asks, but more importantly, we need to do what He asks for the right reasons.

PRAYER: Eternal God, search the depths of my heart to see if I am doing all I can for the right reasons. Lead me to new ways of serving you. Help me to see what is lacking in my life, and support me as I try to change. Amen.

September 22

To do justice and judgment is more acceptable to the Lord than sacrifice (21:3).

Two women chose to serve the Lord. One woman lived in a large house with a swimming pool and a maid. She lounged all day in the comforts of her beautiful home, but each month she sent a generous check to a local church. She specifically designated that her money be used to help poor children wherever they could be found. The other woman joined a mission team and she traveled to some of the poorest areas to dwell with the children and to work to improve their living conditions. She fought for the people, and she grew to love and care for them. Each woman served the Lord. Each did great good. Still, we are called to give all that we can. When we give from our excesses, we sacrifice little, and we do nothing to bring justice and equality to the world. When we give of ourselves, however, we are giving the love of God as He has given it to us. We are avoiding judgment by giving everything we have to the service of God. Our sacrifice is complete, but we are offering up much more than a gift. We are giving our life for others, as Christ gave His life for us, and thus we are becoming the justice of God on our earth right now.

PRAYER: Lord, if I give things, I give very little, but if I give myself, then I have given everything. Help me to turn my life over to you. Take me and make me the person that you need me to be. Lead me to the place I need to be to do the most I can. Amen.

September 23

Whoso stoppeth his ears at the cry of the poor, he also shall cry himself, but shall not be heard (21:13).

"Will you please turn that off? I can't stand seeing those little babies with their stomachs all stuck out and flies all over their faces. It makes me sick. I don't want to have to look at that junk, and listen to those whining people beg me for money. It's all they do. I get tired of everyone trying to spend my money for me."

How different might that person sound if he were on the other end? One of the easiest things we can do is to take a moment to put ourselves in someone else's shoes. Whenever we see someone suffer, our hearts should go out to them. We should not just see a child in pain, but we should see Christ in pain. Our Lord, Jesus Christ is a part of all creation. When we see people starve, we must remember His words, "Inasmuch as yet did it not (offer aid) to one of the least of these, ye did it not to me." We have been called to love one another as we love ourselves, and to love each other as if we were loving God. To do less is to ignore the command of God, and to stray into sin. We are the keepers of our brothers and sisters. If we ignore the pleas of those in need right now, then one day we will have to face the sad reality that our Father in heaven will not hear our own cry when we cry to Him.

PRAYER: Break through the hardness that exists around my heart. Open my ears to the cries of the poor, and open my eyes to the plight of the needy. Remind me to put myself in their place, and let me act accordingly. Amen.

September 24

It is joy to the just to do judgment: but destruction shall be to the workers of iniquity (21:15).

A hush fell over the courtroom. One of the most powerful men in the community had been accused of ignoring federal safety standards. The trial had gone slowly, and there was fear that the executive might somehow buy the judge's favor. It was common knowledge that the man had sent many fine gifts to the judge. It was also known that the judge had returned them all. Now he stood to deliver the verdict, and long months of argument were about to come to an end.

"There comes a time when spoiled children have to answer for the mischief they cause. No one should get away with what is unlawful, especially those who think they can control every situation with the almighty dollar. Money doesn't buy truth, and it cannot stop justice. When something is wrong, it is wrong for everyone, rich or poor. This court finds the defendant guilty of criminal negligence and orders full compliance with the law, and full restitution to those injured parties."

When justice is done, it gives people faith that good really will win out over evil. We need to have hope that everything will be just fine. God has promised that His justice will rule eternally, and we need have no fear that God will allow evil a place in His Kingdom. Only the just will dwell with God.

PRAYER: Lord, I want to be found blameless in your sight. Forgive me my many sins, and allow me to join with you to rejoice in what is right, and fight that which is wrong. Strengthen my will to do good, Father. Amen.

September 25

He that loveth pleasure shall be a poor man: he that loveth wine and oil shall not be rich (21:17).

It was his first real job. He was making a good salary, and he could now afford to live in style. He decorated his apartment, threw fantastic parties, and stayed out all night on the weekends seeking new and different thrills. He moved into the fast lane, and spent money as fast as he could earn it. He had never done so much before in his life. He bought all the things he'd ever wanted, and many things he'd never dreamed of. He traveled and bought expensive gifts for his friends. Everything was as good as it could possibly be. Until he was fired.

He had never believed his party could come to an end, but his lifestyle intruded on his work, and it led to his firing. Now he had nothing. No savings, no support, and no way to pay bills. His dream come true turned into a nightmare. He felt sick.

When we live for fun and self-indulgence, we live for nothing lasting at all. Our lives need meaning. They need a foundation. They need God. If we devote ourselves to Him, then we don't have time for frivolous endeavors which cause us to be selfish and wasteful. God will help us to live wisely and prudently. He will help us to know what is right and what is wrong. He will be faithful to do all of this, if we will only consent to put our trust in Him.

PRAYER: I do want to put my faith in you, God. I know that on my own I will give in to temptations which are selfish and foolish. Protect me from myself, O Lord. Guide me in the paths of what is right and good. Amen.

September 26

It is better to dwell in the wilderness, than with a contentious and an angry woman (21:19).

He felt so lonely. He was surrounded by people, but he still felt very much alone. No one understood him. He was pressured at work, his children were strangers to him, he had no social life, and his home felt more like a prison than a haven of comfort and a fortress against the world. He knew that when he got home, he would be assaulted with insults about his abilities, curses heaped on him about his meager pay, and derogatory comments about his manhood. His wife had once shown him nothing but love. She had stood by him through every bad situation, but that had all ended. His lack of advancement at work and a series of physical ailments had caused her to lose faith in him. She no longer saw him as such a great prize, and she took great delight in letting him know it. He often thought of running away, but he knew that was no solution. Resignedly, he headed for home.

We have been created with a need for companionship and affection, but it is better to remain alone than to dwell with people who take pleasure in hurting us. God wants us to do everything in our power to give each other love. He cries for us when we are mistreated and abused. His mercy goes forth to those who are alone, and His blessing awaits those who shower their love freely on others.

PRAYER: Make me a love-giver, Lord. Help me to watch what I say and do, so that I do not hurt those around me. Bring me from the wilderness of selfishness and pettiness, that I might help those who need it most. Amen.

September 27

A wise man scaleth the city of the mighty, and casteth down the strength of the confidence thereof (21:22).

Long ago, a society built for itself many weapons, and a great wall around their city to protect them. They formed a massive army, and they moved out into the world with the hope of conquering it. They fought with anyone who tried to stop them, and their empire grew. They came to a people, however, who did not arm themselves with any weapons, yet they refused to yield to the powerful war culture. They claimed that they were strong by their faith in God, and that He was the only protection they needed. The army battled them and scattered them into foreign lands. Time passed, and the warring nation fell, leaving no remnant behind. The people of God reunited, and they were strong.

The people of God have never been defeated. Great empires and armies have come and gone, but none have lasted as long as the people who follow God. All else is refuse in comparison with the Lord. Mighty cities will rise, but they will crumble long before the Lord comes to reward His faithful ones. No army comes close to the might of God, and the greatest empire is not bigger than a speck of the love of God. His might endures forever, and His love shines brighter than the sun. Our hope should always be in the Lord, and in Him alone.

PRAYER: My hope and trust is in you, Almighty God. Only you are God. Nothing else even comes close. There is nothing so mighty, nothing so good as you, O Lord. Be with me always. Amen.

September 28

He coveteth greedily all the day long: but the righteous giveth and spareth not (21:26).

His vow had been that when he made it big, he was going to help people like the ones he had grown up around. They had been poor mining people in closed mining towns, and they had small hope for anything but a dismal future. He remembered his vow while he was climbing, but every time he thought of using any of his wealth to help them, he balked. The only way to make money was to invest money, he told himself. The more he made, the more he would be able to give. He never gave. He could never let go of any of his wealth for even a short time. No amount was enough. He could have given a million dollars to the town and never missed it, but the bug had bitten, and greed was the ruling force in his life. He died financially rich, but spiritually and morally poor. All his good intentions went to the grave with him, and the people who so desperately could have used his help found none.

God has blessed us with riches for one reason. It is not because we are deserving, or because He is rewarding us, it is simply that we might give it to others who need it more than we do. Giving is the heart of a Christian. We should take every opportunity that comes our way to give of our time, talents, and resources. God blesses the giver, both in this life, and the eternal life to come.

PRAYER: Take from me the spirit to covet and hold. Open my heart and my mind to the needs that I can do something to fill. I give to you everything that I have and everything that I am. Use me as you see fit. Amen.

September 29

There is no wisdom nor understanding nor counsel against the Lord (21:30).

Lucifer, the most perfect of all of God's creation looked to place himself on the same level as God. He wanted to be worshipped for his perfection, and he conspired against God. He grew jealous of the Lord, and he began to work against Him. He led one-third of the angels in revolt against the Lord, and he and his followers were cast from heaven.

The sin of pride is a dangerous one. It makes us think we are better than we really are. It leads us to judge others, and it makes us resentful of what we are not given. We disregard God's commands, and we begin to think only of ourselves. We close off all that is right and good and we make ourselves out to be our own god. We worship ourselves in subtle ways, and we rebel against the Lord, by denying His will. Just like Lucifer, when we come before God, He will cast us away from Him. There is no place for sin in heaven, and the sin of pride is one of the worst. Sin finds its seed in selfishness, the sister of pride. God knows what is going on inside our hearts and minds. He can see right through us. If we will put our trust in Him, and keep Him always as our Lord, then He will guide us away from pride and into a respect for all His children.

PRAYER: All secrets are open to you, O Lord. You know our comings and goings, and no thought goes by you unnoticed. Forgive my thoughts of pride and arrogance and lead me to a life of humble obedience and worship. Amen.

September 30

The horse is prepared against the day of battle: but safety is of the Lord (21:31).

The neighborhood was getting rougher all the time. The crime rate was sky-rocketing. As much as he hated it, he decided the time had come to buy a gun. He had put a burglar alarm in his home and in his car, and he had built a ten-foot fence around his property, but he still didn't feel safe. His wife told him he was getting paranoid, but he was determined to protect what was his. No one was going to push him around. It felt like war was breaking out, and he was going to be ready.

It's a sad world we live in. So much is done in anger and violence. People are afraid just to walk outside. They lose faith in good, and they put their faith in guns and alarms. They choose to fight the war themselves rather than waiting on the Lord. The world is going to get worse. Bad things are going to happen, but the Lord wants His children to rise above it, not become a part of it. We must put our trust in the Lord, and join with Paul in saying, "To live is Christ and to die is gain." If we are to find our lives at an end, it is much better to feel comfort in the Lord rather than frustration and anger at the fact that we are being hurt. We are Kingdom people, destined for eternity. The troubles of this world have no part in us. We are God's and His alone.

PRAYER: Protect me from this crazy world, Father. I will not fight at the level of those who love evil. I will remain committed to you and your love. Help me to forgive those who would hurt me, and turn my anger aside. Amen.

October 1

A good name is rather to be chosen than great riches, and loving favor rather than silver and gold. The rich and poor meet together: the Lord is the maker of them all (22:1-2).

Everyone loved Mr. B. He was a friendly old man who loved to play with children. Rumor had it that he was a brilliant man who could have done anything he wanted, but one day he walked out on his high paying job, and he never returned. Instead, he stayed home, began playing with the neighborhood children, and that had been how he'd spent his days ever since. If a child was sick, he was right there to visit them. If a child was hurt, he was the first to offer aid. If the familiar ringing of the ice cream truck sounded in the distance, Mr. B was the first in line, ready to treat the neighborhood children, no matter how many of them there were. His only purpose in life seemed to be to spread joy to the children he met. He never had a cross word, and he let them know that he loved each and every one of them. He was legend, and no one who knew Mr. B ever had anything bad to say about him.

When we give of ourselves, we find out what it really means to be rich. Life takes on new meaning, and we are filled with a feeling beyond description. God put us all here, and it is wonderful when we work together to make this life a joy. People who live to love others are a blessing to the Lord. In those people we can understand what it truly means to be happy.

PRAYER: Teach me what it means to be happy, Father. You are the source of all that is good and right. Let me dwell within your love, and let me be a channel for your love in this world that needs it so very much. Amen.

October 2

A prudent man foreseeth the evil, and hideth himself: but the simple pass on, and are punished (22:3).

The sky turned ugly. The clouds looked like they were a thousand feet high. They rolled in a threatening way, and they turned black. The lightning split the sky, and thunder pounded the senses. The horses were locked in the barn, the windmill had been locked, and the windows shut and latched. The family gathered in the cellar to wait for the storm to blow by. That night there would be reports of deaths due to people not paying attention to the signs. Some people never learned. The lightning wasn't enough, the wind wasn't enough; it didn't seem like people had enough sense to be scared sometimes. This was no weather to be out in, but there would be many who wouldn't give it a second thought. Too bad for them.

When we see things which could harm us, we should do everything in our power to avoid them. Sin is one such thing. We have been told what it will lead to, and all the signs warn against it, yet many times we ignore them. If we do not heed the warnings, we are heading to disaster. But if we will wake up to the danger that is possible, then we can avoid it, and live a life of joy and peace. God has given us every opportunity. If we foolishly ignore them, we have no one to blame but ourselves. If we heed them, God will bless us richly, and eternal life will be ours.

PRAYER: The signs are all around me, Lord, but I need your wisdom to see them. Open my eyes to the dangers which lie in my path, and give me the strength I need to get by them safe and sound. Amen.

October 3

Thorns and snares are in the way of the froward: he that doth keep his soul shall be far from them (22:5).

The path looked like it would take forever. The house was just over the ridge, but the path wound all the way around the other side of the hill. The climb looked easy enough to go straight across. They left the path, and started up the incline. The growth was thick and the footing was treacherous. As they reached the top, the way was blocked by thorn bushes and stickers. They were too dense to push through, but when they turned to leave the soft earth shifted, and they pitched into the brambles. The more they struggled, the worse the thorns stabbed and cut. By the time they made it back to the house, they were cut, bleeding and exhausted.

Sometimes, the easy way is not so easy. When we look for short cuts, we need to be aware of the dangers along the way. The path that is laid out before us is there for a reason. With our Christian pilgrimage, we can be sure that God knows the best way for us to go. If we will trust His guidance and help, then we can be sure that the path we are on is the right one. He will never lead us wrongly. The only time we get into trouble is when we go off on our own, exploring places to which God does not lead us. As long as we always know to return to His path, everything will be okay.

PRAYER: I am tempted to walk many roads, not just the one I am on. Many seem to lead to exciting places, and others look so much easier than the one I am on. Help me to know that you have brought me to the best place I could possibly be. Amen.

October 4

He that soweth iniquity shall reap vanity: and the rod of his anger shall fail (22:8).

He knew his competition. This job had opened up suddenly and he wanted it very badly. He had worked with most of the other applicants, and he knew he was better than they were. When he sat down to his interview, he made sure he commented on each one of them. He shared all of their mistakes and shortcomings, and he insulted them all. He continually compared himself to them to show how much better he would be for the job. He left feeling very good about his chances, and treated himself to a drink. Time passed and he didn't hear from the employer, so he gave the firm a call. Someone else had gotten the job. He wanted to know why. After much persistence and bullying, they told him the reason: they didn't want someone working for them who was so ready to stab others in the back. His conceit had turned them off, and his slandering had showed them he wasn't right for the position.

When we plant seeds which are evil or cruel, the only harvest we will receive is worthless. Evil grows evil, and nothing good can come of it. When our motives are evil and selfish, then we will come up empty-handed. God will never bless our actions when they are sinfully motivated. Only by our goodness will we receive reward. God loves to see His children live in love and obedience. He honors His children's good works, and He deals with sinful acts severely. There is no place for evil in the hearts of His own.

PRAYER: Lord, make me like you. Make me love, as you love, and give as you give. Amen.

October 5

He that hath a bountiful eye shall be blessed; for he giveth of his bread to the poor (22:9).

There was great need for a soup kitchen. He had driven all over town, and stopped to talk to people he knew were living on the street. He went out on the streets, and found the people where they lived. He was overwhelmed by the amount of people who were going hungry; he could only do so much. He began visiting area churches and charities to see what support he could drum up for the kitchen. With widespread support he knew great things could be accomplished. The need was there. Now, all that was needed was the commitment from others to do something about it.

There are two kinds of givers. There are those who give when they are asked, and there are those who go out and find ways to give. When we give only when we are asked, there is a danger of falling into an attitude wherein we hope no one will ask, and we will not be called upon to give. When we open our eyes and search for ways to give, however, we will not have to look too far, and we will find a way that we can serve. God wants us to follow the example of Christ, who went to where the people were. We can shield ourselves from the poor if we try hard enough, but when we are honest we know that they are there. They are waiting for us, and God urges us to take our duty seriously and do something now.

PRAYER: Where there is need, that is where I want to be, O Lord. Help me to give not only when it is convenient. Help me to look for need that I might give all the time. Amen.

October 6

Foolishness is bound in the heart of a child; but the rod of correction shall drive it far from him (22:15).

The little boy couldn't see into the pan, which sat perched on the edge of the stove. He hoped it might be icing, or pudding, or maybe mashed potatoes. His mother had said to stay away from it; that it was a no-no. Still, there might be something good in it. He moved closer, ever so slowly. As he got to the base of the stove, he began to reach up toward the pan of boiling water. Just as his little fingers began to grab, his mother swept him up from behind, and gave him a firm spanking. Hopefully, the next time she said no, he would remember that she meant it. She hated to spank him, but the pain and shock he received from that act was small sacrifice in the face of the pain and shock he would have received from the scalding water.

Punishment is rarely offered out of cruelty or meanness. It is given out of love, to dissuade us from actions which might hurt us worse. God punishes sinners to show them that there is a better way. He imposes rules on us, not to make our lives less than they can be, but to make them the very best that they can be. His rod is stern, but it is applied only in love, so that we might have life and have it more abundantly. God deals with all of His children with love and grace. If we will know that, then we will grow in the ways of God, and be happy.

PRAYER: Do not allow me to walk in the way that leads to destruction. Do whatever you need to so that I might live a full and happy life. Amen.

October 7

Rob not the poor, because he is poor: niether oppress the af-flicted in the gate: for the Lord will plead their cause, and spoil the soul of those that spoiled them (22:22-23).

A man walked by a newsstand and looked over the magazines. He selected a couple of titles and prepared to pay for them. When he pulled out his wallet, he realized that the proprietor was blind. He looked at the stack of magazines and papers and he selected a couple more. He then told the man that he had selected one, and that the price was $1.75. He paid the man with two one dollar bills, grabbed the four magazines, and strode away whistling. He called back over his shoulder, "Keep the change," and continued on his way, happy at the deception he had just pulled off.

There are people who look for ways to take advantage of anyone and everyone they can. They take delight in kicking others when they are down. They are cunning, and ruthless, and merciless. God will have nothing to do with anyone who lives by abusing the poor and helpless. God is on the side of the meek, and when they are attacked, God is attacked. The poor may not be able to defend themselves, but God certainly is. He will remember those who work to spoil the afflicted, and He in turn will spoil their souls. God is love, and those who live by hatred and evil will have no reward from Him.

PRAYER: You have blessed the meek and the poor and those who mourn. Let me be among your blessed, Lord. I rejoice when your will is done. Let me spread your love wherever I roam. Amen.

October 8

Make no friendship with an angry man; and with a furious man thou shalt not go; lest thou learn his ways, and get a snare to thy soul (22:24-25).

Their boy had always been a good one. Even until high school he had helped around the house, he had been respectful, he had cared for his younger sisters, and he never talked back. He was the perfect boy, and he seemed to be happy. Then, in high school, he had started hanging around with a pair of boys from the center part of town. They were always in trouble or causing it. They cursed, and fought, and they vandalized town property. Everyone knew the kind of trouble they caused. And it was rubbing off on their son. He had started talking back and throwing his weight around, and he was impossible to speak with. Thirteen years of upbringing wasn't enough to protect him from a couple of months of bad company. It was hard to see him so bad after he had been so good.

As Christians, the company we keep is extremely important. If we spend our time with people who embrace sin, then we will be more tempted to do likewise than if we dwelt with others who are trying to live good, righteous lives. There is safety in numbers. Fellowship is a way that we can grow strong in our faith. With others to support us, and for us to support, we find additional strength during difficult times. Where two or more are gathered, there the Lord is with them.

PRAYER: Thank you for giving me friends who feel the same way about life that I do. I need support in this life, because it feels like the world is against me. I grow homesick for heaven, and it is comforting to have friends to share and wait for your glory with. Amen.

October 9

Remove not the ancient landmark, which thy fathers have set (22:28).

When the neighbors decided to sell their land, they thought little of it. Now, it was a major dispute. The neighbors were claiming that they had ownership of part of their land. It would have been a moot point twenty years before. His father had set large stone pillars on the property line, and a fence stretched from one to the other. They had marked the boundaries clearly and concisely, but they had been removed long ago, and now there was nothing to show where the line was. The property deeds had somehow been lost, and it looked like the court might find in favor of the neighbors.

Sometimes we devalue the things our parents have done. We assume they acted impetuously and without cause. We lose touch with their wisdom and their desires. We destroy their legacy to us, bit by bit. This is most true of the teachings they gave us when we were young. Parents do their best to bring up their children in the best way possible. They do what they can, and hope that some of it sticks. Our heavenly Father does the same thing. God has given us a legacy which has stretched over thousands of years. The tales of the Bible should give us instruction on how we should live our lives and what we should avoid. Often we choose to ignore the instruction, thinking that it is outdated. God's truth never grows out of date, and His instruction is as a lamp unto our feet.

PRAYER: Lord God, forgive me when I think that I know more than those who have gone before me. Help me to see the wisdom of history, especially my personal history, that I might discern all the treasures that have been left for me. Amen.

October 10

When thou sitteth to eat with a ruler, consider diligently what is before thee: and put a knife to thy throat, if thou be a man given to appetite. Be not desirous of his dainties: for they are deceitful meat (23:1-3).

It wasnt' fair. He worked hard for his money, yet that no-account brother of his hardly did anything and he was rich. He hated going to his brother's house because it made him feel so useless. The house was huge, and it had all the best furniture. His brother's cars both cost more than he could make in a year. His wife and kids were dressed in designer clothes, and they ate steak almost every meal. He envied his brother that he had everything a person could want. What he didn't know was that his brother was on the verge of a fatal heart attack, caused by too much pressure and not enough time. He also didn't know that his brother's wife wanted to leave him, and that his home life had been rotten. All the glitter of his brother's gold blinded him so that he could not appreciate what he had himself. He only saw the good; none of the bad.

We need to be careful what we are envious of. God calls us to live our lives day by day. It is wrong to live in the past, and it is dangerous to live for the future. Better by far is to live in the present and to learn to appreciate the blessings which we have, not mourn for all the things which we have to do without.

PRAYER: I am surrounded by so much good. Help me not to begrudge those who have more than I do, for I do not know what their life may be like. Happiness has nothing to do with what we can own, but who we are. Amen.

October 11

Labor not to be rich: cease from thine own wisdom. Wilt thou set thine eyes upon that which is not? for riches certainly make themselves wings; they fly away as an eagle toward heaven (23:4-5).

His entire life he had wanted to be rich. He saved every penny he made, and invested wisely. With money came power, and he aimed to be one of the most powerful men around. Over time he came to desire money with all his heart. His investments became more and more risky as he tried for fast profit. All his life he had seemed to have a Midas touch, but then it turned to brass. A series of ill-advised investments ate up his wealth. In panic, he tried to recover his losses, but in his haste, he lost the rest of what he had. He had given himself totally to making money, and after a long life he had absolutely nothing to show for it.

It is better to give ourselves to something which cannot be taken away from us. Money is here and then gone, but faith in God endures forever. The treasure He gives us is eternal. Joy, peace, strength, love, and a thousand other precious gifts can be ours if we will pursue God with all our heart, mind and soul. He is the only thing worthy of such devotion. Everything else is a deception. It may seem worthwhile, but in reality it is without value. Give your heart to God, and He will reward you beyond your wildest dreams.

PRAYER: I am surrounded by temptations which are temporary. They seem permanent, but they are frauds. Only you last forever, and in your love I will find true wealth. Fill me with a treasure which cannot diminish. Amen.

October 12

Let not thine heart envy sinners; but be thou in the fear of the Lord all the day long. For surely there is an end; and thine expectation shall not be cut off (23:17-18).

The class erupted into chaos. The teacher had been called to the phone, and after she left the room, the children went wild. A few sat quietly, watching the antics of the others. One boy watched as papers flew across the room. Some boys were having a snowball fight with wadded up paper. They were laughing and having a wonderful time. The temptation became too much for the child, and he jumped from his chair, picked up a paper wad and drew back his arm to let it fly. Just then, the teacher returned, and she caught the boy before he ever got his throw off. When the punishment came, it was as severe for him as it was for all the children who had been naughty from the beginning.

No one knows the hour or the day when the Lord will return. It could be tomorrow or a thousand years from now. What is required of Christians is that they live each day as if it were the day Christ was returning. We cannot let down for even a minute. Sin may be appealing, but we must realize that the reward for sin is death. Only by remaining steadfast in our pursuit of righteousness may we hope to attain the life which never ends.

PRAYER: Keep me constant, Lord. I often want to do the things I know I should not, and I need your help to steer clear of things which are not good to do. Forgive me when I fall prey to sin, and lift me up so that I might live a life which is pleasing to you. Amen.

October 13

Buy the truth, and sell it not; also wisdom, and instruction, and understanding (23:23).

It looked like a great deal. He had wanted a new camera for a long time, and when he saw the one he wanted for $300 less than any other price he had found, he jumped at the chance. It had worked well for a couple of weeks, but then the shutter stuck. After that, the pictures came out foggy. The lens didn't seat properly on the face of the camera, and the film started jamming. It didn't take long to realize that he had been taken. The camera he bought was nothing but junk. He had paid a foolishly low price, and he had been made a fool of.

There are so many things in our lives which look good, but they are really inferior. Fame, wealth, prestige, looks, all seem like they are wonderful things to have, but they fade away and leave us with nothing. Truth, wisdom, and understanding are costly, but they are worth anything we have to give. They fill us with an inner treasure which does not fade. There is nothing greater for us to devote ourselves to. God will guide us to wisdom and understanding if we will ask Him to. He blesses anyone who sincerely tries to find truth. With God on our side, we can rest assured that we will attain our goal. Once attained, we will never let go of the riches we have been blessed with.

PRAYER: There is a lot in this world that has no value. Keep me from giving myself to those things. Make me desire truth, wisdom, instruction and understanding. I love you, Father, and I want to do what is right. Bless my efforts. Amen.

October 14

Who hath woe? Who hath sorrow? Who hath contention? Who hath babbling? Who hath wounds without cause? Who hath redness of eyes? They that tarry long at the wine; they that go to seek mixed wine. Look not thou upon the wine when it is red, when it giveth his color in the cup, when it moveth itself aright. At the last it biteth like a serpent and stingeth like an adder. Thine eyes shall behold strange women, and thine heart shall utter perverse things (23:29-33).

Everyone was into drugs of some kind at the theatre where she worked. She had resisted for quite some time, but finally she gave in. She tried many things, and found that some of the pills made her feel wonderful. She kept telling herself that she was in complete control, and that she could do without the stuff, but as time passed she began to admit that she was kidding herself. She looked in the mirror, and saw a much older woman staring her in the face. She was broke because her habit cost so much, and she realized that she was close to ruin.

The same is true of anything we get hooked on. Drugs, alcohol, money, success; these all have the same destructive power. They drain us of our spirit and they leave us as empty shells. Only one thing is worthy of our souls, and that is God. If we give ourselves to Him, He will give us back better than before. We can come to true wholeness and potential only in the Lord.

PRAYER: Destroy what is wrong within my heart, dear Lord. Take me and teach me to live a life which is good and strong. Support me through my weak moments, and fill me with your holy might. Amen.

October 15

Through wisdom is a house builded; and by understanding it is established: and by knowledge shall the chambers be filled with all precious and pleasant riches (24:3-4).

She loved visiting her friends. Their whole family was wonderful. It was a joy to enter a place where there was so much love and affection. They spoke to one another with respect, and they showed kindness beyond belief. Even when the girls did something wrong, they were treated with love and care. She wished she could live in a home like that, and she swore that when she was a parent, she would try to be as fair and loving as her friends' parents were.

Families should be havens of love and support. We should learn what love is all about from our families. We should also learn what it means to truly love others, whether they deserve it all the time or not. Unconditional love means love which doesn't ask anything in return. Christians are called upon to love all people, regardless of whether they are worthy of it. This is the love which God gives to each one of us, and it is a love that He hopes we will use in our relationships here on earth. A house which is built upon kindness and understanding is a fortress against all the evil in the world. A good home is a blessing beyond words. Establish a home in true love, and its benefits will last forever.

PRAYER: Teach me what it means to love unselfishly, dear God. Help me to judge no one, and to love everyone that I can. Forgive me when I am unloving, and fill me with your spirit, that I might grow in your ways. Amen.

October 16

A wise man is strong; yea, a man of knowledge increaseth strength. For by wise counsel thou shalt make thy war: and in multitude of counselors there is safety (24:5-6).

The story of David and Goliath is a comforting one. Its moral says clearly that might does not always make right. If we will use our heads we can overcome seemingly impossible odds. There was no question that Goliath was more powerful than David, but David proved to be the better warrior because he knew how to use his head, and he knew how to use his faith.

There are times in the lives of each of us when we feel like we don't stand a chance. We are overwhelmed by the immensity of our troubles, and they bury us under feelings of futility and despair. If we try to face these problems on our own, we will probably fail. The wise person seeks support in difficult times. There is no better place to turn than to the Lord. He will support and strengthen us in every situation. His counsel is solid and true. If we will join forces with God, then there is nothing on earth which can defeat us. The Lord is a sure foundation, and the evil of the world is powerless in the face of His might. Like David, we can rest assured that God will stand beside us. Through faith we can be made victorious over even the most powerful forces on earth.

PRAYER: I am weak, Father, but I have no fear for I know that you are strong. I have nothing to fear in this life, so long as I listen for your wise counsel and have the wisdom to heed your loving advice. Be with me, I pray. Amen.

October 17

If thou faint in the day of adversity, thy strength is small (24:10).

They had rehearsed the play a hundred times. A month of hard work was quickly coming to its pay-off. The play opened to a packed house, and the actors and actresses waited anxiously for the curtain to rise. The lines had been memorized, the costumes fitted, the make-up put on and taken off repeatedly, the lights were in place, and the performers were in their places. The production went smoothly most of the way, but one actor completely forgot his lines. Instead of covering for himself, he froze. The other actors covered as well as they could, and the play finished without further incident. The actor was replaced after a few more bungled performances, and the play went on to receive rave reviews.

The Christian life is a preparation for the glory which is to come. We rehearse our parts every time we follow in the footsteps of Christ. It is important that we know our parts well before we go to the judgment seat of Christ. Those who know their parts well have nothing to fear. But if we freeze, and we are found lacking, then we will be unfit for the Kingdom. Good actors and actresses dedicate themselves totally to their craft. Christians must do the same. Our faith must completely guide our lives. If that is true, then we too will meet with rave reviews in the last days.

PRAYER: I want to be skilled in the ways of righteousness and light, Almight God. Help me to know how you would have me to walk. Help me to be faithful to practice my faith continually. Amen.

October 18

If thou forbear to deliver them that are drawn unto death, and those that are ready to be slain; if thou sayest, Behold, we knew it not; doth not he that pondereth the heart consider it? And he that keepeth thy soul, doth not he know it? And shall not he render to every man according to his works (24:11-12).

A hunter set traps to catch animals so he could sell their pelts. When his son was old enough, he took him out to teach him how to trap. It was not long until he began having trouble catching any animals. One day, after setting the traps, he saw his son go out into the woods, so he followed him. The boy went from trap to trap, springing those which were empty, and freeing the animals from those which had done their job. The father stepped into the view of his son and asked him why he was doing such a thing. The boy responded that he couldn't stand to think of the creatures being killed, so he was setting them free. The father ceased taking his son with him, but he never forgot the sympathy and compassion that his son displayed.

Sinners are caught in traps of their own design, but they are deadly nonetheless. As Christians we have an obligation to do everything we can to free them from their traps, and save them from certain destruction. If we will endeavor to bring the truth of Christ to those who desperately need it, God will find favor with us and He will bless us all the days of this life, and the next.

PRAYER: Lord, make me an instrument of your grace and love. Make me to spread your truth to everyone who is in need, before it is too late. Bless my efforts to bring your light into this dark age. Amen.

October 19

Rejoice not when thine enemy falleth, and let not thine heart be glad when he stumbleth: lest the Lord see it, and it displeases him, and he turn away his wrath from him (24:17-18).

A popular kind of movie these days has a rough and rugged cop or detective wage war on crime. The bad guys are doubly bad, and the good guys are cunning, smart and powerful. They speak with their fists and their guns. The movie makers work hard to get the audience on the good guys' side, and there is great cheering and applause when the bad guys get theirs in the end.

It's sad that we feel like that when the bad guys meet their end. God's people should feel bad when sinful people die in their sin. When any child of God dies, it is a tragedy, never a reason for celebration. God loves all His children, no matter what they do. He wants them to come back to Him, and when they die in their sin, it breaks His heart. As we learn to feel with the heart of Christ, and to think with the mind of Christ, then we also feel great sadness at the death of a sinner.

As long as we live, we should dedicate ourselves to sharing the truth of Christ. We may be responsible for leading people out of the darkness and danger of sin into the light and protection of God's love. God rejoices at our efforts to bring our brothers and sisters into His love. If we will do so, He will bless us richly.

PRAYER: I am sorry that I often feel good when I hear of evildoers who have met with their own destruction. Help me to learn to love the sinner while hating the sin. Let me feel and see and act as you would, Lord. Amen.

October 20

Fret not thyself because of evil men, neither be thou envious at the wicked; for there shall be no reward to the evil man; the candle of the wicked shall be put out (24:19-20).

It made him so mad sometimes. He worked diligently at his job, doing everything in his power to make sure that each thing was done right. However, the man he worked with could have cared less. If things were substandard it didn't bother him at all. What made it really bad was that the rest of the company respected the work that the pair produced. No one knew that it was all because of him that things were done well. His partner was more than willing to share the glory, but he wouldn't carry his end of the load. It was infuriating to do all the work and then share the credit.

His efforts were not in vain, nor did they go unnoticed. When promotions came around, he was moved up into a managerial position, while his former partner stayed right where he was.

Often, it seems like the wrong people get all the glory. We try to do our very best, and we receive no credit at all. It is good to know that our Father in heaven knows everything that is going on, and one day we will be promoted to our heavenly reward. God blesses those of His children who do what they know they should. Those who slack off can hope for nothing more than His wrath, for He will not abide by the person who gives less than their very best.

PRAYER: I want to do the best in every situation. Help me to find my full potential and to use it in your service. Lead me where I need most to go, and show me how I can be of the most usefulness. Amen.

October 21

These things also belong to the wise. It is not good to have respect for persons in judgment. He that saith unto the wicked, Thou art righteous; him shall the people curse, nations shall abhor him: but to them that rebuke him shall be delight, and a good blessing shall come upon them (24:23-25).

There was a faithful church woman who was renowned as a gossip and tale-teller. She would go to others to share with them "in Christian love." What she was really doing was talking about others behind their backs. She prayed for people by saying they were possessed by evil, when in fact their only sin was to disagree with her. Some perceived her to be holy, but most people knew of her terrible hypocrisy. Finally, they came to her and let her know that what she was doing was completely un-Christian and destructive.

We have no right to judge anyone, and we should not use our piety in order to put others down. Our prayers should be prayers of love for God's guidance and protection, not for selfish and judgmental concerns. We accomplish nothing by talking ill of any other person, and we sin grievously when we try to mask it in Christian piety. We should try to help others understand God, but we must enter into that quest as equals. We need to make sure that our motives are always pure when we seek to help another person.

PRAYER: Lord, help me help others without feeling proud or vain. You have changed my life, and I am better off now than ever before, but do not let that change cause me to feel superior in any way to any of my brothers or sisters in Christ. Amen.

October 22

Be not a witness against thy neighbor without cause; and deceive not with thy lips. Say not, I will do so to him as he hath done to me: I will render to the man according to his work (24:28-29).

It had started innocently, but then before he knew it, he was in a fight. He hadn't wanted to fight, so he had only made a half-hearted attempt to defend himself. He realized now that he had looked bad in front of all his friends. The more he thought about it, the angrier he got. He kept thinking of ways that he could get even. It began occupying all his time. Revenge was all he wanted. He was going to teach the other guy a lesson he would never forget. He wanted to make him regret that he'd ever started anything.

When we think a lot of ourselves, we cannot stand to look bad in others' eyes. When we are hurt and embarrassed, we want to strike back. We think that by repaying injury with injury it will make us feel better. We believe that justice means an eye for an eye, a tooth for a tooth. Nothing is further from the truth. If we set aside our pride, we find that it is not so difficult to practice forgiveness. Forgiveness heals injuries, instead of opening new wounds. It makes us feel better, it makes others feel better, and it is pleasing to God. We should strive to pay God back for His grace, rather than pay back our enemies for their evil.

PRAYER: Lord, I do not want to pay back evil with evil, but with good. Help me to love my enemies, and pray for my persecutors. Let me know how to love everyone, whether they love me or not. Amen.

October 23

I went by the field of the slothful, and by the vineyard of the man void of understanding; and, lo, it was all grown over with thorns, and nettles and covered the face thereof, and the stone wall thereof was broken down (24:30-31).

Everyone remembered the property in its glory days. The house was enormous, and it was beautiful. The lawn had always been well-groomed, and there was a magnificent garden in the back. Now it was a disgrace. The lawn looked like a field, the house was dirty and the mortar was crumbling from between the bricks. Vines covered the face of the building and the back yard looked like a garbage dump. The new owners were rarely home, and they did little to keep the property up. In the three years they had lived there, they had not mowed the yard once. The neighbors complained, but the residents said they had the right to live any way they chose.

Although it is wrong to judge a person based on appearance, often we can get an indication of what people are like on the inside by watching from the outside. If we live a holy life, it will be apparent in the way others see us. If we are slothful, others will be able to tell just by looking at us. Sometimes there are extenuating circumstances which cause even the most upright people to be negligent, but usually a person who is disciplined and committed to God will make every effort to put forth a good example.

PRAYER: Father, let what is in my heart be obvious to all who might look. Let my outside reflect the goodness which you have put inside. Amen.

October 24

It is the glory of God to conceal a thing: but the honor of kings is to search out a matter. The heaven for height, and the earth for depth, and the heart of kings is unsearchable (25:2-3).

He loved mysteries. He would lock himself in his room and read detective stories for hours. He would take notes so that he could outsmart the detective and solve the mystery first. Any kind of puzzle fascinated him, and he threw himself into whatever mystery lay before him.

Most people are fascinated by a good mystery. We like to be challenged and to give our minds exercise. There is no greater mystery in this life than the mystery of God. He is a puzzle beyond our comprehension, but His greatest desire is that we will try to know Him as best we can. He longs for us to devote our lives to an understanding of His will and ways. He has given us the holy Scriptures to read and contemplate, and they hold both questions and answers which can occupy a lifetime. If we will work to unlock the mysteries of God, He will help us and lead us to ever greater understanding. We must spend time daily with the Lord in order to know Him more. We need not expect answers immediately, but we can live with the questions and struggle out their solutions. No greater challenge awaits us, but its reward is finer than the purest gold if we will face it.

PRAYER: For every answer I receive, there is another question to take its pace. Grant me the determination to pursue you with all my heart and mind. Give me the key to unlock the mystery of your love and grace, O Lord. Amen.

October 25

Take away the dross from the silver, and there shall come forth a vessel for the finer (25:4).

He worked the clay with skill, smoothing and turning it. It began as a lump, but in his hands it took shape. He crafted it into a fine pitcher, but as he worked he noticed that some of the clay was lumpy, so he started afresh. He reworked the clay, adding water and kneading it back and forth. He flipped the clay back onto the potter's wheel and began again. This time as he worked, he discovered a small stone in the clay, and once again he started over. He worked the clay thoroughly, making sure that all of the impurities were out of it, and once satisfied he crafted his earthen vase.

In the case of clay, or of silver, it cannot be used unless it is pure. If it is used in its imperfection, it will be flawed and worthless. We are like clay in God's hands when we give our lives back to Him. We ask Him to take us and shape us and to remove all our imperfections. Only by being perfected in His hands may we ever hope to have a place in heaven. God will not settle for less than what is perfect. In His hands, we will be recreated, as God intends us to be. He will take away all that is bad or imperfect, and He will create from us a vessel acceptable and worthy to have a place in His Kingdom.

PRAYER: I am filled with imperfections and flaws. Left as I am I cannot hope to have a place with you, Almighty God. Take me and start anew. Reshape me into the person you want me to be. Create in me a holy and good spirit, and bless me all of my days. Amen.

October 26

Go not forth hastily to strive, lest thou know not what to do in the end thereof, when thy neighbor hath put thee to shame (25:8).

The owner of the service station had sent warnings, but without reply. The bill had not been paid for ten months. At six months he had turned it over to a collection agency, but they, too, had been ignored. Finally, he had them summoned to small claims court. It seemed open and shut until the judge asked why they hadn't paid. The defendants brought forth copies of letters they had sent saying that the repair work that was supposed to have been done had not been done properly. It had caused further damage to the car, and they had taken it elsewhere. The service station owner refused to give them satisfaction, so they refused to pay their bill. They offered a notarized statement from the second service station attesting to the fact that the original work had been poor at best. The judge found in favor of the defendants and ordered the service station owner to pay for the damages his negligence had caused.

When we accuse someone of wrongdoing, it is wise to make sure that we have done nothing that we should be ashamed of. No one is without sin, and we have been told not to cast stones unless we are without fault. It is better to look at our own lives and work to improve them before we try to improve others around us.

PRAYER: Lord, before I look to others to criticize them, let me look at myself to see that I am no better. Make me concerned with my own growth, so that I might continually strive to grow and mature in your love. Amen.

October 27

As the cold of snow in the time of harvest, so is the faithful messenger to them that send him: for he refresheth the soul of his masters (25:13).

There was no doubt about it, harvest time was the hardest time of year. The planting and tilling and weeding were difficult, but harvest required every ounce of strength and stamina a soul could muster. When the days were cool, it made the job so much more pleasant, but when it was hot there was no worse job on earth. The fields baked in the hot sun, and you baked also. Many a farmer came to his end out in the fields at harvest time when the sun was hot. This year was great. The snow was moving south from the hills, and the air off the plains was cold and brisk. Working in weather like this made you feel alive. It was refreshing and made you feel like you could work forever without stopping.

The breath of the Lord is like that. When we live without it, we are amazed at how hard this life is. We feel completely drained and exhausted by the simplest of tasks. When we have the Lord in our lives, however, He gives us strength and renews our stamina. With God all things are possible, and when His Spirit is in our hearts, we feel as if we can last forever without pausing. We are made conquerors with Christ, and nothing can defeat us.

PRAYER: Renew me, Father, in those times when I feel that I cannot go on. Forgive me when I try to live life all by myself, turning from your loving care. Give me your Spirit that I might rise above the struggles of this life and claim the victory won for me by Christ. Amen.

October 28

Confidence in an unfaithful man in time of trouble is like a broken tooth, and a foot out of joint (25:19).

The deeper the group moved into the woods, the more they knew they were lost. They had separated from the larger group to go exploring, and they hadn't been able to find their way back. It was beginning to get dark, and they were getting scared. Three of the group had confidence that the others would find them, but one wasn't so sure. They decided to just stop and wait where they were in hopes that someone would come along. As they sat, the skeptic of the group kept saying that they should keep moving. He wanted to go off toward the east, saying that doing something was a lot better than doing nothing. He had little faith in the ability of the rest of the group to find them. When the other three were resistant to his suggestions, he said he would go off by himself, and return later with help. He struck out on his own, and it wasn't long until the rest of the group happened along to where the three waited. They told the group about the fourth person. It was not until the next morning that he was found, but not before he had suffered through the fear and anguish of being lost alone.

Without faith, we do terribly foolish things. Only through faith will we develop the confidence we need to make it in this crazy and frightening world.

PRAYER: Help me to have the confidence in you that I need, Father. Strengthen my faith that I might trust in your power in every situation. Destroy the spirit of doubt which often creeps into my heart. Amen.

October 29

As he taketh away a garment in cold weather, and as vinegar upon nitre, so is he that singeth songs to a heavy heart (25:20).

A woman lay in her hospital bed, crying. The diagnosis had been cancer, and it was inoperable. While she was sobbing, a friend came in to see her. She asked the woman what was wrong, and the woman told her. Her friend patted her hand and said, "Where is your faith? Everything will work out just fine, as long as you have faith. God must have some reason for letting this happen, so just sit back and watch Him work."

The woman felt a strange anger in her heart. She knew her friend was trying to be helpful, but her words stung and were terribly unfair. She had plenty of faith. That had nothing to do with it. She had cancer, and that was something she wasn't prepared to deal with. Her friend acted like she hadn't even heard.

God never causes bad things to happen. He does indeed take bad things and turn them into good, but we have no way of knowing what He has in mind. When we try to comfort others we need to connect with their pain and suffering. Offering them easy answers and platitudes does not help at all. We merely add to the person's suffering. We end up giving nothing of value and, in fact, it is as if we pour vinegar into their wounds or take from them a cloak in the cold of winter. We do more harm than good.

PRAYER: Lord, let me listen to the cries of others and respond from my heart, where you are Lord and Master. Make me a compassionate, loving friend when others suffer. Amen.

October 30

If thine enemy be hungry, give him bread to eat: and if he be thirsty, give him water to drink: for thou shalt heap coals of fire upon his head, and the Lord shall reward thee (25:21-22).

The air was strangely silent. The last of the mortar shells had exploded, and the gunfire had ceased. The skirmish had gone on for hours. A patrol moved forward to check for the enemy, and as they rounded a bend, an enemy soldier lay bleeding in the path. One of the soldiers raised his rifle to shoot the man, but his partner told him to stop. The man was in bad shape, and he needed help. All the killing was senseless, and it seemed criminal to shoot someone who had one foot the grave. The soldiers carried the hurt enemy toward his own side and they bandaged his wound. They left him with water and food, and went their way. In the center of a terrible war, the two men felt like they had found something right to do and they had done it.

If someone would do us harm, that is something that they will have to answer for. God has said we should love everyone and we are called to serve not only our friends, but our enemies as well. We will answer to God for our actions, as will our enemies. It is vital that we have nothing to be ashamed of in that final time. We must not act like those who would hurt us. When we treat them with love, we make their sin doubly dark, and the Lord rejoices in our loving kindness.

PRAYER: I have difficulty loving those who love me, Father, so I definitely need your help to love my enemies. Show me what is good in them that I might respond with concern and affection. Amen.

October 31

He that hath no rule over his own spirit is like a city that is broken down, and without walls (25:28).

The evening had begun with the usual Halloween pranks. Smoke bombs and toilet paper for trees, soap for windows, and an occasional water balloon for unsuspecting passers-by. Then, the older boy from down the street had joined in. He had grown tired of the pranks and suggested they try some more exciting tricks. Under his guidance the band of kids slashed some tires and broke glass in driveways. They poured oil on people's front steps and they threw rocks at windows. What had started as an evening of mischief turned to adolescent terrorism. The children went wild with their destruction, causing the residents to dread the idea of Halloweens yet to come.

Even the most innocent prank is still going to hurt someone. When we make another person a victim, we take from them their rights to security and comfort. When pranks get out of hand because we lack self-control, they can be dangerous and cruel. If we don't have any self-control, then we don't have the will to say "no" when we should. We need to pray to God for His strength and wisdom so that we resist the temptation to do the things we know we shouldn't. Discipline is an important part of the Christian life, and if that is what we lack, then we must seek it with all our heart.

PRAYER: Help me to resist evil, O Lord. I know that I am sometimes weak, and I need your strength to get me through. Help me to develop self-control and discipline in my life, Father. Amen.

November 1

As the bird by wandering, as the swallow by flying, so the curse causeless shall not come (26:2).

The memorandum said that the front office was displeased with the performance of some of the employees. One of the girls became really upset when she read the notice, but the girl next to her seemed unconcerned. She walked over to the girl and asked why she was untroubled by the message.

"The only people that the message is speaking to are the ones who are giving less than their best effort. I come in here every day and give 100 percent. I know that I'm doing the best job I can. As long as I know I'm not goofing off, then I don't care what they have to say about it. If you're doing all you can, then relax. If not, take the memo as constructive criticism and do better."

When an insult or comment is directed to us we need to weigh it carefully. If it is valid, we should act on it, but if it is unfair, then we need not be troubled by it. God asks that we try to be the best we can be. If we are true to our abilities, then He will be pleased with us. To the person who does all that they are able, an insult is like a bird that never lands, that never hits its target. While it is aloft it can do no harm.

PRAYER: When I do all that I can, make me secure in that knowledge. When I am doing less, help me to see ways to improve and grow. Help me to handle insults with grace, and let me not be troubled by comments which are not true. Amen.

November 2

Answer not a fool according to his folly, lest thou also be like unto him (26:4).

It had gotten all over the school that Andrew's mother had gone to a mental institution. Most of the children were sympathetic, and they didn't tease him, but there were some who went out of their way to torment him. He tried to ignore their insults, but finally it got to be too much for him. Whenever one of the children would say something cruel, Andrew would strike back, saying terrible things in return. His anger overwhelmed him and he found himself getting into fights to defend his mother. Even the children who were sympathetic didn't want to be around him, because of the anger he showed. He looked for weaknesses and skeletons in the closets of his classmates, and whenever he found out something that they would be ashamed of, he spread it around school.

Some people can be very cruel, but that is no reason for us to reply in kind. Jesus was tormented and ridiculed by many people in His lifetime, and He let the insult bounce right off. There was no way that Christ would ever have returned an unkindness. We are called to be loving, giving people, even to those who would try to hurt us. God blesses those who will remain loving in the face of cruelty, and His anger will be against those who do wrong.

PRAYER: Evil is contagious, O Lord. When one person does something cruel, and another person replies cruelly, then a cycle begins which can only be broken by love. Give me the love to heal anger and cruelty, Father. Amen.

November 3

Answer a fool according to his folly, lest he be wise in his own conceit (26:5).

She kept telling her friend not to cheat. The test was a big one, but it really wasn't worth cheating. Her friend had done it before and had always gotten away with it, but the English teacher they had now was a watchdog. Nothing got past her gaze. The teacher was as good at catching cheaters as her friend was at cheating. Nothing the girl could say would sway her friend from cheating on the test.

The day of the test came, and her friend attempted to cheat. She got caught and received an "F" for her grade. The girl got a good grade, and she tried to explain to her friend that she didn't have to cheat to do well. Her friend listened carefully, and with the help of the first girl, she was able to pass her classes without further deception.

When we know someone who is trying to live life by sinful ways, we need to try to tell them, but it is wise to remember that most people only learn by making their own mistakes. When they do, we need to be there to support them and help them understand. We need to speak out against the folly of the foolish, and hope that they learn their lesson, whether it is the hard way or not. Only by being caught can some people ever learn that the sin they commit is stupid.

PRAYER: Help me to be a good support to my friends. Even though they do not listen to everything I say, Lord, help me to be there to help them whenever I can. Amen.

November 4

The legs of the lame are not equal: so is a parable in the mouth of fools (26:7).

The discussion always came around to religion. She was a devout woman who read her Bible daily, prayed morning and evening, and went to church weekly. He, on the other hand, was neither a believer nor a non-believer; he just liked to argue. The problem was that he had read the Bible and he knew it inside out. She would try to explain her beliefs to him, and he would tear them apart using Scripture as his support. It always made her angry to the point of tears. She knew he was twisting Scripture to make it say what he wanted it to say, but she didn't have the knowledge she needed to combat it. He took the Bible and made it into a joke.

When foolish people get ahold of the Bible, they can do some pretty terrible things with it. They twist its meaning and they use it for selfish reasons. Non-believers love to take the Bible apart and quote it out of context. They like to misinterpret it in order to make believers appear foolish. How much moreso they will look before the judgment seat of God when they are called upon to explain themselves. God gave us the Bible as a comfort and a support, not as a topic for debate. If we will spend time in Scripture, it will prove a faithful friend, and no one will be able to take its riches from us.

PRAYER: I fall into the trap of defending my faith, Father, when I have nothing to defend. Christ defended Himself with His resurrection, and He needs no further defense. Help me to remember not to argue my faith, but to live it. Amen.

November 5

As a thorn goeth up into the hand of a drunkard, so is a parable in the mouth of fools (26:9).

He couldn't believe his friends. He had only had a little bit to drink, and they wouldn't let him drive his own car home. He'd show them. He didn't need his car, because he could walk. He turned a corner and walked halfway up the street before he realized he didn't recognize any of his surroundings. He decided that he was a block wrong from where he wanted to turn, so he cut through a yard which he felt would be adjacent to his own. In the dark, he stumbled and fell into a hedge of rosebushes. He climbed out of the bushes, cursing and shouting. The residents of the house called the police to report a disturbance, and when they came they were able to take him home.

Alcohol dulls the senses and makes people feel they know exactly what they are doing. It gives them a false sense of security, and makes it nearly impossible for them to admit they are wrong. Usually, they have no idea what they are doing. The same is true of a parable in the mouth of a fool. The fool may think that he or she knows what it is about, but without the wisdom of God in their lives, they haven't the slightest idea. God will disclose His great mysteries to everyone who will come to Him in humility and love. All we need to do is ask.

PRAYER: Lord, help me to keep my wits about me in every situation. Help me to avoid doing things which make me less than you want me to be. Guide me with patience and love, Father. Amen.

November 6

As a dog returneth to his vomit, so a fool returneth to his folly (26:11).

All his friends thought that he was crazy. He loved to dodge cars as they sped along the highway. He would wait behind a bush until the car was too close to stop, then he would take off running across the road. The drivers would usually hit their brakes and come to a screeching halt, and to date he had never even been scratched. After it was over he would laugh and brag about it to all his friends. No matter how much they pleaded with him, he insisted on playing his stupid game. He called it bravery, but they thought he was a fool. One day he wouldn't be so lucky, and then who would he brag to?

God gave each of us a measure of common sense, and He expects us to use it. We have no right to do things which are a danger either to us or the people around us. God expects us to use the brains He has given us for constructive purposes. A dog vomits and then eats the vomit because of not knowing any better. We should have a bit more intelligence than the canine. When we do something which is foolish or wrong, we should know not to keep repeating it until disaster strikes. God blesses those who will use their talents and gifts for what is right and good, not what is foolish.

PRAYER: I know that I do plenty of silly things, O Lord. Help me to stop being foolish, and empower me to use the mind and body that you have given me for good works. Let me see the errors I make, so that I do not repeat them. Amen.

November 7

The sluggard is wiser in his own conceit than seven men that can render a reason (26:16).

He stood in the long line of the welfare office waiting his turn. When he got to the window he was asked the usual string of the same dumb questions. He answered them, feeling very smug inside. He had been applying for jobs that he knew he was unqualified for. He didn't want to have to work any more than was absolutely necessary. He could tell them that he was looking for work, but that nothing had come up. Plus, he was doing some auto repair on the side that nobody knew about. He certainly wasn't going to say anything. He felt very good about being able to outsmart all these stuffed-shirts. They thought they were pretty smart, but they weren't anything compared to him.

It is difficult to deal with deceptive people, because they are convinced that they are right in what they do. They think they are getting away with things, just because they don't get caught. The Lord in heaven sees everything, even that which is hidden. He will judge us based on how we live our lives, and what we believe. If our lives have been lies and deceptions, then we can have no hope of dwelling with God. God blesses those people who are honest and intelligent to use the gifts and talents that they have in order to be the people He wants.

PRAYER: I often look for shortcuts, for ways of getting something for nothing. Help me to know that when I do that, eventually I lose. Make me an honest and dedicated child of yours. Amen.

November 8

He that passeth by, and meddleth with strife belonging not to him, is like one that taketh a dog by the ears (26:17).

A man was passing by a store when he saw two other men fighting. At first, it was just a quarrel, but as tempers flared, both men took to scuffling. Blows were exchanged, and the man threw himself into the middle, trying to break the combatants apart. A knife was drawn, and in the confusion, the innocent man was stabbed. He fell to the ground, and the other two men took flight.

Our inclinations might be to intervene in matters which we feel are wrong. In many cases we can be of some service, but often we should mind our own business. We can get ourselves into trouble which is unnecessary. It is as foolish to enter into a fight that is beyond our control as it is to try to take hold of a rabid dog. The only result will be that we will come out losers.

God gives each person a freedom to choose. Some people will abuse that freedom, and they will try to hurt others with it. They will have to answer for that before God. Each of us needs to ask what Christ would do in a similar situation. Christ knew when to leave well enough alone. He knew when to enter in, and when to stay back. God wants us to be useful, but He wants us to use our reason before we leap in where angels would fear to tread.

PRAYER: Lord, open my eyes. I so often act without reason and without foresight. Help me to know when to act and when to wait. Amen.

November 9

As a mad man who casteth firebrands, arrows, and death, so is the man that deceiveth his neighbor, and saith, "Am not I in sport" (26:18-19).

A man had the habit of making fun of people as a joke. He would often lapse into extremely poor taste, and he offended regularly. When people would react in anger he would accuse them of not having a sense of humor, and he would say, "Hey, I'm only kidding. You know how much I think of you." Then he would turn around and insult them all over again. He thought that he was being immensely humorous, and many people laughed at his jokes, just so long as they weren't the target of them.

There is no such thing as a harmless joke at the expense of another human being's feelings or dignity. Christ calls us to respect and love one another, and we have no right to do anything which might prove hurtful. Our words should build each other up, not provide a stumbling block. A lot of cruelty has been masked as jokes throughout the centuries, but one day God will judge what was funny, and what was evil. It is the duty of every person of God to weigh the impact of their words and to speak in ways which are a blessing rather than a curse. The Lord rejoices when our words are sweet and gentle, but His wrath is kindled by words which burn and cause anguish.

PRAYER: Lord, fill my mouth with the sweet sounds that are pleasing to you. In a world of such unkindness, let my speech reflect a love and caring that is foreign to most, and a haven of peace to all. Amen.

November 10

Where no wood is, there the fire goeth out: so where there is no talebearer, the strife ceaseth. As coals are to burning coals, and wood to fire; so is a contentious man to kindle strife (26:20-21).

The foreman was always finding fault with everything that was done. Nothing was ever good enough. Even when it was done exactly as he specified, it still wasn't correct. Everyone lived in fear that they would be his next victim. Some people dreaded coming into work for the fear of having to face him. That was why everyone breathed a sigh of relief when he went on a two-week vacation. From the first day the atmosphere changed in the office. People could breathe easily, and they got along much better. They stopped being defensive, and production increased greatly. When quality control came to find out why, they decided to replace the foreman, and the office became a joyful and peaceful place to work.

Some people live to stir up trouble. They cause so much pain and anxiety that they are despised. If we will be steadfast and endure the burden of such people, God above will see it and He will reward us. There is no place with God for a person who intentionally inflicts pain on other people. A fire cannot burn without fuel, and so it goes that anxiety cannot continue without a cause. God will be faithful to remove the source of our pain if we will but rely on Him.

PRAYER: My Lord, I hope that I have caused no one pain this day. If I have, I ask your forgiveness, and ask you to lead me to a way that I can make amends to the person I wronged. Let my witness be one of peace. Amen.

November 11

Burning lips and a wicked heart are like a potsherd covered with silver dross (26:23).

Every head turned toward the door when she walked in. She was breathtaking. Her hair was long and beautiful. Her face had fine, gentle features, and she was tall and slender. She moved with a quiet grace, and she knew all the right moves. Many people gravitated toward her, and she basked in the attention. One young man walked up to her and tried to engage her in a conversation. She took one look at him and began laughing.

"Go away, you worm. I don't want to even be seen talking to you!"

Throughout the evening, she repeatedly dealt with people with equal measures of contempt. Her gorgeous exterior merely covered an evil and corrupt interior, blinded with self-love and conceit.

We can take garbage, dress it up on a silver platter, and when we are finished, it is still garbage. What is on the outside matters very little. It is what is on the inside which is most important. God created each of us with a spirit which is in His image. Looks, dress, actions have little to do with who we are. It is what is in our hearts which matters most. Wickedness can be masked, but God will see right through the facade. The pure in heart and right-minded are a joy to God, and it doesn't matter one bit what those people look like on the outside.

PRAYER: Lord, cleanse me inside. Make me a new creation in your love and grace. Help me to put aside vanity over looks and appearances. Let my only concern be what is in my heart. Amen.

November 12

Whoso diggeth a pit shall fall therein: and he that rolleth a stone, it will return upon him. A lying tongue hateth those that are afflicted by it; and a flattering mouth worketh ruin (26:27-28).

She couldn't believe what was happening. She had accepted a date for Friday night from a man she was seeing off and on. Then, out of the blue, her boss had asked her out. She had dreamed of that happening ever since she got the job. She reluctantly called her date for the evening and told him that she had become very ill, and that she wouldn't be able to go out. Then she prepared herself for her evening with her boss. It was a wonderful evening, and she kept trying to tell herself that what she had done was perfectly fine. They were riding the elevator up to her floor, and she was anticipating a nice ending to the evening in her apartment. When the elevator doors opened, her sometimes-boyfriend was sitting across from it. He had come to spend the evening with her, because he felt sorry for her. Suddenly, the guilt of what she had done swept over her, and she began to cry.

Each time we tell a lie, we set a trap. Someone might find out. Most lies have the potential of hurting someone. We do not have the right to do anyone harm. God watches each of us to see whether we will commit ourselves to living lives of truth or not. When we choose correctly, He rejoices, and blesses us richly.

PRAYER: I want to be an honest person, showing my love and respect for other people by my honesty. Help me to destroy that part of me which is prone to lie and deceive. Give me a portion of your truth by which I might live. Amen.

November 13

Boast not thyself of tomorrow; for thou knowest not what a day may bring forth (27:1).

He thought of all the times he had promised his little boy that they would do something together soon. Play ball, sail boats, go to the zoo; it really didn't matter. He was always too busy, and so he said they would do it soon. He always figured they had a world of tomorrows, and he had really believed that they would do all the things his son had wanted to. It didn't seem possible. One day his boy was running and laughing, and the next day he was dead. Why hadn't he spent more time with his child? Why did he always say, "later," instead of "now"? The pain and guilt rested heavy on his heart, and he knew that he could never know the joy of sharing those times with his little son.

We live our lives as if we have all the time in the world. That is so foolish. The only thing we are sure of is that we have today, this minute. It is the wise man or woman who learns to live each day to the fullest. We must strive to be as good as we can be, and to give as much as we are able every single day, for we do not know which one might be our last. God richly blesses those people who will live fully and for the day. His pride is in His children who act wisely and don't waste any of the precious time He has given them.

PRAYER: Lord, help me to make the most of this day. Teach me to live a full life, and to do everything in my power to please you. Bless my life, Father, and make me a blessing in the lives of others. Amen.

November 14

Let another man praise thee, and not thine own mouth; a stranger, and not thine own lips (27:2).

The quarterback stood before the reporters, giving them his views of the upcoming game.

"I really don't think we have much to worry about. We have prepared for this game, we have a stronger defense, a stronger offense, and I am definitely a better quarterback than my opponent. My statistics speak for themselves. I've out-performed him in every category. He's good, but I'm better."

The interview ended, the game was played and it was an upset. The opposing quarterback threw rings around his adversary, and the words he had uttered hours before were spread far and wide through all the major news services.

When we compliment ourselves, we open ourselves to disaster. Pride comes before the fall, the saying goes, and it is true. We cannot fall if we never set ourselves up above everyone else. When we do something well, we should content ourselves with the appreciation of others, and not fall into the trap of conceit and arrogance. God loves humility, and His blessing is upon all who will think more highly of others than they think of themselves. Our praise should be for God and for others, but never for ourselves.

PRAYER: Lord, teach me humility and grace. I too often think that no one else can do things as well as I do. I get a wrong picture of my importance. Put my life into perspective, that I might live as I ought to. Amen.

November 15

A stone is heavy, and the sand weighty; but a fool's wrath is heavier than them both (27:3).

The old building had stood for over a century. It had weathered many storms, a dozen tornadoes, and a few minor earthquakes. Over ten thousand people had lived in its frame during its century of existence. It was a landmark, but it was still coming down. The trucks moved in, the wrecking ball leading the way. The huge crane pulled back, and then swung toward the structure, the ball connected a punched a huge hole in the side. A few more swings and the entire wall collapsed. Within hours, all that remained was a mountainous pile of rubble.

Words spoken in anger, without forethought, can have the same effect on people's lives. Cruel words spoken in rage can destroy a relationship, and their impact is more powerful than the weight of the wrecking ball. Wise people learn to control the passions which can maim and destroy. It is the fool who will speak without restraint and inflict the greatest pain. As Christians we must always watch the words of our mouths. We have promised God that we will be people of love, and words spoken in anger have no place in love. The words of our mouths spring forth from our hearts, reflecting what is really inside.

PRAYER: Search my heart to its very depth, Lord, and cleanse me of my iniquity. Help me to walk in a way that is good and helpful. Make my lips issue forth praise and peace instead of venom and fire. Amen.

November 16

Faithful are the wounds of a friend; but the kisses of an enemy are deceitful (27:6).

Jesus waited in the garden. His disciples had dozed off and He was alone to speak with God. He prayed hard and long, and when He finished He looked up to see the approaching torches of soldiers and magistrates. He awakened His disciples, and to their amazement, one of their own was leading the aggressors. Judas looked upon Christ, and he felt icy. He moved forward to embrace the Lord, then kissed Him on the cheek, as if to say goodbye, and that he was sorry. Jesus pulled back, and said through pain and anguish, "A kiss? You come and you betray me with a kiss?"

Have you ever thought how painful that action was to Christ? An act usually associated with love was used to signal destruction. Someone that Christ had trusted and befriended paid Him back by turning Him over to the authorities, and he did it with a kiss.

There are times when a friend will strike us in order to wake us up to danger, or to bring us back to reality. Those blows are a blessing. But when someone hurts us under the pretense of love, that is the worst kind of pain. God wants us to deal with each other honestly. We cannot have things both ways. If we are not for God, we are against Him, and we should never compound our crime with hypocrisy.

PRAYER: Each time I sin, Father, I betray you with a kiss. I claim to love you, but then I do the things which I know you hate. Please forgive me, Lord. Help me to be better, I pray. Amen.

November 17

Ointment and perfume rejoice the heart: so doth the sweetness of a man's friend by hearty counsel (27:9).

The day had been so hot and tiring. All she could think of was soaking in a nice tub full of bubbles. It was the least she deserved. She stepped into the warm, fragrant bath and immediately the tensions and heat of the day were banished. As she soaked, her muscles loosened and she relaxed. There was very little in life which was as nice as a good soak in a tub after a trying day. She felt like she could face anything the world would throw at her after her bath. It didn't take a whole lot, but she was refreshed and ready to meet life again.

A good conversation with a trusted friend can be every bit as refreshing as the aforementioned bath. There can be nothing quite so gratifying as spending time with a good friend, just talking things over. We need someone with whom we can share secrets and dreams. That is why prayer is so powerful. Any time, anywhere, we can have a talk with God which will strengthen and renew us. He can give us the strength to meet the world head-on, and He will never leave us. He so wants for us to come to Him to share our lives with Him. It pleases Him to know that we love Him enough to want to spend time with Him.

PRAYER: I come to you knowing that you will not judge, or condemn, or mock. Thank you for being so close whenever I need you. I could not want a better friend in my life. I love you, Lord. Amen.

November 18

He that blesseth his friend with a loud voice, rising early in the morning, it shall be counted a curse to him (27:14).

It was not always easy being a night owl. Staying up late was only a pleasure when she was allowed to sleep in late. Since they had moved to the new neighborhood she had met a few people, and they all arose around 6:00 a.m. That was fine if that's what they wanted to do. The problem was that they called her up after breakfast, which for them was 7:00. She knew that they were just trying to be friendly, but sometimes she wanted to scream at them. She had tried nicely to tell them that she like sleeping in, but they still called by 8:00. She didn't know how long she would be able to tolerate their friendliness until it drove her completely crazy!

Consideration is an important Christian quality. If we love and respect other people, then we will want to know what is pleasing to them, and we will try to accommodate them. If we force ourselves on others, then we are being selfish. God doesn't want anyone to force their will on anyone else. Instead, He wants us to do for others everything in our power to make them comfortable and happy. To serve means to do what other people need and want. We do not get to set the rules, but we follow the rules of love set down by God.

PRAYER: Lord, I sometimes think I know what is desired of me, but I don't always ask. Help me to be sensitive to the needs of others, that I might serve them and bring them joy and comfort. Amen.

November 19

As in water face answereth to face, so the heart of man to man (27:19).

It was nice to get away from the city to spend a day at the lake. The sky was crystal clear, and the bright sunshine felt wonderful. The trees were in full color, as the cool days came on. They walked along the lake, which was smooth as glass. The view across the lake was mirrored perfectly on its surface. The reflection caused the beauty of the view to be doubled. The image on the lake was just slightly out of focus, and in places it rippled. The colors weren't quite as brilliant, but it was still exhilarating.

The image reflected back from water is slightly imperfect and it is not as clear as the object it reflects. The same can be said of one's soul. It is merely a reflection of the soul of God in which it was created. As we grow closer to God, the image comes into sharper focus and it more closely resembles the soul of our Creator. The goal of Christians should be to become as much like God as is possible. It isn't complex, though that doesn't make it easy. All we have to do is let God finish the work He has begun in us. If we turn our lives over to God, then He will make us over in His image, and He will fill in the details which are lacking. He wants nothing more than for our souls to merge with His, so that both object and reflection are one.

PRAYER: Lord, I want to be one with you in soul, mind and being. Help me to be the creation you want. I am alive to serve and to bless. Work through me that others may know your great love and power. Amen.

November 20

Be thou diligent to know the state of thy flocks, and look well to thy herds (27:23).

A man was entrusted with a fine herd of cattle, and he was hired to transport them across the plains. Each morning he gathered the riders together and they began the long day's ride. Each night they settled in and left no one to guard the herd. By the time they arrived at their destination they found that they were missing almost a hundred head. The owner of the herd refused to pay the man, because he had been so careless in his duty.

When we take on a responsibility, we are obligated to do the very best we can. We have no right to take liberties with possessions that do not belong to us. When someone is counting on us, we owe it to that person to give everything we can to serve them. God wants us to serve others with as much devotion as we serve Him. When we give anything less than our best, we cheat ourselves, we cheat the people we serve, and most importantly, we cheat God. If we have an obligation, we must fulfill it or else we become liars and sluggards. God blesses those who will always give everything they have to the service of others. He is anxious to bless His children, and He gives great reward to those who will be obedient.

PRAYER: Lord, teach me how you want me to live. Whenever I can, help me to serve others. Let me be steadfast and trustworthy, and let my integrity be a sign that you have made me new, in your image. Amen.

November 21

The wicked flee when no man pursueth: but the righteous are bold as a lion (28:1).

Ever since he had taken the money he had been unable to sleep. Every noise made him jump. He was positive the police would show up at his door. So far no one had said anything about the shortage at work, but he suspected that they were toying with him. He thought maybe they had found out somehow. Coming home the night before he was pretty sure that someone was following him. He wished that he had never taken anything. Everyone was just waiting for him to make a mistake. Why hadn't anyone come? He lay awake, completely silent, listening to hear the footsteps when they would finally come up the stairs.

When we do something wrong, our consciences nag at us mercilessly. We await our punishment in anguish and fear. If we will live upright and faithful lives, we will have nothing to dread. The wise man is careful to do what is right, then he never has to worry. The wicked are constantly on the alert, for they fear being caught. The righteous can stand firm in their actions for they have nothing to answer for. They are as bold as lions, but the evildoer is timid and scared, and has to hide in fear.

PRAYER: Sin destroys peace of mind, security and confidence. Lead me in paths of righteousness, that I might never have to fear punishment. Make me pure in heart and mind, and keep me from going where I should not go. Amen.

November 22

A poor man that oppresseth the poor is like a sweeping rain which leaveth no food (28:3).

The crops were almost in ruin. If rains didn't come soon, the people in the village would face another year of starvation. The forecasts had been dismal for so long, that the people could hardly believe it when rain was predicted. They waited in excited anticipation. The clouds began to form, the wind to blow, and the blessed moisture began to drop. But the storms kept building, and the winds increased. The water pounded the ground, and it beat upon the crops. The food supply which had so desperately needed water was completely wiped out by storms and flooding when the rains finally came. It had been like a cruel joke played upon the people.

We see the rich of this world oppressing the poor, and it seems almost natural, but when the poor do things to hurt each other it is amazing. It is as if they forget their poverty themselves and inflict worse on their neighbors. It is senseless and cruel, and it strikes with the force of a terrible storm. It is hard to defend or deal with, because it is so unexpected. We feel that the people most like us will relate to our plight and be sympathetic. Evil strikes in every place, though, and it is by God's grace that those who are faithful will at last be saved.

PRAYER: I do things which are cruel to the people I should be most kind to. Forgive me when I do such foolish and hateful things. Father, help me to be thankful for your grace and love. Let my thanks be shown through my love for others. Amen.

November 23

Evil men understand not judgment: but they that seek the Lord understand all things (28:5).

They waited until the family had gone to bed and all the lights were out. Quietly, they tip-toed to the door and listened. Once assured that everyone was asleep, they quickly dressed and slipped out the back door. They walked to the corner, and caught a bus into town. Both girls had plotted this trip for a long time. They were going to see what the nightlife was really like. They stayed out all night, going from place to place and experiencing the town at night. They returned home, exhausted and weary, to find that their parents were waiting for them. When they found out what had happened, they grounded both girls and took away all their privileges. Neither girl felt their punishment fair, nor could they see what they had done that was so terrible. Both chose to ignore the dangers they could have met and neither admitted the foolishness of what they did.

Wrongdoers are never willing to admit that what they do is really wrong. They come up with some excuse that they feel makes everything okay. When they are caught in their folly, they resent being punished, and they cannot understand why they are being persecuted. Wise persons realize the dangers and problems, and avoid them. When they fall into temptation, they readily understand why they have been punished.

PRAYER: Lord, I know that you never punish without cause. If I need to be taught my errors, then I ask you do it as gently as possible, but always in the best way so that I can learn how to be better. Amen.

November 24

Better is the poor that walketh in his uprightness, than he that is perverse in his ways, though he be rich (28:6).

It was the offer of a lifetime. He had the chance to invest in a project which was sure to make money. His brother brought the proposal to him to let him in on it. He was tempted, but there was a drawback. The project entailed driving some people from their homes in order to get some building done. There were some shady dealings going on, and the people were being robbed by the company doing the building. None of the homeowners was even remotely aware of the value of their property. He thought long and hard about the offer, but he eventually decided against it. Anything which made him money at other people's expense wasn't worth the guilt. Better to stay poor and be able to look yourself in the eye in the mirror, than to be rich, and hate yourself for it.

Some things just aren't worth the compromise they entail. If we have to give up too much, then we find it harder and harder to live with ourselves. The poor person who feels good about himself is far richer than a wealthy person who lives with shame and guilt. God will bless the person who holds fast to values by granting peace and comfort.

PRAYER: Lord, I feel good that I have a chance to serve you. Help me never to compromise my values and beliefs. Let all of my actions reflect the love and devotion that I feel toward you. Amen.

November 25

He that turneth away his ear from hearing the law, even his prayer shall be abomination (28:9).

He was always late to every meeting. His superiors tried to get him to play by the rules, but he resisted. His work was usually good, so they let him go. Lately, though, they had entrusted him with some vital work, and he showed no sign of trying to get it in on time. He worked at his own pace, he skipped the progress meetings, and he refused to talk about it to anyone. When he finally produced the package to his firm, it was a week late, and they were no longer interested. He was let go without so much as an explanation.

When we turn away from the instruction of our superiors, then we must be willing to suffer their wrath. We are answerable to God in this life, and if we choose to ignore Him, we cannot be surprised when He chooses to ignore us. We cannot live any old way we want to, and use God only when we want something from Him. Our lives must be devoted to Him, and we are called to walk in all His ways. We must heed His instruction and guidance, and when we do that He will be faithful to hear and answer our prayers. He is so happy when His children listen for His voice, and He will listen to us when we call out to Him.

PRAYER: I am a proud person, Lord. I think that I know what is best, and I sometimes ignore the suggestions of others. Teach me to listen, to trust, and to obey. Hear this prayer, this day, O Lord. Amen.

November 26

The rich man is wise in his own conceit; but the poor that hath understanding searcheth him out (28:11).

He had built for himself an empire. He was a powerful man. He controlled the lives of thousands of people. He manipulated millions of dollars, and literally had the power of life and death in his hands due to foreign investments. His home was a mansion, and he hadn't driven for himself since he got a chauffeur ten years earlier. He had everything, and he prided himself on the brains he had used to get where he was.

We sometimes confuse cunning and craftiness with wisdom. We think that the ability to out-think and out-maneuver other people makes us more intelligent. Intelligence has nothing to do with it. A truly intelligent person would know that you don't treat other people like pawns in a game. Wisdom would tell a person that money was not the path to happiness. Wisdom would tell even the richest and most powerful man that he did not get all his blessing on his own. God created this world, and everything in it belongs to Him. We possess it for a short time, but the Lord owns it forever. God gives us material wealth so that we can use it for the good of others. Abundance is for sharing, not for hoarding. The one who prides himself on the wisdom that brought him wealth has no real idea of what wisdom is.

PRAYER: Almighty God, you are the author of all creation and the owner of all that is. Help me to remember that without you, I would have nothing. All good things come from you, and I am thankful. Amen.

November 27

He that covereth his sins shall not prosper: but whoso confesseth and forsaketh them shall have mercy (28:13).

The little boy took his crayons and colored in one of his mother's favorite books. After he was finished he realized how angry she would be, so he ripped out the page and hid it under the sofa. In the days that followed he felt very bad about what he had done. Finally, in tears, he went to his mother with the mutilated page. His mother took him up into her arms and confided, "I knew what you had done, but I left everything where it was because I knew that you would want to tell me eventually. I am glad that you were honest, and I want you to know that I love you just as much now as I ever have."

It is hard to tell someone when we have done something we know we should not have done. We're afraid that the victim might not forgive or love us. It is good to know that God will forgive us anything if we will only come before Him to honestly repent. He loves us so much that we cannot turn His love away. If we try to hide our sins from God, He will know it and will punish us for our deception, but when we confess, we please Him so much that He will bless us with peace and joy.

PRAYER: I am ashamed of myself, Lord, and I have difficulty coming to you. I am unworthy of your love, and I am embarrassed by my weakness. Let me know that I can come to you at any time with anything. Thank you for your acceptance and your grace. Amen.

November 28

As a roaring lion, and a raging bear; so is a wicked ruler over the poor people. The prince that wanteth understanding is also a great oppressor: but he that hateth covetousness shall prolong his days (28:15-16).

The jungle was silent. The animals sensed the presence of their Lord. A thundering roar cut loose and sent the animals scurrying for cover. No animal dared confront the lion who ruled over the jungle land. His presence commanded respect and worship. However, it was a respect built on fear, not on love. As long as the beast had ruled, he had never known love. His subjects bowed to him, and they ran in fear, but he had never known what it meant to be well thought of.

Our Lord is a Lord of both power and love. It is well to fear the Lord, for He alone holds the power of true life and death. But we cannot have a relationship with anyone based on fear. There must be love, and our God makes it easy to love Him. He has given us a wonderful gift by giving us life, and He has proven His love for us by sending His only Son our Lord, Jesus Christ, to take the punishment for our sins so that we might one day be reunited with Him. Only a loving God gives so much to His children. We can rejoice that we do not serve a tyrant or a hateful master, but we serve the source of all that is good and right. His goodness shall endure forever, and we will be a part of it.

PRAYER: Thank you for not controlling me or forcing me to love you. I could not worship a God who made His children fear Him. Please help me to be the person you created me to be, so that I might return the love to you which you have given to me. Amen.

November 29

He that tilleth his land shall have plenty of bread: but he that followeth after vain persons shall have poverty enough (28:19).

She had made a difficult choice and she had regretted it almost every day since she had made it. All her adult life she had dated one man. He was hardworking, but he didn't have any aspirations. He was content just to stay where he was and do what he was doing. He hadn't seen any reason to improve himself because he was perfectly happy with himself just the way he was. Then David had come along. He was handsome, a real smooth talker, and he dreamed big. He told her that he would give her everything and anything that she desired. She had believed him, but after they were married she found out that he had been all talk, no action. His dreams were merely idle wishes, but he had no commitment, and no desire to hold down a job. She often wished she had never left the man who had been good to her for so long.

We are in danger, sometimes, of trading what is lasting and secure for what seems better. It is not. Good things come to those who work hard and are devoted to doing what is right. God calls us to be steadfast and righteous. Only by following in this way can we hope to find a life which is fulfilling and joyful.

PRAYER: I am blinded by many bright dreams which seem so tempting, but there the danger lies. In my blindness I lose sight of what is good and true. Shield my sight from the false attraction of earthly treasure. Keep my eyes focused on the treasure which never fails. Amen.

November 30

He that rebuketh a man, afterward shall find more favor than he that flattereth with the tongue (28:23).

A gifted tennis player rose to the top of her team with ease. She was hailed as a potential star on the pro circuit. All of the publicity went to her head, and she began to believe all the hype. She got to the point where she thought she was too good to associate with her teammates. She basked in the glory of her success, and grew conceited. As she prepared for semi-finals, she broke curfew and the coach sat her down and refused to let her play. She raged and fumed at the treatment, but the coach said, "I don't care who you think you are. You play for my team, and so you follow my rules. I don't treat you any differently than any other of the girls. You need to learn real fast that being good at a sport doesn't make you a better person than everybody else. The quicker you learn that the better."

The girl never forgot the experience, and the words of her coach stuck with her, and saved her from a lot of pain and frustration in the future.

True wisdom is a friend throughout our lives. The truth is often not pleasant to hear, but if we will accept it, it will help us through many situations. The flatterer gives nothing of lasting value. It is the person who is willing to offer rebukes as well as praise who will give the greatest gift.

PRAYER: The truth is hard to hear many times, but that doesn't mean I don't need it. Open my heart to the truth, and let me always be accepting of your guidance. I count on you to help me through the tough times, and to share in my good times. Amen.

December 1

Whoso robbeth his father or his mother, and saith, It is no transgression; the same is the companion of a destroyer (28:24).

Her boyfriend really needed money badly. She had asked her parents for it, but they had told her that they wouldn't give it to her. She was getting desperate, but then she remembered some silver her mother had stored in the attic. Her mother had said that one day it would be hers anyway, so she was just taking it a bit early. She removed the silver from its resting place and took it to a pawn shop to sell. The next time a financial emergency arose, she ransacked the attic for more valuables to sell. It became a regular practice, and she told herself that she was entitled to the things since it was her house, after all. When her parents found out they went into a rage. The girl could not understand their anger, and she resented their concern in the situation.

When what we want becomes more important than anything else, we are blind to what we do to others. We will do anything to satisfy ourselves, and that is all that counts. That is selfishness; the seed bed of all sin. Christ was sent into this world to lead us away from selfishness. God gave the greatest gift of all so that we might know that truth comes to us not through taking, but only through giving, and giving all that we have and are.

PRAYER: Giver of all that is good, all that is right; create in me a spirit of love and care. Let me see when I am doing what is wrong, and teach me what I can do that is right. Thank you for teaching me what giving is all about. Amen.

December 2

He that trusteth in his own heart is a fool: but whoso walketh wisely, he shall be delivered (28:26).

It had been years since he had gone ice skating. As he looked out across the frozen pond, he was overwhelmed by a wave of nostalgia. He tested the ice with a boot, then took a few more steps onto the pond. He remembered the warnings of his mother when he was young. She had always told his younger brother and him to be careful and to test the ice before they went out on it. He had always remembered the rule. Too bad his brother hadn't. His brother never listened to mom and dad. He acted like he knew what was best. One time they had gone out to skate, and his brother had just waltzed out onto the ice. It was too thin, and before anything could be done, his little brother had drowned.

When we think that we always know best, we open ourselves to disaster. Wisdom comes from learning to listen to the counsel of others. When we are mature, we realize that others offer warnings and advice to protect us, not to control us. The wise listen to friends and elders, and are made stronger. The foolish decide that their wisdom is all they need, and so wander alone down the road to destruction.

PRAYER: Help me not to trust so much in my own wisdom, heavenly Father. Let me see that there are many things I have yet to learn. Give me patience and perseverence that I might come to know that which will save me from my own foolishness. Amen.

December 3

He that giveth unto the poor shall not lack: but he that hideth his eyes shall have many a curse (28:27).

There was a poor family who decided it was beyond their means to celebrate Christmas. They told their children not to expect presents, they planned a simple meal for Christmas day, they decided not to decorate, and they told the children the less said about Christmas the better. Some friends heard of the situation, and they pooled resources to give the family a Christmas they would never forget. On a day when the family went out, all the neighbors pitched in and decorated the house, putting up a tree, and surrounding it with presents. The refrigerator was stocked with wonderful treats and a feast fit for royalty. No indication was left of where the things had come from. When the family returned home they understood what Christmas was all about, and they truly did have a Christmas that none of them would ever forget.

It is important that we look for ways to give to those people who are in need. When we give unselfishly and totally, we begin to understand what God wants of us. God gave us the life of His Child Jesus, and it is when we give of ourselves to others that we please God the most. We can never pay God back for His great gift, but we should try whenever possible.

PRAYER: Show me ways that I can do good things for other people who are not as fortunate as I am. If nothing else, I can pray for them and give them my care and love. Help me to give what I can whenever I can. Amen.

December 4

When the righteous are in authority, the people rejoice: but when the wicked beareth rule, the people mourn (29:2).

In a small New England town, a bank and a library prepared for the holidays. The week before Christmas, the library announced that there would be a party to celebrate a good year, and a Merry Christmas. The bank made no such announcement. The president felt that a Christmas party was beneath the dignity of a bank. He said that business would be carried on as usual, and that was that. The people in the library felt that Christmas had come early. They were appreciative of the consideration, and the atmosphere was happy and festive. At the bank, the people felt a sadness. The Christmas spirit had been stifled, and the atmosphere was heavy and gray.

It takes very little to make people happy. A little giving goes a long way. When we deny people even the smallest kindnesses, they lose spirit, and there is no joy. People rejoice under kind leadership, but harsh and unthinking leadership gives rise only to mourning. God loves a cheerful giver, and He doubly loves givers of joy. If we will remember the great love that God has shown us, it will be easy to show a little of that love to the people we deal with day in and day out.

PRAYER: Let me sow seeds of kindness, Lord, that people might know of my great love for you. You have given so much, now help me to give a little. Being kind is not hard, and it costs so little. Help me to give it freely and abundantly. Amen.

December 5

The righteous considereth the cause of the poor: but the wicked regardeth not to know it (29:7).

Growing up black in a large city wasn't easy. If you were black you didn't get the breaks. If you were born poor there was a good chance you would die poor. What made it even worse was that it was just a few blocks to a rich white neighborhood. The children would go and stare through the fences at the white homes. It was cruel, because they were just seeing all the things that they could never have. Most of the black families weren't even asking to be rich, they just wanted a little bit more than they had. They watched the white people go about their business and sometimes they felt like they weren't even there. Many of the white people had learned to look through the poor blacks like they were non-existent.

In America there is a hidden people. They are stuck away out of sight so that others don't have to deal with them. They are the poor. They make the well-to-do feel guilty, and so they learn to ignore them. If we ever ignore one of God's children, we may expect that He will ignore us. God wants us to be aware that things are not equal and fair. The test of a true Christian is whether or not one is willing to sacrifice of oneself in order to change the way the world is. If we will give of ourselves, God will bless us and keep us close to Him.

PRAYER: Lord, I don't ever want to shut my eyes to any of your children who are in need. If I have anything to give, I will try to give it. I know that when I give to the least of your children, in reality, I am giving to you. Amen.

December 6

The bloodthirsty hate the upright: but the just seek his soul (29:10).

The headlines screamed of the atrocity. A young woman had been killed while she was home for the holidays. She had been assaulted and beaten and then killed. It was shocking any time it happened, but there was something which made it worse at holidays. The woman's family would remember this every year when the season rolled around, and it would place a cloud over the celebrations.

The killer was caught just before Christmas, and the parents of the girl wanted to see him. They went into a room where a guard brought in the accused. For a moment they sat looking at each other, then the father said, "I don't know why you killed our baby, and I don't really care. I want to hate you, but I can't. God gave His Son so that I might have life, and now I've given my daughter. I hope that her life makes a difference. We came to tell you that we're praying for you, and we hope you really repent of what you have done. We won't stop praying until you're dead or saved." With that, the couple left.

How can we learn to love those who try to hurt us? Christ did it through the grace of God. God will supply us with the same power if only we will seek Him out.

PRAYER: Your gift to me in the life of your Son is greater than I can comprehend. I want to know that love in my life. Help me to pray for the evil people in this world, that they might know the truth and love that you freely give. Amen.

December 7

If a ruler harken to lies, all his servants are wicked (29:12).

The cold weather always meant more work for the police. Accidents increased and so did shoplifting and domestic squabbles. The calls came in and they had to check each one out. For that reason, the Christmas season always brought the most crank calls. Kids got out of school and didn't have anything better to do, so they would report fights, fires, accidents, and crimes that really didn't exist. Once one kid found out he could get away with it, all the kids had to try it. At a time of year when it would have been nice to relax, everyone on the force had to work double time.

Sometimes lying can be fun. Just like every sin, there is something attractive about it. Lies can be masked as practical jokes, and they then seem harmless, but someone pays the price when a lie is told. It may be done in fun, but it hurts someone. God wants us to neither accept lies nor lie to other people. He wants His children to embrace what is true, and to live accordingly. When we stick to the truth, we show that we respect it. We believe that truth is good and that we should follow the truth of God in our lives. God is truth, and in Him there are no lies at all.

PRAYER: Father, I do not want to lose the truth. I want my life to be filled with truth. I want to share your truth with everyone I meet so that they can know how wonderful you are. Thank you for blessing my life so richly. Amen.

December 8

The poor and the deceitful man meet together: the Lord lighteneth both their eyes (29:13).

He hated having to walk to work. His office was in the center of a poor part of town. The beggars sat along both sides of the street, and he couldn't stand to smell their smell, to see their faces, or hear their pitiful begging. He hurried through the streets, and the question ran through his mind why God made him suffer like this? He wished the poor would go off and find some other street to haunt. It bothered him that he even had to share the sidewalk with some of these characters.

As he approached his office, he saw, from the corner of his eye, yet another group of poor people clustered outside a church. He walked past them, feeling outraged that they even littered the lawn of the church. He decided enough was enough. He turned to speak his piece to the group, but what he saw made him stop. His heart sank and he felt a pang of guilt and shame in his stomach. The group on the lawn was the nativity scene. The poor were Mary, Joseph and the Babe, and suddenly the evil of his thoughts was made clear to him.

God has made us all, and He has made us equal. If we reject poor people because they make us feel guilty or uncomfortable, then we must remember that we would reject Christ Himself, who never made a claim to prominence or wealth.

PRAYER: Let me accept all people just as they are. Open my eyes so that I can see the Christ which exists in all of your children. I love you, Lord; I want that love to grow as large and strong as is possible. Amen.

December 9

When the wicked are multiplied transgression increaseth: but the righteous shall see their fall (29:16).

The mall was extremely crowded. In the course of a few hours, they saw a purse snatcher, a car thief, a fight, a drug sale and at least ten cases of shoplifting. It was enough to make you lose faith. Christmas used to be such a good time, but it seemed like all of the bad element came out to spoil it. It felt like the good, decent people were far outnumbered by the thugs, junkies, thieves, and muggers. Evil was all around. You couldn't escape it, even at Christmas. It caused the couple to go into a deep depression throughout the season. Then, one afternoon, they looked out their window to see a smal girl walking hand in hand with an older woman. The child was leading the woman, for she was blind. The pair had beautiful smiles on their faces, and there was an innocence and joy which was startling. Just watching the two; young with old, made the couple know that there was still good in the world. As long as there was some good, there was also some hope. The gift of Christ in our lives assures us that evil does not stand a chance. It may multiply over time, but innocent joy is more powerful than all the evil in the world. As long as we know that, everything will be just fine.

PRAYER: There is good in your world, Lord, if I can only have the eyes to see it. Bless my sight so that I might see the good wherever it exists. I grow weary of the evil. Let me know that in the end, evil will be no more, and good will reign eternally. Amen.

December 10

Seest thou a man that is hasty in his words? There is more hope of a fool than of him (29:20).

The rush was on. The woman stood bewildered in the department store. Her husband had asked especially for a certain razor, and she was determined that she would get it for him. She finally got a sales clerk to wait on her, and she told him what she wanted. He looked at the counter, and then went into a fast sales pitch for a razor that was on sale. Five times she repeated what she wanted, and five times he tried to sell her something else. In frustration she walked a way to try another store.

Sometimes it feels like no one listens to us. We try to communicate what we mean, but it never gets through. It is frustrating when we deal with people who will not listen to what we say, and they themselves never quiet down. There is much to be said for the person who learns to listen instead of talk. When we listen, we learn. When we talk, we block learning. A fool loves to hear the sound of his own voice, but the wise person rejoices in what can be heard. We need to learn to listen, so that we can honestly help the people who come to us for our aid. If we talk, we will close people out and they will never come back. We deal foolishly, and we present an example that we cannot be proud of. God wants us to deal with people in love, and most people need to feel like they are being heard.

PRAYER: I know that you listen to me, Lord. Teach me to listen that I might be a blessing to those whom I serve. I want to learn all I can, and it is in silence that understanding comes. Amen.

December 11

Whoso is partner with a thief hateth his own soul: he heareth cursing, and betrayeth it not (29:24).

The two girls went into the record store to browse. The store was packed with the Christmas rush, and one of the girls picked up a tape, and stuffed it into her friend's bag. The friend began to protest, but the girl ushered her quickly out of the store. The two girls had an argument and parted company mad at one another. For the next few days, the innocent girl spent her time feeling guilty and evil for what she had been a part of. She kept telling herself that it wasn't really her fault, but she felt badly anyway.

Many times we feel guilty about things which are not our fault. We know other people who make us feel guilty. Some of these people call us friends, but they don't really treat us like they mean it. They use us and take advantage of us, and we all too often let them get away with it. God doesn't want us taken advantage of and He would prefer that we not associate with people who do it. When we spend time with them we stand the danger of following their example. God is a friend who never takes advantage, and is always there for us when we need Him. He doesn't use us or manipulate us, He only loves us and wants our very best. If we will trust Him, He will bless our lives and let us know that we are loved.

PRAYER: I need to be loved, Father, and I do not need to be taken advantage of. I need to be able to trust my friends, and know what they think and feel. Lead me to people who feel and believe as I do, that we may be a strength and support to one another. Amen.

December 12

Every word of God is pure: he is a shield unto them that put their trust in him. Add thou not unto his words, lest he reprove thee, and thou be found a liar (30:5-6).

The television was packed with commercials which insulted the senses and the intelligence. Christmas decorations had been up since before Halloween. The radios blasted rock Christmas carols, and every time you turned around someone had their hand out or in your pocket. If a person wasn't careful, they might just forget what Christmas was all about. Thank goodness for the church. That was the one place she could go where the world couldn't cheapen Christmas. God knew that she needed a port in the storm. She needed a place where the truth of Christmas could still shine forth, and she didn't have to worry about any intrusions.

The house of God can indeed be a haven of safety from the whirl of the world. God knows that we need a place where we can feel safe and secure. We are shielded in our faith in God, and once shielded, nothing in this world can penetrate. God loves us so much, and He protects us when we need it most. He is faithful to those who come to Him seeking rest. He cradles us in His loving arms and shuts out the assaults of the world. In Him we can know peace and tranquility beyond our wildest dreams.

PRAYER: Most holy God, be a refuge in time of trial and a constant support as I deal with the pressures of this world. I feel lost and unprotected often, and I need you to shield and strengthen my life. Amen.

December 13

Remove far from me vanity and lies; give me neither poverty nor riches; feed me with food convenient for me (30:8).

The line for the soup kitchen was blocks long. The people had come from all over the city to share in a hot meal. So many different kinds of people came, but most all of them were appreciative. It was nice to be able to do something for people who were in such desperate need. One woman came up and told the workers, "Last year I wasn't happy at Christmas, and I didn't thank God for a thing. This year I've got something to thank Him for. I thank Him for you, and for the good meals you make for me. I don't need much. I just need a little. You give me more than I need, and thanks to you I can give thanks to God."

Often we feel like if we can't give a lot we might as well not give anything. That's sad, because it is the little things which often mean the most. We have within our power the ability to give a blessing to someone this very day. We need to look for ways to show our love to everyone around us. If we will do that we will make God happy, we will make others happy, and we will come to know peace and joy which defies description. There is no greater feeling in all the world than to touch the life of someone who is in real need.

PRAYER: If I do anything this day, O Lord, let it be to touch a life in such a way as to make you known to them. Help me to see the multitude of ways that I can serve others. Bless me, I pray. Amen.

December 14

Accuse not a servant unto his master, lest he curse thee, and thou be found guilty (30:10).

"Timmy was sneaking through the closets looking for presents!"

Timmy's little sister stood with her hands on her hips as she ratted to mom and dad.

"How do you know?" asked their father.

"I saw him do it," she replied.

"And just what were you doing in our room?" he further asked.

A frightened look crossed the little girl's face, as she realized that by accusing her brother she had also accused herself.

When we try to get someone else in trouble, it is rarely out of a sense of honor or duty. More often it is a case where we cannot mind our own business. Jesus Christ told His followers to be unconcerned with the actions of others until they made sure that all of their own actions were upright and holy. His point is this: If we spend our time minding our own business, there won't be any time left over for us to stick our noses in where they don't belong. God wants to see each of us grow, but we need to be responsible for our own lives, not the lives of other people.

PRAYER: Help me to examine my life to see what my strengths and weaknesses are. I want to develop my strengths, to correct my faults, and to grow in every way possible. Amen.

December 15

There is a generation that curseth their father, and doth not bless their mother. There is a generation that are pure in their own eyes, and yet is not washed from their filthiness. There is a generation, O how lofty are their eyes! And their eyelids are lifted up. There is a generation, whose teeth are as swords, and their jaw teeth as knives, to devour the poor from off the earth, and the needy from among them (30:11-14).

His parents were such an embarrassment to him. They were old world Italians, and they just didn't fit in with his image. He had worked all his life to beat the stereotypes, and he'd done his best to deny his heritage. He lived in fear that his parents would show up at the wrong time and spoil everything. He was rich and popular, and he was ashamed of being associated with his garlic-eating parents.

There is nothing more sad than a person who rejects who he is and where he comes from. When we get so proud that we deny our families, then we have very little character or compassion. We should be proud of where we come from. Whether we are Italian, American, Russian, Black, White, Christian, Jew, or any of a thousand other categories, we come from a single source, and that is God in heaven. We should be proud of that heritage. If we are proud of our heavenly Father, He will be proud of us, and we will know a happiness that will never, ever end. We are made holy through the love of God.

PRAYER: I am proud of you, Lord. How could I be otherwise? Without you nothing which now is could ever be. You have created everything, and you have made me special and unique. I am your child, and I will love you forever. Amen.

December 16

The horseleech hath two daughters, crying, "Give, Give." There are three things that are never satisfied, yea, four things say not, It is enough: the grave; and the barren womb; the earth that is not filled with water; and the fire that saith not, It is enough (30:15-16).

The store was open late on Christmas Eve. All of the clerks had been told that they had to work regular hours if they wanted to have a job after the holidays. The owner had come to them and said that they could make a killing if they would stay open late. Someone asked the owner if he didn't think he would make enough money without the few extra hours. His reply?

"There is no such thing as enough money. I will do everything I can to get every penny out of the purses and wallets of the people in this town. If I have to grab them off the street I will do it. We stay open, and we will do our very best. Am I understood?"

The man was understood probably better than he wanted to be. God knew the man immediately, and his name is "Greed." There are very few things as unlovely as a glutton, someone who takes more and more and more and gives nothing back. Greed is a form of selfishness which believes that we deserve whatever we can get, therefore we should get as much as possible. God blesses those who give, not who take. The greedy have already received their reward; it is the poor and persecuted who will have their reward come to them in heaven.

PRAYER: I wish to pursue you with everything I am. Take my life and shape it into something good. I want to make you pleased with me, Father. Lead me to do what you would have me do. Amen.

December 17

There be three things which be too wonderful for me, yea, four which I know not: the way of an eagle in the air; the way of a serpent upon a rock; the way of a ship in the midst of the sea; and the way of a man with a maid (30:18-19).

The sky was lit up by a million pinpoints of light. The wonder of it all was too much. It was hard to imagine that once a star shone brighter than all the rest which led people to a stable in Bethlehem. There a Babe was born who changed history. Standing outside looking up at all the stars made you know that there was indeed a God, and that He was good. The world was full of wonders which attested to His greatness. All the different creatures of the sea, the beauty of a ship on the ocean, the deep wonder of love. All of these things seemed magical, and indeed they were. They were full of a magic which was God. His handiworks were testimony of His beauty and might.

And yet, more wonderful still was the knowledge that amidst all of this beauty and power, God had really one desire, and that was to love and be loved by me. How could that be? He had so much. He is so much. At times I feel very insignificant and small, but then I think of God's great love, and I realize that I am somebody special, for I am the Lord's.

PRAYER: How can I thank you for what you have done for me? How can I thank you for all I have been given? How can I ever hope to be worthy of your love? All I can do is praise You and love and give You my life. Amen.

December 18

For three things the earth is disquieted, and for four which it cannot bear: for a servant when he reigneth; and a fool when he is filled with meat; for an odious woman when she is married; and a handmaid that is heir to her mistress (30:21-23).

It was hard to watch. The woman had never worked a day in her life. She had messed around all through college, not learning much of anything. She had wandered around the country and had never contributed much anywhere she went. She finally came home to where her father lived, and he supported her. Now, he was dead and she was rich, and she lorded it over everyone. She acted like this was the life she was entitled to. For people who had to slave for everything they got, it just didn't sit right.

It looks at times like evil will triumph over good, and that injustice is the rule rather than justice. We live our lives the best way we know how, and it is a struggle. Others do nothing good, living lives of selfishness and sin, and they seem to have it all. The problem is that we see with short sight. It appears that they prosper for a good long time, and in the course of a lifetime, that is true, but when we think in terms of eternity, the evil only prosper for a short while, and we have the assurance of a life everlasting which will be full of blessings. All our trials will end, and we will find reward beyond our wildest imaginations.

PRAYER: Help me not to be jealous of the prosperity of the evil. Let me remember that their success is short-lived in the course of time. They will flower, then fade away, while I will blossom eternally with the power and glory of your love. Amen.

December 19

There be four things which are little upon the earth, but they are exceeding wise: the ants are a people not strong, yet they prepare their meat in the summer; the conies are but a feeble folk, yet make they their houses in the rocks; the locusts have no king, yet go they forth all of them by bands; the spider taketh hold with her hands, and is in kings' palaces (30:24-28).

The palace was kept immaculate. The servants worked night and day to keep it clean. And even with all their efforts, still a small spider wove a fine web in the corner of the king's chambers. Each day the servants would come in and sweep it away, and within just a few hours it was rebuilt anew. The lowest of creatures dwelt all of her days with royalty, surrounded by the finest fare, and on occasion, she would travel into the king's bedclothes, and while he slept she would make a meal of the royal flesh, and in the morning, she would be satisfied, but her bites would cause the king much anguish. So small a creature has power to influence the lives of the people she comes in contact with. How amazing she is.

Yet, we too, in our seeming insignificance, have great power to affect the lives of the people we meet. We can influence by good or by evil, but we can do it with a slight amount of effort. God wants us to strive always to help others in every way we can. The smallest of insects and bugs can do what seems impossible. We should at least try to do as much.

PRAYER: I do not want to be stopped by limitations I put on myself. Help me to realize that with you all things are possible. Your power exceeds any of my doubts. Make me aware of your presence with me, that I might do all things. Amen.

December 20

There be three things which go well, yea, four are comely in going: a lion, which is strongest among beasts, and turneth not away for any; a greyhound; a he goat also; and a king, against whom there is no rising up (30:29-31).

She felt safe when she was with her father. She remembered the time that the wolves came around. He had taken his gun out and had shot them all. Everyone else in the town had been afraid, but not her father. He stood up for everything that was right and good, and if there was something which had to be done, he did it. That was just the kind of person he was. Whenever she came home, the same old feelings of safety and comfort were there. As long as her father was there, everything would be just fine.

It is good to know that we are loved, and sheltered and cared for. It is comforting to know that in this harsh and hard world someone will stand up and not let anything happen to us. That is what faith in God is all about. When we come to know God, we realize that we are never out of His sight, and that He will watch over us and protect us and care for us all the days of our lives. This assurance turns our lives from burdens into joys. He has given us the gift of life, and it is a blessed gift which He rewards time after time. His love knows no bounds, as evidenced by His greatest gift of all; the Christ, the Babe of Bethlehem.

PRAYER: My God, you are with me in all of the dark hours and hard times. I do not know what I would do without you. You give me so much, and when I am afraid, you comfort and support me. Thank you for being with me, Lord. Amen.

December 21

If thou hast done foolishly in lifting up thyself, or if thou hast thought evil, lay thine hand upon thy mouth. Surely the churning of milk bringeth forth butter and the wringing of the nose bringeth forth blood: so the forcing of wrath bringeth forth strife (30:32-33).

For every action, there is an equal and opposite reaction. When we do something wrong, we can expect that we will have to suffer for it. Every day, the little boy had stopped to throw stones at the birds which roosted along the fence. He had never been much of a shot, and they always flew away before he could come close. One day, he hefted a rather large stone, and let it fly at the unsuspecting birds. The rock flew straight, and hit a bird, knocking it from the fence. In shock and horror, the boy raced up to the fence and picked up the lifeless bird. He began crying, telling the bird he hadn't meant to hurt it. He felt sick inside, and helpless as he looked at his own handiwork.

Why is it that people tempt fate, and then they are so shocked when something goes wrong? If we play with fire, we will eventually get burned. If you strike someone hard enough on the nose, it will bleed. If you churn milk long enough, it will turn to butter. If you dwell in wrong and sinful acts, then you will have to encounter the wrath of God. It is not speculation, it is reality, and the wise understand this and do everything they can to avert the disaster which must result.

PRAYER: O Lord, help me to keep from living so foolishly. I act as if I am immortal, without doing the things which are required of me. I have much to learn, and only you can teach me. Please do so, Lord, I pray. Amen.

December 22

It is not for kings. O Lemuel, it is not for kings to drink wine; nor for princes strong drink: lest they drink, and forget the law, and pervert the judgment of any of the afflicted (31:4-5).

The promotion was what he had dreamed of. He had worked all his life to get where he was, and he intended to celebrate. But the celebration had gone on too long. He found that the drinks which had originally been intended as self-congratulation turned into a way of dealing with pressure. As the stress built, so did his dependence on alcohol. He began drinking at the job. His performance slipped, and his work grew sloppy. Eventually, he was fired. All his hard work had been for nothing; thrown away by a dependence on a crippling crutch.

In our weaknesses we do foolish things. We try to find our own ways to make it through life, and we turn from the only good way there is: Jesus Christ. Christ was sent to earth to conquer death, and to give people a source of strength and courage by which they could live. The gift of Christ is more powerful than anything the world can throw at us. All we need is the wisdom to see its power and take hold of it for our lives. God will bless our lives, and He will help us through every hard time. His love for us has been proven time and again, and there is nothing on earth that will ever turn Him from us.

PRAYER: I walk dangerous paths, Father, and I am not wise enough to avoid all the pitfalls. Guide my steps with your divine light, that I might not stumble, but walk surely, bringing glory and honor to you. Amen.

December 23

Open thy mouth for the dumb in the cause of all such as are appointed to destruction. Open thy mouth, judge righteously, and plead the cause of the poor and needy (31:8-9).

I watched the young woman at the counter. She seemed lost, confused and agitated. After a couple of minutes, I realized that she was retarded. I walked over to where she was and asked her if I could help her. She said she wanted to buy a present for her mother, but didn't know what things cost, nor how much money she had. I helped her count her change, and then we picked out a scarf. It was much more than the girl had, so I called the clerk over. I asked him if he would sell the girl the scarf for what she had, and after she was gone I would make up the difference. He agreed, and the girl went off happily clutching her gift.

There are so many people in the world we can help if we will only do it. Christmas is a time for giving and sharing, but it shouldn't be for only a few days a year. The gift that Christ gave us lasts every day, and so should our kindness and love. We have an obligation to try to love others as much as Christ loves us. That is a full-time job, but a more fulfilling duty cannot be found. When we see others in need, our hearts should go out to them, and we should do everything in our power to assist them.

PRAYER: Lord, I want to do your will each and every day, not just at Christmas time. I have thousands of opportunities to give aid throughout the year. Guide me to do what is most helpful and good. Amen.

December 24

Who can find a virtuous woman? For her price is far above rubies. The heart of her husband doth safely trust in her, so that he shall have no need of spoil. She will do him good and not evil all the days of her life (31:10-12).

The trip was so long and hard. The burro kept staggering from side to side, and Mary felt as if she were going to burst. She and Joseph knew that the baby was coming soon, and they were trying desperately to find a place to rest. She never said a word of complaint. She knew that her child was to be blessed, and she trusted in God that He would protect and shelter them. She did not know why she had been selected of all women to bring God's Son into the world, but she was filled with pride and excitement.

Joseph looked upon her and he felt glad. He was proud of Mary and he felt doubly blessed by the Lord. He was entrusted to bring up the Son of the Most High God, and to care for his own lovely wife. The pair moved on to Bethlehem joyful and at peace, for they knew that God was with them.

God is with us each day. When we live our lives according to His will, then we become a blessing to those around us. Wives become blessings to husbands, and husbands to wives, children to parents, and sisters to brothers. A life well lived is a gift, not only to God and ourselves, but to everyone we meet.

PRAYER: Make my life virtuous and good. Help me to bless the lives of my family and friends. Shine your love through my life, that I may be a beacon of your light. Help me to glorify you in all things. Amen.

December 25

She is like the merchants' ships; she bringeth her food from afar. She riseth also while it is yet night, and giveth meat to her household, and a portion to her maidens (31:14-15).

The town lay in silence. It was late, and the people had closed up their homes and settled in. In the shed, the animals were making low, soft sounds. In their midst were very special people. A young mother cradled her Son, and the father looked on with great love and pride. Another Father looked on with pride, and His bright light shone upon them. Mary had watched all the things which had happened this evening, and she kept all the things in her heart and pondered them. Her life would never be the same. Her life would be dedicated to being the best mother she could be for the Son of God. Pleasing God became her sole purpose for being. Her life was transformed, and her glory would shine throughout the centuries. Throughout time, people would look at Mary and know that she was more blessed than any other woman. For she not only carried the spirit, but had carried the body of God within her.

A virtuous woman is a joy to the Lord. Mary proved to be not only virtuous, but holy. Her holiness came from nothing she did, but it was bestowed upon her by God. Once blessed, she could do nothing less than bless the lives of all she met.

PRAYER: You have made my life so much different than it was before. I cannot thank you enough for all you have given me. I ask that the love you sent so long ago be reborn in me this day, and every day to come, that I might proclaim, "Christ is with us. Hallelujah!" Amen.

December 26

She girdeth her loins with strength, and strengtheneth her arms. She perceiveth that her merchandise is good: her candle goeth not out by night (31:17-18).

She was an organizer. Everything had to be done in a particular order at a particular time. She knew she was a perfectionist, but it had always paid off. She usually got what she set her sights on, and everyone knew that she was dependable and trustworthy. If there was a job that they needed done by a specific time, they came to her. She was proud of her accomplishments, and it gave her a deep satisfaction to know that other people looked at her work to improve their own. She was an example and she vowed that as long as she lived, she would be a good one.

In this day and age, too few people are concerned with quality and integrity. Many try to get by with exerting the least amount of effort possible, and they refuse to give more than they are asked for. It is the wise person who knows to give all they can. God is hoping that we will be bright and shining examples of truth and goodness. When we give less than one hundred percent, we provide a shoddy example, and we are an embarrassment to God. When we live our lives to the fullest, then we do God honor, and His glory is spread through our lives. God will bless us richly, if we will only strive to be the creations He intended us to be.

PRAYER: Lord, I sometimes let down and don't do all I should to make you proud of me. Help me to see ways that I can improve myself, and in so doing, bring honor and glory to you each day. Amen.

December 27

She stretcheth out her hand to the poor; yea, she reacheth forth her hands to the needy (31:20).

The back door was always opening to some stranger. Years ago she had developed the reputation of loving kindness and concern. Whenever a poor person happened through town, they knew that they could receive a warm meal and a kind word at her house. The poor came from all over to visit her, but they never took advantage of her kindness. They were so impressed by her concern for them, that they respected and revered her. While they ate, she would talk to them about her faith, and she was deliberate in letting everyone know that if it weren't for her trust in God, they would not be receiving this meal. God made her love everyone, and she found the power to give of herself through His love. She witnessed to hundreds of people in her life, and her kindnesses stayed with them wherever they went.

Love is such a funny thing. We tend to think in terms of it being something which sweeps us off our feet. But love doesn't have to be big to be powerful. Small acts of kindness can change lives. We can reach out to so many people, not with a lot, but with everything that is important. That is, God's precious love. There is nothing finer.

PRAYER: Guide me to do what needs to be done, O Lord. Wherever I can bring love, let me do so. Help me to see the needs around me, and then give me the resources and the desire to do everything I can. Amen.

December 28

She is not afraid of the snow for her household: for all her household are clothed with scarlet (31:21).

She looked back over her life and she was satisfied. Never once had they been rich. Never once did they have more than they knew what to do with. That didn't mean they'd ever been poor. Her children had always had clothes to wear and shoes for their feet, and food enough to satisfy their bellies. They had all had to pitch in to make things go, but families ought to do that. Her children loved each other. Other families got tied up with gadgets and things, but hers had spent their time in love and sharing. The family would spend long hours talking and sitting around the fire. Those were the good times. Those memories were more precious than gold.

We can provide our family and friends with many things, but we have nothing greater to give than our love. If we will deal with people in love and kindness, we give them something worth more than the finest possessions. Money can't compare with a love that carries through our lives. God gives us such love. We may think that we are poor, that we don't have all the things we want, but if we have His love then we are richer than kings and queens. Nothing compares with the love of God, and the person who knows such love will never know want.

PRAYER: Father, I adore you. You have been so good to me and have shared so much. Help me to share what you have given to me with others. Let me share the treasure which is in my heart. Amen.

December 29

She openeth her mouth with wisdom; and in her tongue is the law of kindness (31:26).

She didn't believe in spanking the children. If they couldn't be made to understand the difference between right and wrong by reasoning with them, then other ways could be found without striking them. Nothing good would come of even the most well-intended violence. Her children knew that they had nothing to fear from their mother. She would never hurt them for any reason. Her only desire was to give them the best life possible. They knew they could talk to her, and she would listen as a friend, not judging or condemning. She had learned long ago that kindness was the key to respect and obedience. It was not through fear that people came to know the love of God, it was through his tender mercy and loving grace.

God gives so much to us, His children. He tries to lead us through a life which is good and joyous. His instruction is often hard, but if we will learn to follow it, we will find great blessing. He does not try to strike us down, or condemn us, He only tries to help us see our errors and make things right. God loves us and gives us a promise of a life everlasting which is rooted and grounded in love and grace.

PRAYER: Give to me a gentle spirit, that I might deal in love with those I try to help. Fill me with consideration and comfort, so I can give it to people who are in desperate need. You have given such to me, I only want to do the same for others. Amen.

December 30

She looketh well to the ways of her household, and eateth not the bread of idleness. Her children arise up, and call her blessed; her husband also, and he praiseth her. Many daughters have done virtuously, but thou excellest them all (31:27-29).

Emma sat encircled by friends and family and she was at peace. Looking around at her family, she felt that God was pleased with her. Her sons and daughters, grandsons and granddaughters, great-grandsons and great-granddaughters were all fine people, who knew what it meant to love, and knew what it meant to have faith. Her family had been brought up in the fear of the Lord, and it was worth it. In a world which was full of hurt and fear, her family was full of hope and love. There was a crowd of people here to celebrate with her, but most importantly she knew, God was here, too. She looked forward to meeting Him face to face.

When we have lived well, we can stand before God unashamed. He will look upon us, and the radiance of His face will warm and comfort us. He will tell us that we have run the race well, and that we have been good and faithful servants, and all the hurts, frustrations and disappointments of this life will fade away to nothingness. In our meeting with our Maker, we will understand fully, just how wonderful the gift of life really is.

PRAYER: I look at the beauty and wonder in this world, and something deep inside tells me that I haven't seen anything yet. I look at the evil and pain in the world, and something cries out inside that I don't belong here. Be with me all of my days, Lord, and bring me at last to your eternal glory, I pray. Amen.

December 31

Favor is deceitful, and beauty is vain: but a woman that feareth the Lord, she shall be praised. Give her of the fruit of her hands; and let her own works praise her in the gates (31:30-31).

The sun was setting and evening quiet settled in. A fire burned in the hearth, and its light was the only source in the room. Life seemed so difficult sometimes. You did your best, gave it your all, and it seemed like you got nothing for your troubles. Nothing good ever seemed to last, but still, she had hope. Tomorrow would be a new day, and she looked forward to seeing what it would bring. True, not everything had gone right in her life, but she had lots to be thankful for. She worked hard, but that made her feel good. She felt like she had accomplished something. She wasn't beautiful, or popular, but she was at peace with herself and that was what was important. She was loved by her husband and children, and she knew that they would always be there with her. She could complain a lot, but down inside she knew that she was a really lucky woman. Her feelings of futility gave way to a feeling that everything was going to be okay. And so it was. As long as God was in heaven, and His sight was on His children, everything would be just fine. In His will and His infinite love, all things were possible. Life was good. She leaned back into the chair, and smiled. The new year was going to be great.

PRAYER: My Lord, shine your light in my life, and give me the strength I need to face whatever comes my way. I look forward to tomorrow, and all the blessings it will bring. Thank you. Thank you for life, for love, and for being my God. Amen.

Inspirational Library

Beautiful purse/pocket size editions of Christian classics bound in flexible leatherette. These books make thoughtful gifts for everyone on your list, including yourself!

The Bible Promise Book   Over 1000 promises from God's Word arranged by topic. What does God promise about matters like: Anger, Illness, Jealousy, Love, Money, Old Age, and Mercy? Find out in this book!
Flexible Leatherette $3.97

Daily Light from the Bible   One of the most popular daily devotionals with readings for both morning and evening.
Flexible Leatherette $4.97

My Daily Prayer Journal   Each page is dated and features a Scripture verse and ample room for you to record your thoughts, prayers, and praises. One page for each day of the year.
Flexible Leatherette $4.97